MW01259917

Comic (and Column) Confessional
First Edition

© Dave Astor

First published by Xenos Press in 2012.

Xenos Press
300 N. LaSalle, 49th Floor
Chicago, IL 60654

ISBN: 978-1-105-79286-1

Typeset in 9pt Palatino Linotype
By Outsider Editorial Services

Book Design by Interloper Designs

Cover Photo of Dave Astor (in 1988) by Sharon Freedman

To my wonderful wife Laurel, and my wonderful daughters Maggie and Maria, with love.

Comic (and Column) Confessional

Table of Contents

Preface

By Heloise

David Astor knows more about newspaper syndication than almost anyone I know. He did my first interview for *Editor & Publisher* when I took over the column after my mother died. How lucky for me! David always reported fairly and accurately. He understands the business side and the creative side — that means the talent! David is simply the best in our business and here is a "Hint from Heloise" ... this book should be a textbook for anyone who wants to be in the newspaper business, or learn about it! Plus, it's an interesting read about the industry and the people who are involved.

Reading this book is like a voyage through the eyes of someone who has been in the newspaper field for decades. You will learn about "the other side" of the business, including reporting, editing, personalities (that sometimes don't mesh!), newspaper syndication, column writing on a local or national basis, and much more. David Astor knows most of the major and minor players personally and has had access to them.

When David did his research, he was always careful to dig a little deeper and add just the right tidbit of information that made a story interesting. He has seen and reported on the good, bad, and ugly — while maintaining a professional stance as well as a human one! Reading this book will give you insight into our business as well as the intricacies of how many newspapers and media syndicates are run.

Columnists and cartoonists are a special breed and David understands that! Dip into this book for just a few pages, which are filled with stories of personalities you may have grown up reading, and you will want to finish it in one sitting. You will never look at a newspaper column or cartoon the same way again!

INTRODUCTION

Covering the (Non-Mafia) Syndicates

Before I started a new magazine job in 1983, probably the most famous person I covered as a journalist was President Ford. That was in New Jersey in 1975, when I was a student at Rutgers — a public university with a private-sounding name.

But covering a speech by Ford for the *Targum* campus newspaper was hardly a life highlight when you consider that the guy pardoned Richard Nixon and had future Iraq War architects Dick Cheney and Donald Rumsfeld in his administration. If only the Betty Ford Center could cure people of addictions to invading countries....

Then I joined *Editor & Publisher* magazine in '83. *E&P* covers the newspaper business, and I was given the syndication "beat." You know — the world of comic strips, editorial cartoons, columns, and crossword puzzles that get harder as the week goes on. (Monday's clue: Name two Iraq War architects.) Suddenly, I was meeting the likes of "Peanuts" legend Charles Schulz and advice titan Ann Landers.

This book will include my recollections of Schulz, Landers, and many other notables I covered for *E&P* until my time there ended in 2008.

Was I laid off? Did I leave for another job? Did I go back to school to earn an MBA (Master's in Books Autobiographical)? The answer will be in the last chapter of this memoir. I, for one, am eager to find out what happened with me in '08.

Yes, yours truly spent 25 years at one place in this era of transient employment — was I nuts? But even a non-job-hopper can amass many memories in a quarter century. In 1987, for instance, Landers was irked when her twin sister — "Dear Abby" writer Abigail Van Buren — published a letter of mine about a tragedy involving my daughter. Several years later, Schulz took me aside at a convention to express annoyance with a story I wrote reporting that "Garfield" might have passed "Peanuts" in total newspaper clients (Jim Davis' cat comic was always first in lasagna portions). Clearly, several syndication superstars had quite the competitive streak.

Other people I encountered included some still living, some now dead, and some existing in an in-between state (Ohio?). Among them were online magnate Arianna Huffington, hints expert Heloise, lifestyle maven/columnist Martha Stewart, Microsoft co-founder/columnist Bill Gates, humorist Dave Barry, and TV stars/columnists Walter Cronkite, Bill O'Reilly, and Dan Rather.

Also: now-retired cartooning great Gary Larson ("The Far Side"), not-retired cartooning great Garry Trudeau ("Doonesbury"), *partly* retired cartooning great Lynn Johnston ("For Better or For Worse"), the amazing Stan

Lee ("Spider-Man"), the legendary Mort Walker ("Beetle Bailey"), editorial cartooning colossus Herblock (yes, he coined the term "McCarthyism"), from-the-political-world columnists Hillary Rodham Clinton and Coretta Scott King, and nothing-to-do-with-syndication speakers such as Al Gore and actor/National Rifle Association guy Charlton Heston.

You can see why my *E&P* job — until things soured — would've had to be pried from my cold, deadlined hands.

Do you like anecdotes? This book has plenty of them. For instance, there was "Calvin and Hobbes" cartoonist Bill Watterson's desperate 1986 effort to stop his photo from running in *E&P*. My awkward 1989 car ride with Jesse Jackson. Columnists challenging English professors to an intense spelling bee when the two groups happened to share the same Utah hotel in 1996. And a 2005 Texas talk by Jim Leavelle, the cowboy-hatted detective in the iconic 1963 photo of Jack Ruby shooting Lee Harvey Oswald. When some columnists and I gathered around Leavelle after his remarks, he pulled from his pocket something *very* interesting.

I'll also tell you something about myself in this book. Perhaps the most important fact I should convey right now is that I'M NOT RELATED TO THE WEALTHY ASTORS! My paternal grandfather went through the name-change thing when he emigrated from Eastern Europe, and I grew up in a lower-middle-class family fed with the help of food stamps after my parents divorced. My short-tempered father eventually disappeared from my life.

Having an unstable dad and an economically insecure family were among the things that made me a painfully shy person well into adulthood. I didn't even go on a date until college! Given that kind of personality, becoming a journalist was either a way to fight my shyness or an exercise in masochism. Perhaps both. But I do love to write!

Did working for *E&P* help me feel better about myself? You'll see in this book. You'll also see how the esteem thing had a huge effect on my personal life.

But this memoir will cover more than my personal life, my celebrity encounters, and my fabulous cats (I realize the words "fabulous" and "cats" are redundant). I'll also discuss how changes at *E&P* and throughout the media world had a big impact on me and other journalists.

One watershed development was the dawning and never dusking of the digital age. This online revolution, while bringing many positive things to the table, also had its troubling aspects. The rise of the Web (as well as America's economic downturns) helped cause daily newspapers to lose lots of circulation and ads. This led to many dailies going out of business and most dailies shrinking their staffs — with not enough online journalism jobs replacing the print ones lost.

Newspapers made things worse for themselves by offering content that was often staid and boring — whether in print or on their Web sites. "Non

Sequitur" cartoonist Wiley Miller even did a hilarious 1997 comic placing newspapers in the "sleeping aids" aisle of a store!

And many dailies and their parent companies continued trying to rake in so much profit that they didn't plow enough money back into improving their product — making the (usually free) Internet an even more appealing alternative for many readers and advertisers. One way newspapers maximize profits is by often paying their writers low wages.

With many of their newspaper clients budget-crunched or gone, syndicates saw a reduction in their comic and column sales. So they also reduced their staffs, went out of business, or got bought by bigger syndicates. Not surprisingly, syndicates and newspapers also greatly reduced their ad buys in *E&P*, which starved the magazine of revenue.

Meanwhile, the Internet forced journalists — many of whom write for a print publication's Web site for no extra pay — to hyper-quickly do many more stories than in the pre-digital days. The result was exhaustion — while context, accuracy, and excellent prose often got lost in the shuffle.

Don't get me wrong, I love many aspects of the digital age. It opens up new (albeit often unpaid or low-paid) work possibilities; you can communicate easily with friends, relatives, and business colleagues via email and social media; and you can watch YouTube videos of rock groups (I'm partial to 10,000 Maniacs, whether fronted by Natalie Merchant in the band's early years or Mary Ramsey in recent years). Also, you'll see in this book how an online encounter profoundly changed my life. So I and many other digital-agers are stuck between a rock and a hard drive.

Another media change — this one with almost no redeeming value — was increased consolidation and corporatization. Many family-owned newspapers were gobbled up by chains. And the mergers of several syndicates not only resulted in layoffs of employees but also the jettisoning of some cartoonists and columnists. If you have 10 big syndicates that each distribute a gardening columnist, and then you have six big syndicates after consolidations, four gardening scribes might be weeded out.

Meanwhile, staffers at chain-owned media outlets tend to get laid off more than staffers at family-owned ones do. Both entities are profit-conscious, but most corporatized chains are profit-*obsessed*.

E&P eventually got sucked into the conglomerate vortex, and the consequences were … interesting.

CHAPTER ONE

1983:
Discovering Beetle
Bailey's Sister

In 1982, the U.S. economy wasn't as bad as it would become in 2008, but it was bad enough. I was so desperate to leave my job as senior editor at the now-defunct *Marketing Communications* magazine that I sent out more than 100 résumés before getting a whiff of new employment. That was when job-seekers composed a cover letter on a typewriter, stapled it to a résumé printed at a print shop, stuffed those pieces of a paper into an envelope, walked to a mailbox, and then stood there paralyzed when they couldn't find the "send" button.

I wanted to leave *MC* because Ronnie Telzer, the great person and editor who hired me four years earlier, had departed — as had Les Luchter and other staffers with whom I enjoyed working. The exodus came after the company owner gave *MC*'s reins to a consumer-products executive who had little magazine experience and spouted elitist bromides like "we will write about the big wheels making the big deals."

From mid-1982 into early 1983, I vented during my spare time by writing a never-produced play about the weird doings at a fictional advertising publication modeled on *MC*. The comedic work was called, appropriately enough, *Ad Nauseam*.

Then I got lucky. *Editor & Publisher* staffer Bill Gloede, a gregarious guy I had worked with at the *Passaic* (N.J.) *Herald News* in 1978, told me about an opening at *E&P* and put in a word with managing editor Jerry Walker.

Jerry interviewed me over lunch in a beer-and-burger pub near *E&P*'s Manhattan office on Lexington Avenue at East 51ˢᵗ Street. I was nervous as hell, partly because Walker seemed so outgoing while I was much shyer than the average journalist.

"You want a beer?" he asked.

"No, thanks," I stammered, because I don't drink and — even if I did — imbibing isn't the best idea during a job interview.

"If I hire you, Brown and Teubner aren't going to like your hair," said Jerry, referring to *E&P*'s editor (Robert U. Brown) and publisher (Ferdinand Teubner) and my longish Caucasian afro.

"Should I cut it?"

"Fuck 'em. You're hired."

Despite my hair, I'm actually a rather straitlaced guy who has never even smoked a joint. I'm almost a Mormon — with the slight differences of not being religious, not living in Utah, not having conservative politics, and not having polygamous ancestors. My grandfather might have been married to both his job and my grandmother, but that was kept hush-hush.

I cannot tell a lie: I started at *E&P* on George Washington's birthday — Feb. 22. That 1983 morning, I was plunked in front of one of those video display terminals that connected to a central computer. Though the VDT looked old enough for Washington to have tossed it across the Potomac, I was thrilled that my "beat" would involve covering syndicated cartoonists and columnists. Tough gig — I would *have* to read the comics every morning. Research, you know.

My first story, about the *Pittsburgh Press* temporarily dropping "Dondi" because a character in that comic called a mentally challenged boy a "retard," disappeared from my VDT screen when I hit the wrong button.

"No!" I groaned, not enjoying my first-ever computer encounter.

"Write it again," Jerry advised after he stopped laughing.

Gee, why hadn't I thought of that?

The *Pittsburgh Press* disappeared a decade later, becoming one of dozens of daily newspapers to fold during my 25 years at *E&P*. The demise of those dailies and my tenure at the magazine were not related, I think.

E&P's six-person newsroom reeked of tobacco smoke. It was long before cancer sticks were banned from offices, and two of the six puffed enough to keep the other four wishing that our open cubicles were hermetically sealed.

Unfortunately, I was too new and unassertive to ask my co-workers to light up less. So my lungs started job-hunting, but they ended up staying at *E&P* as long as I did.

At least the receptionist never smoked as I signed in at the front desk. In those pre-voice mail days, she would hand me pink slips of paper with phone messages on them. It wasn't until years later — when I started covering the never-ending layoffs of editorial cartoonists and other newspaper people — that "pink slips" made me think of something besides messages.

Jerry the managing editor could be curt and crusty. But I and the other four reporters knew how to do our jobs, so he mostly left us alone — a great change from the latter days at *Marketing Communications*. The five of us were actually called associate editors, perhaps because that title made us "managers" ineligible for overtime pay.

And overtime I worked on occasion, partly because *E&P* had no copy editor and no art/layout person — meaning writers also had to do that work. More profits for the wealthy Robert Brown, who inherited the magazine from his father. The 70-something Brown, *E&P*'s editor since 1944 but more owner than editor by 1983, had pricey homes to maintain in tony Old Greenwich, Conn., and elsewhere.

But Brown was actually a very nice guy — though a bit paternalistic. And in that not-so-corporate time, *E&P* didn't have a parent company with endless layers of management and bureaucracy. There was also a decent pension plan rather than one of those measly 401(k)s so prevalent today, and each *E&P* employee received a bonus check at the annual holiday party that was direct-deposited into the hand that wasn't clutching a drink (in my case, water).

Of course, the bonuses were nothing like the federal bailout money financial institutions would receive in 2008. During the holidays that year, one bank spent its $15 billion in taxpayer largesse on three $5-billion fruitcakes, or maybe I made that up.

As I alluded to a few paragraphs ago, I copy-edited my own stories, obtained and sized photos that accompanied those articles, sketched out where the stories should go in the magazine, and did other things for the 1983 *E&P*. It was actually fun to juggle a variety of tasks, because it gave my brain an occasional break from writing.

And the writing workload, though large, was not overwhelming. In those ancient days before publications had Web sites, there was a finite print space to fill. And the only deadline was *E&P*'s weekly magazine deadline, so you didn't have to work 13 hours in one day to get a piece online that night if a big story broke. You could take a lunch break — and leave the office at a decent hour to have a family life (if you had a family).

But, as I said earlier, I sometimes stayed late to finish things up.

"Go *home*!" Bill Gloede would urge good-naturedly. "You're making the rest of us look bad!"

My reaction was to blush.

When I was the last person in the office, I turned off the main computer by flipping almost a dozen switches. But not before I made hard copies of my stories on one of those primitive printers that spooled out a continuous roll of paper with little holes on each side.

Many of the early stories I did for the 1884-founded *E&P* were trend pieces. It was a good way for me to learn what was going on in the syndication biz while imparting useful information to *E&P*'s readers — who included newspaper editors and publishers (duh!), reporters, ad managers, circulation directors, cartoonists, columnists, syndicate executives, journalism professors, and my mother (if I mailed her a copy).

One March 1983 trend story was about the increase in stuffed animals, greeting cards, and other licensed products picturing comic strip characters such as Snoopy from Charles Schulz's 1950-launched "Peanuts" and that fat cat from Jim Davis' 1978-launched "Garfield." Syndicates make a good chunk of their profits via licensing, and a few cartoonists become rich indeed. Schulz — and later his estate — often earned more than $20 million a year.

"What are syndicates?" my friends would ask in 1983.

The answer: They're non-*Sopranos* companies that receive submissions from cartoonists and columnists eager to see their work in newspapers. Syndicates sign a handful of these aspiring creators, then market and sell their features to as many newspapers and other media outlets as possible.

When I say "a handful," I mean a handful. A large syndicate might receive 10,000 submissions a year and sign fewer than a dozen. This means syndicates are "gatekeepers" that choose the best content to offer newspapers and other clients. But there are many excellent submissions that syndicates *don't* choose, perhaps because these features are deemed too controversial, not mainstream enough, etc., to sell to a wide pool of newspapers based in locales ranging from liberal to very conservative. That's why some people feel syndicates choose only the best of the content that's sort of "white bread."

Syndicates also collect feature fees from their media subscribers, and then give most creators roughly 50% of that money. Small-circulation clients usually pay less (say, $5 a week) than large subscribers (say, $50 a week) for a comic or column. So selling a comic to the huge *New York Times* is a real coup. Oops — bad example, given that the *Times* doesn't have a comics section....

And syndicates, which seek out creators in addition to signing creators who seek out syndicates, edit the work of the people they represent.

Meanwhile, some syndicates have sister units involved in things like book publishing and the aforementioned licensing — both of which bring in revenue that helps make up for the low feature fees I just discussed. (One reason fees aren't higher: The shrinking number of multi-paper towns leaves fewer dailies to bid against each other for the rights to run certain comics and columns.)

One big book operation is Andrews McMeel Publishing, a sister unit to the James Andrews/John McMeel-founded Universal Press Syndicate (renamed Universal Uclick in 2009). AMP is known for its comic collections, gift books, and more.

Among the other major syndicates besides Universal are King Features Syndicate, Tribune Media Services, Creators Syndicate, the New York Times Syndicate, and the Washington Post Writers Group (WPWG).

As you can see, some syndicates are affiliated with large media companies. These syndicates distribute features that originate in their companies' newspapers (for instance, WPWG has some columns from *The Washington Post*) but also distribute features that originate elsewhere.

Syndication allows feature-buying clients to publish America's best columnists and cartoonists for just a few dollars a week. And if a newspaper has a homegrown creator who gets syndicated, the paper shares that national spotlight with its syndicated columnist or cartoonist.

In 1983, the trend story I remember most was an April piece focusing on the depiction of women in comics. Given the fact that men back then did about 98% of the 200-plus comics distributed by major syndicates, the depiction wasn't always enlightened. Too many stereotypes of nagging housewives and bad female drivers. But there were signs of progress in '83, such as former stay-at-home mom Lois of "Hi and Lois" working part-time in real estate — thus displaying much more energy than her lazy brother Beetle Bailey (yes, they're siblings!).

The "Beetle" comic, by the way, began in 1950 with the title character as a college student. But the strip didn't take off until cartoonist Mort Walker — a heckuva nice guy — sat down at his drafting table to draft Beetle into the Army during the Korean War.

But back to women. As of 2008, females would comprise about 8% of the comic cartoonist rosters at major syndicates — not great, but progress. Meanwhile, the number of female *editorial* cartoonists with big distributors was still miniscule in '08, barely better than in 1983. After wading through the testosterone, I found only two syndicated female editorial cartoonists — Etta Hulme and Kate Salley Palmer — to interview for a November '83 story.

"Why so few?" I asked Etta.

"Durned if I know," replied the *Fort Worth Star-Telegram* staffer in her Texas accent.

The reasons for this paltry representation have been debated for years: Men more interested in cartooning? Not enough female cartoonist role models? Sexism at syndicates and newspapers? Women smart enough to avoid newspaper cartooning as newspapers declined? All I know is that editorial cartooning is also called political cartooning, and that political cartooning has an even lower percentage of women than political bodies such as Congress. Then again, this memoir is 100% male-written, so who am I to talk?

At least King Features in 1983 syndicated the *Sunday Woman* weekly newspaper supplement ably edited by Merry Clark.

But whatever the failings of the industry I now covered, I was very grateful to have a job at which I could do stories about things that mattered to me.

CHAPTER TWO

1954-1982:
A Flashback Near
This Book's Front

I was born in the Bronx, and lived the first year of my life not far from Yankee Stadium — where A-Rod hit so well that he started swatting homers 20 years before his parents conceived him.

My parents crossed the George Washington Bridge in 1955, becoming yet another white New York City couple moving to the mostly white New Jersey suburbs. But their car, a 1950 Oldsmobile the size of a Brontosaurus, was black.

As a kid growing up in Teaneck, N.J., I read the comics in my parents' favorite newspapers: *The Record* of nearby Hackensack and the New York *Daily News*. But I wasn't a rabid "funnies" fan during the years prior to covering comics — being more into *The Wizard of Oz* than "The Wizard of Id." I do remember liking story strips such as Chester Gould's "Dick Tracy" (with its over-the-top villains) and George Wunder's "Terry and the Pirates."

I had no idea back then that a much better version of "Terry" was originally done by Milton Caniff, who quit his own comic in 1946 when his syndicate wouldn't give him ownership rights. So Caniff started "Steve Canyon" and the syndicate gave Caniff's "Terry" to Wunder.

But although there were things I was clueless about, yours truly did manage to avoid casting a presidential ballot for Barry Goldwater in 1964 — an easy decision given that I wasn't old enough to vote.

One reason for my shyness as a kid was my ridiculous skinniness; I weighed just 130 pounds when reaching my full height of 6'2" before adding another 50 pounds as an adult (given the level of my parents' income, our refrigerator wasn't exactly filled to the brim). And I had a smart, older half-sister named Linda whose looks, self-assurance, and dating success made me and my also smart younger brother Robert feel as insignificant as Charlie Brown did whenever he encountered Lucy (who was partly based on "Peanuts" cartoonist Charles Schulz's take-charge first wife).

But it was the dynamics of my parents' marriage that really did a number on my confidence. My father was an unhappy person — partly because he disliked being a TV/radio repairman and partly for reasons I don't know. My long-retired mother, Thelma, doesn't like to talk about him to this day.

My father ran his own repair service when he wasn't working for someone else, so there were TVs, radios, record players, and other devices stuffed on shelves in our basement and garage. Our family's devices included a DuMont black-and-white TV built inside a blond-wood cabinet, on top of which sat a weird-looking turntable my father had put there. I used it to listen to vinyl 45 rpm "singles" such as "Monster Mash" by Boris Pickett and the Crypt-Kickers, "She Loves You" by the Beatles, and … the "Peanuts"-inspired "Snoopy vs. the Red Baron" by the Royal Guardsmen.

My father often took out his frustrations on my mother. I remember him chasing her around the dining-room table and then hitting her, with "conversations" like:

"You fucking whore!" he shouted.

"Get away from me!" she nervously yelled back.

"You goddamn bitch."

"Don't hit me!"

Sometimes he did. And I remember the police being called. None of the officers had jaws quite as square as Dick Tracy's.

My parents divorced when I was 13, and my father often didn't send alimony and child support. This was a major problem, because my mother had been a "homemaker" during part of the marriage and now worked a bookkeeping job that didn't pay enough. It was hardly the idyllic life depicted in "The Family Circus" comic, but at least we had normal-shaped heads.

One low point was when my mother asked me to testify against my father at a court hearing to make him pay what he owed. Although we needed that money, and although I disliked my father much of the time, I still feel guilty remembering the look he gave me when I was on the witness stand. I don't think something like that ever happened in "Judge Parker."

After the hearing, I and my friends Lon and Kevin played our usual baseball game in Teaneck's Terhune Park, where we rotated as pitcher, hitter, and left-fielder. I swung so viciously that my bat kept missing Kevin's lob throws. If I had known the meaning of metaphors back then, I was trying to smack the stitches out of my miserable life.

"I'm sitting down!" shouted the bored Lon from left field. And he did.

In high school, I built up a little self-esteem by doing fairly well at cross-country and track. I had gotten my mile time down to 5:06 when my right knee began to feel sore during a self-scheduled Sunday run on the hard pavement near my Oritani Place house. I stupidly didn't rest the knee — I guess I was hooked on my modest athletic success and those exercise endorphins — and soon I was out for the season. By the time 11th grade rolled around, my right leg had grown longer than my left one — adding back trouble to the mix. If I was a cartoon character, I would have consulted Rex Morgan, M.D.

I quit running, concentrated on my studies, squeaked into Rutgers College on the waiting list, and funded my four years there mostly by working summer jobs — including a stint on the assembly line of a lighting-fixture factory. I was lucky to attend college during a time (1972-76) when less-crazy tuition costs gave students a fighting chance to pay their own way.

Actually, I had saved some money in the years before college by working odd jobs and *very* odd jobs (including spraying insecticide into sewers for Teaneck's municipal department). But my mother had to empty my bank account to help pay household expenses after the divorce. I didn't blame her; she was a determined woman making sure the family survived.

Despite possessing the social skills of a paper towel, I found a niche at the Rutgers *Targum* newspaper. I eventually became its editor-in-chief as well as the campus "stringer" for *The New York Times* — which paid modestly, but I would have done it for free. One illustration of how different technology was back in the '70s involved the way I sent each story to the *Times*. I called a phone number and read the article into a recording device for someone to later keyboard. You even had to say the punctuation marks!

I'm still not sure how I moved up the *Targum* ranks, because I was too introverted to be an inspiring leader. But I wrote well, and spent much of my editorship composing daily editorials — on a manual typewriter, of course. When mistakes were made, I blotted them out with white stuff. Mashed potatoes worked best.

One *Targum* tussle I remember was an effort to replace Charles Schulz's "Peanuts" in the newspaper with Garry Trudeau's "Doonesbury." I was in the "Doonesbury" camp, but "Peanuts" won — showing how much clout I had! I also recall that the *Targum* ran editorial cartoons by Pat Oliphant, whose fun drawing style was a revelation to me and other readers accustomed to the more somber-looking art of Pat's older peers.

I had no idea I would later meet Oliphant, Trudeau, and Schulz.

After graduating from Rutgers with a major in English and a minor in Eye Fatigue from reading long Dickens novels, I joined *The Daily Register* of Shrewsbury, N.J., with not-so-great expectations. The $130-a-week pay was lousy and the Monmouth County locale near the ocean shore was too suburban for me at a time when I longed for what U2 would later call the "City of Blinding Lights" (Manhattan).

One story I wrote in June 1976 covered the "Operation Sail" parade of "tall ships" that would mark the nation's bicentennial on July 4. People were so worried about the possibility of traffic gridlock from cars driving to see the ships that I renamed the event "Operation Snail" in the story's first paragraph.

"Clever lead," said one of my editors.

"Thanks," I replied, not sure if he was being sarcastic.

"You know you're scaring people, don't you? They might not go to the event."

"Should I change the lead?" I asked, prepared, as was usually the case in those days, not to stand up for myself.

"Hell no!"

I wrote my *Register* stories on an electric typewriter (technology was marching on!) and then put the pages in a bin for bureau chief Bob Bramley to edit with a pencil.

I resigned from the *Register* in 1977 to start a master's degree program at Northwestern University's Medill School of Journalism, after having been rejected by Columbia University's more prestigious j-school. I loaded up the rust-spotted Volkswagen Beetle I had bought for $150 in '76, and drove that '69 jalopy from New Jersey to Evanston, Ill. Given that my family had little money for vacations, it was by far the longest trip I had ever taken. I was living the "Go west, young man" dream of famed 19th-century newspaper editor Horace Greeley, who did not have a GPS device on the dashboard of his horse.

It was fun being out of the Northeast and near Chicago while going to a school that had some stimulating professors. But there were a couple of Northwestern negatives that stick in my mind. (As you've probably noticed by now, I'm often a "glass-half-empty" guy who also worries about breaking the glass and stepping on the pieces barefoot.)

One negative was the brutal winter of 1977-78. Chicago's near-suburbs had more than 80 inches of snow, and the temperature dipped below zero so often that Lake Michigan partly froze — becoming Lake Superior if you feel ice is superior to water.

The other Northwestern negative involved the son of a famous journalist getting a summer 1978 internship at a well-known magazine even though I and various other Medill applicants had better credentials at the time.

"Is that fair?" I nervously asked the editorial department chair, after screwing up the courage to enter her office.

She looked daggers at me, and I quickly left. It would not be my last brush with nepotism.

After a quick five months at the *Passaic* (N.J.) *Herald News*, I broke every rule of job-hunting etiquette to land the aforementioned *Marketing Communications* position. I accidentally overslept the morning of the interview, and thus arrived 15 minutes late. Then there was this exchange between *MC* editor Ronnie Telzer and myself:

"Why would you like to work here?" she asked.

"Well, uh, actually, I'm not sure I want to work for a marketing magazine."

But after acing a copy-editing test, I was offered the job anyway — and happily accepted it. I didn't want to write about ads that make people desire stuff they don't need, but I *did* want to work in Manhattan rather than continue reverse-commuting into New Jersey. Yes, my desire to live in New York City was so strong that I had moved there when I got the job in Passaic, N.J.

But my Manhattan project ultimately didn't work out — and it wasn't because of the rents, which were affordable at the time for young singles if they shared an apartment. In my first place, on West 98ᵗʰ Street, the actress/dancer holding the lease departed for a couple of months to perform in an out-of-town gig — and left hundreds of dollars worth of calls on the phone bill. Like an idiot with a "kick me" sign on his back, I had agreed to have the phone in my name a few months earlier. When I meekly asked her to mail the money, she hung up — and mailed me an eviction letter instead!

That was in 1979, the debut year of "For Better or For Worse" by Canadian cartoonist Lynn Johnston. I then found a room four blocks closer to Canada (on West 102ⁿᵈ Street) in an apartment rented by a friend of my sister Linda. But Linda and Judy eventually had a falling out, so Judy booted me from *that* apartment in 1981. Clearly, the cartoon characters residing in "Apartment 3-G" had more housing stability than yours truly.

Then I left Manhattan for Brooklyn, where I rented the top floor of a modest three-story building with my former Rutgers pal Mark Arzoumanian. We got along great as apartment mates (Mark is an exceptionally nice guy), and remain close to this day. I also became friends with another great guy, Mark Teich, who used to date the Judy who jettisoned me from Manhattan! So it goes to show that even a strong believer in diversity can like two people with the same first name. But I think the "Mark Trail" comic is kind of clunky.

CHAPTER THREE

Still 1983: The Year of the Cat and the Croc

Perhaps the most fun part of being at *Editor & Publisher* involved writing profiles of syndicated creators. After covering post-*Mad Men* marketers in my previous job, it was wonderful to interview people who wanted to entertain and educate readers — not just sell stuff.

One of my first profile interviews was with the *Chicago Tribune*'s Dick Locher, just after he won the Pulitzer Prize for editorial cartooning in April 1983. I soon discovered that Dick was one of the most likable guys in the newspaper biz.

"How the heck are you, my friend?" he would say when I phoned. "I'm delighted you called."

"I'm fine. How are you?"

"I'm doing *super*, thank you."

Dick and I would later share the not-super experience of having something awful happen to a child.

In June 1983, I profiled "Garfield" creator Jim Davis to mark his strip turning five (35 in cat-comic years!). He was the first syndication mega-celebrity I interviewed, and boy was I nervous — even though we talked by phone rather than in person. I was trembling so much I almost gave myself a concussion with the phone receiver as it bounced against my left ear.

Davis' strip was already in 1,400 newspapers by 1983 — though, like "Peanuts" in 1950, it hadn't sold that well initially. In fact, "Garfield" had only about 50 clients after a year of syndication. Ironically, one thing that jump-started the comic's phenomenal popularity was the *Chicago Sun-Times* dropping it to save money. The *S-T* received more than 1,300 angry phone calls and hundreds of letters in those pre-email days, so papers elsewhere realized that "Garfield" had quite a fan base among millions of cat lovers. (And Odie the dog needed a CAT scan every time Garfield knocked him off the table.)

Born in 1945 in Indiana, Davis grew up on a small farm that had as many as 25 ... you guessed it ... cats. Because of asthma, he spent a lot of time inside doing ... you guessed it ... drawing. Jim later worked for an ad agency, and then spent several educational years as an assistant to "Tumbleweeds" comic creator Tom Ryan before going out on his own with "Garfield."

Davis told me in the 1983 interview that he came up with his cartoon cat's part-feline, part-human persona by imagining what a person would be like "if he had all his primal instincts intact." Then Jim added a dash of Archie Bunker (from the show *All in the Family*) and Morris the Cat (of TV commercial fame).

"Why did you name your character 'Garfield'?" I asked.

"It was my grandfather's middle name."

Hmm ... makes one wonder about the middle name of "Funky Winkerbean" cartoonist Tom Batiuk's gramps.

Even an individual strip like "Garfield" can be affected by corporatization. Over the years, Davis assembled a team at Paws Inc. to help him do "Garfield" so he'd have enough time to work on things like the thriving licensing business spawned by his comic. From all reports, Jim's employees love their good-natured boss. But some readers feel the comic-by-committee approach helped turn "Garfield" from a nicely edgy strip in its early years to a less quirky feature by the 1990s.

Davis was not the first cartoonist to drop the solo act after becoming highly successful, but Charles Schulz wasn't in that group. The "Peanuts" creator resolutely did all the writing and drawing of his comic, though he had plenty of help with his licensing empire and animated TV specials.

"Bloom County" cartoonist Berkeley (then known as Berke) Breathed certainly felt "Garfield" became somewhat watered down, because he created his hilariously ragged Bill the Cat character partly to tweak Davis' funny-page feline.

I interviewed Breathed in June 1983. His part-silly-humor/part-sociopolitical-commentary feature was four years away from becoming only the second comic strip to win an editorial cartooning Pulitzer (after "Doonesbury" in 1975), but "Bloom" star Opus the penguin was already as well-known as President Reagan. I might add that Opus had better politics.

"Why a penguin?" I asked Breathed.

"There are too many cats and dogs on the comic pages," he replied, adding that penguins are popular at zoos and walk upright — which visually looks good for a critter in a newspaper strip. Fans who didn't read "Peanuts" from the start might be interested to know that Snoopy the dog walked on all four legs from 1950 to 1958.

Breathed was born in 1957 — a year before Snoopy became bipedal — and got his start as a regularly published cartoonist with the "Academia Waltz" comic in the University of Texas newspaper. That *Daily Texan* strip attracted the attention of the Washington Post Writers Group syndicate, and "Bloom County" was launched when Breathed was only 23.

A week after interviewing Breathed, I talked with "Cathy" creator Cathy Guisewite, one of the few women on funny pages in 1983. "Cathy," like "Garfield" and various other comics, would lose some of its zing after many years in newspapers. But its humorous depiction of an unmarried career woman was kind of groundbreaking at the time — though the nose-less Cathy character was often insecure and angst-ridden. The 1950-born Guisewite told me that her comic covered the "four basic guilt groups: food, love, mother, and career."

Guisewite's mother helped launch her daughter's career by urging Cathy to seek syndication for her drawings. The younger Guisewite, an Ohio native who graduated from the University of Michigan, ended up signing with Universal Press in 1976.

By the way, there's no truth to the rumor that the cartoon Cathy's missing nose was laid off during a recession.

To complete a cartoonist-profile bonanza, I did a July 1983 story about "The Far Side" creator Gary Larson — a great guy whose shyness and modesty struck a chord in me. I deeply admire successful people who don't get too enamored with themselves.

Gary didn't invent the offbeat-cartoon genre, but he's a humor genius who popularized that genre in newspapers — inspiring the creation of many other "way-out" syndicated comics by the mid-'80s and seeing his "Far Side" client list eventually approach 1,900 papers. But at the time I interviewed Larson in '83, he had only 92 clients.

Many of Larson's surreal comic panels stick in readers' brains to this day. One cartoon I remember shows a suitcase-toting, sunglasses-wearing crocodile (or alligator?) emerging from a taxi to visit his niece and nephew in a swamp. One of the country crocs says: "Well, for crying out loud! It's Uncle Irwin from the city sewer!"

Gary — who loved putting anthropomorphic animals in his feature — himself traveled from Seattle to the Bay Area in 1979 to drop off his portfolio unsolicited at the *San Francisco Chronicle*. The cartoonist told me he then "wandered around San Francisco getting depressed and homesick" while waiting for a response to his work. It was quite a response: a five-year contract that included syndication via Chronicle Features starting in 1980.

"How did you feel about *that*?" I asked.

"Like Cinderella," Larson replied. "I've never been an assertive guy. If I hadn't gotten lucky as soon as I had, I probably wouldn't have been a cartoonist. I don't think I could have stood the rejection."

On such a tenuous string does creative immortality sometimes hang. I'm a fan of poet-turned-novelist Sir Walter Scott, and recall reading that he got less-than-encouraging comments after showing the first chapters of *Waverley* to someone he knew. So Scott stashed the partial book in a drawer, and stumbled upon it only by accident several years later. *Waverley* was published and became a smash hit, and Scott went on to write *Ivanhoe* and other classic novels.

It's hard to imagine a cartoonist today making an unannounced visit to a newspaper or syndicate and leaving with a contract. But the newspaper biz was less corporate in 1979, and Chronicle Features was the kind of smaller syndicate that would have trouble surviving as the 21st century grew closer. In fact, Chronicle was bought by the much larger Universal Press in 1997 — 13 years after Larson left Chronicle to join Universal.

"The Far Side" creator agonized over that 1984 decision, even seeking my advice over the phone; I was mostly noncommittal for "objective reporter" reasons.

But Universal possessed a much bigger sales force than Chronicle as well as the Andrews McMeel division that had already published two best-selling "Far Side" collections (and that employed the talented executive Tom Thornton, who Larson liked). Perhaps you have some "Far Side" anthologies on your shelves, because more than 40 million copies were eventually sold.

Larson was born in 1950, grew up in Washington state, and eventually drew cartoons for several Seattle-based publications — including the *Seattle Times*. Gary's weekly "Nature's Way" comic for the *Times* morphed into the daily "Far Side" after that fateful San Francisco trip.

Of the comics entering syndication in the 1980s, the three most-admired were "The Far Side," "Bloom County," and Bill Watterson's "Calvin and Hobbes." Those features had laughs, attitude, and art that ran the gamut from whimsical to brilliant. And I got to talk with the creators of two of them during my first months at *E&P*!

People I interviewed in 1983 often sent letters praising the writing and accuracy of my stories — which was balm to my shaky self-confidence. I always wrote back, just as I always returned phone calls and always gave out syndication advice and other info to those requesting it.

I wish more journalists would be as responsive when people contact them. It can help get or keep readers and, more importantly, it's the right thing to do.

Positive letters poured in despite — or perhaps partly because of — my somewhat shaky interviewing technique. Especially during those early days at *E&P*, my shyness often caused me to stammer out questions with many "ums" and "ahs." But that tended to put interview subjects at ease. Too many journalists come off as arrogant know-it-alls, which helps explain why a number of them have a popularity level somewhere between poison ivy and Satan.

"You have a great talent for helping people feel relaxed and conversational," was a much-appreciated compliment I once received from Jillian Gilliland, who beautifully illustrates the "Tell Me a Story" syndicated feature written and edited by Amy Friedman.

Whatever my verbal shortcomings, I thoroughly researched people and topics before doing interviews, and carefully prepared questions before asking the subjects of articles to tell me their story.

CHAPTER FOUR

Still 1983:
Mr. Will Finds a
Way to Shill

Did the previous chapter make it seem like I only interviewed cartoonists? That wasn't the case. Soon after my early summer talk with Gary Larson, I called columnist Carl Rowan — who was credited with helping to save the 1955-56 Montgomery Bus Boycott by none other than Martin Luther King. He also served in the Kennedy administration as deputy assistant secretary of state for public affairs and ambassador to Finland, and was with JFK the night before that fateful Texas trip.

"I remember specifically that after we talked about Finland I asked him why he was going to Dallas," Rowan told me. "A lot of mean and nasty things were being said about him down there. He said it was the president's job to set the mood for the nation, and that if the president didn't stand up against meanness and bigotry, who else would do it?"

If only JFK had also stood up against womanizing....

"How did you help save the bus boycott?" I asked Rowan, awed to be speaking with someone who was there at such a watershed moment.

"Well, I don't know if 'save' is the right word," he replied modestly. Then Rowan explained that he had sat in on a boycott planning meeting as a Minneapolis *Tribune* reporter and filed a story. A different story subsequently came over the wire reporting that three African-American ministers not involved in the planning had said the boycott was off. Rowan said he immediately phoned King, who responded: "What?!" King quickly called another meeting, and people were told the no-boycott story was wrong. The bus action that launched the modern civil-rights movement would happen.

The Tennessee-born Rowan (1925-2000) emphasized that covering poor people was important to him. "You really appreciate having written a word or two for somebody who can never say anything to Congress or the White House," noted the liberal commentator, who was a rare black columnist in the "mainstream media" at the time his feature began in 1965. That was after Rowan became class president and valedictorian of his high school, graduated from Oberlin College, earned a master's in journalism from the University of Minnesota, and worked for African-American newspapers in Minneapolis and St. Paul before joining the *Tribune*.

When I was a Rutgers student in 1973, I became interested in singer/actor/athlete/scholar/activist Paul Robeson — a 1919 Rutgers graduate shunned by the university for about 20 years after he was smeared during the McCarthy era. Learning about Robeson's life helped spark my interest in African-American history, and I ended up writing a long obituary of Robeson for the Rutgers *Targum* in 1976 before attending a funeral-home viewing the next day in New York City.

I was driven to Harlem by a *Targum* photographer who, somewhat inappropriately for the solemn occasion, played tapes of Bruce Springsteen's two pre-*Born to Run* albums in his car while giving me a full tutorial on the music of the then-young "Boss."

"You *gotta* listen to this!" John told me again and again, swerving the car in his excitement along the New Jersey Turnpike like a character in a Springsteen song.

"Uh-huh," was my murmured response, too timid to ask that the damn thing be turned off. I'm a Springsteen fan, but on that day I would have preferred to hear Robeson's stirring bass-baritone.

Though I obviously admired some people more than others, I strived at *E&P* to be objective (most of the time!). I interviewed plenty of conservative creators — including columnists Kathleen Parker and Cal Thomas, and editorial cartoonists Chuck Asay and Rick McKee — who liked my stories about them. For instance, after I did a 1983 profile of "Ethics & Religion" columnist Michael McManus, he wrote my editor to say: "If all of your empire is filled with people as competent — both in reporting and grace — as David Astor, *Editor & Publisher* is in for a new era of greatness." I can vouch that Mike's statement is correct in two ways: the spellings of my name and magazine.

Next on my 1983 story list was Heloise, who inherited the 1959-launched "Hints from Heloise" column from her late mother in 1977. But it was initially a reluctant continuation.

A few years prior to '77, mother had told daughter: "I'm going to retire, and then you're Heloise."

"I don't want to be Heloise," replied daughter, who was okay with her name but reluctant to take over the daily column on which she was helping. The 20-something assistant had seen how hard her mother worked keeping up with thousands of letters a week, appearing on TV, giving speeches, and writing books.

Then Heloise I died, and King Features Syndicate told Heloise II that it needed to issue a press release about the future of the column within 24 hours.

The possible heir apparent agonized, and finally told King: "I will do this for a year. But you cannot make me do TV shows, speeches, or a book. If I don't want to do the column after a year, we'll be done."

Heloise II went on to appear many times on TV, give countless speeches, and author more than a dozen books as she continued to "columnize" to the present day.

My 1983 interview with the "Hints" legend took place at the King Features apartment while the Texas-based Heloise was visiting New York City.

"Hi," I croaked, so nervous I might have sounded hoarse. A nobody like me was meeting Heloise, a household name in 500 newspapers!

"Why hel-lo, David!" she replied, as friendly and outgoing as can be. Meanwhile, I thought to myself: "I'm glad I can write well, or my nervousness would make syndicated people think I'm an idiot."

The prematurely gray Heloise — who was just three years older than the 1954-born me — discussed how she had retained many aspects of "mother's" feature (including household hints submitted by readers) while also putting her own stamp on things (such as introducing theme days — food, pets, etc. — and offering more advice for time-stressed women who work outside the home).

The "Hints" column has a utilitarian "how-to" vibe that only hints at how whip-smart and funny Heloise is. And I was impressed to learn in '83 that Heloise spent some of her free time piloting a hot-air balloon and riding dirt bikes.

"What can I tell you, David? I like to have fun," she said. Clearly, Heloise's knowledge of life encompasses more than using vinegar to remove stains.

By the way, the first Heloise's given name was Eloise, but the "H" was added for the alliteration with "Hints."

Also in 1983, I wrote about a widely read columnist involved in a major ethics flap (reporting on controversies was another staple of my E&P work). That columnist was George Will, the conservative pundit who entered syndication with the Washington Post Writers Group in 1974 at the tender age of 32.

The Illinois native also became a contributing columnist to Newsweek magazine in 1976 and is one of the few political columnists to ever hold a doctorate in politics (from Princeton University). Indeed, Will is an intellectual commentator who — like William F. Buckley Jr. — periodically uses big words that could flummox even the smartest reader.

Will's controversy? It was revealed in 1983 that he had helped prep Ronald Reagan for his 1980 debate with Jimmy Carter and then went on TV to tell viewers what a fine job Reagan had done.

Can you say "conflict of interest"? Eight of Will's 400 papers could: They dropped the column.

Will defended himself by stating that people knew he supported Reagan, that he gave minimal help to the Republican, and that columnists have a somewhat different relationship with politicians than reporters do. Reagan — who later told Soviet leader Mikhail Gorbachev to "tear down this wall" — was undoubtedly pleased that Will tore down this journalistic wall.

Gorbachev eventually wrote a syndicated column. Among the other non-journalist notables to do that during my E&P tenure were Benazir Bhutto, Jimmy Carter, Hillary Clinton, Bill Gates, Jesse Jackson, Coretta Scott King, Henry Kissinger, George McGovern, Chuck Norris, Oliver North, Mister

Rogers, and Martha Stewart. Even Pope John Paul II wrote a syndicated column — sort of. I'll explain that in a later chapter.

Many syndicates sign celebrities because they may have interesting insider insights and can be easier to sell in a corporate age where plenty of profit-conscious newspapers lack the patience to wait for a "no-name" feature to develop a following. But as *Daytona Beach* (Fla.) *News-Journal* columnist Mark Lane once told me, many celebrity columns are "deadly boring, grossly self-serving, and enjoy only short runs." I might add that these features — which leave less space for columns by trained journalists — are at times ghostwritten.

I do have to admit that some celebrity columnists are fabulous wordsmiths from another writing genre; author Isaac Asimov was one example.

Anyway, don't be surprised if the Obamas' Portuguese water dog starts opining for editorial pages one day!

CHAPTER FIVE

Still 1983: A Cartoon Clown on Death Row

Not every Spider-Man fan knows that the worldwide-web-slinging star of comic books and blockbuster movies also occupies newspaper space. Stan Lee, who co-created the superhero in the early 1960s, began writing "The Amazing Spider-Man" newspaper strip in 1977.

I nervously phoned the 60-year-old Lee six years later — in August 1983 — to ask why Spidey had found success as a syndicated star. "The big trap that some adventure strips fall into is that they concentrate just on adventure, with hollow characters going from one pitfall to another," the California-based Lee said in his enthusiastic voice. But Spider-Man, he added, "is treated like a real human being. I tried to give him the problems any normal guy would have."

After the *Editor & Publisher* story ran, Lee mailed me a Spider-Man poster and thank-you note. "I hope you've got some fading plaster on a wall somewhere that the poster might cover up for you," he quipped. Given that I was living in a cheap Brooklyn apartment poorly maintained by the landlord, this was a very practical gift!

Lee later sent me an original Sunday "Spider-Man" comic. The signed strip showed Spidey fighting a brute named "Destructo," who may have been one of the private-equity investors with a stake in *E&P*'s future parent company.

Lee — who also co-created iconic characters such as Iron Man, the X-Men, the Incredible Hulk, and the Fantastic Four — was born Stanley Lieber in New York City. During his long and varied career, he also served as a Marvel Comics executive and made cameo appearances in Hollywood films featuring characters such as Spider-Man.

The newspaper version of "Spider-Man" was among the last story strips successfully launched in comic sections dominated by "gag-a-day" features. Once a huge category — think "Brenda Starr," "Dick Tracy," "Gasoline Alley," "Little Orphan Annie," "Mary Worth," "Prince Valiant," "The Phantom," and the Dr. Nick Dallis-created "Apartment 3-G," "Judge Parker," and "Rex Morgan, M.D." — story strips have struggled in recent decades because profit-conscious newspapers shrank comics to reduce newsprint costs even though the funny pages are popular. (One of the alienate-our-readers moves newspapers excelled at.) This comic shrinkage left little room for the detailed art most story strips need.

"It's a major problem for the 'every wrinkle must show' school," was what "Terry and the Pirates"/"Steve Canyon" cartoonist Milton Caniff once told me.

Also, most modern-day Americans don't want to wait weeks for a plot payoff, and many readers don't see a newspaper every day — meaning they can miss parts of a story.

But some "gag-a-day" comics successfully include story lines. Among these hybrids are Lynn Johnston's "For Better or For Worse," Tom Batiuk's "Funky Winkerbean," and Greg Evans' "Luann." The first two cartoonists were rewarded with Pulitzer Prize finalist nods in 1994 and 2008, respectively.

It was also in 1983 that I met the Manhattan-based Jerry Robinson, who, like Stan Lee, was born in 1922.

Jerry started working on Batman comic books as a Columbia University journalism student in the late 1930s. The young Robinson created one of the great cartoon villains — the Joker, later brought to vivid life on movie screens by Jack Nicholson in 1989 and Heath Ledger in 2008 — before becoming a newspaper cartoonist, author, and founder of the Cartoonists & Writers Syndicate (eventually run by his son Jens) that has a roster of creators from dozens of countries.

"How'd you come up with the idea for the Joker?" I asked, tickled to be talking to a guy with an early connection to the Batman comic books I had read as kid.

"I wanted to create a protagonist worthy of Batman," replied Jerry. "In my reading of literature, every great hero had his opposite — David and Goliath, Sherlock Holmes and Moriarity. And I thought it would be interesting to have a villain with a sense of humor."

"How did you get the Joker's 'look'?"

"When I thought of the character, I searched frantically that night for a deck of cards."

I'm glad Pokemon cards didn't exist 70 years ago....

It should be noted that Bob Kane contended he and his Batman co-creator Bill Finger dreamed up the Joker (who made his comic book debut in 1940), with Robinson involved in the process. But I talked with Jerry many times over the years before his 2011 death, and believe he's telling the truth. Kane did acknowledge that Robinson coined the name Robin for Batman's sidekick — deriving that moniker not from Jerry's last name but from the Robin Hood stories Jerry read as a kid.

Meanwhile, back at the *E&P* office in September 1983, owner/editor Robert Brown "accepted the resignation" of longtime managing editor Jerry Walker "following a disagreement over policy," according to a tiny blurb in the magazine. Apparently, there were questions about whether or not Jerry had accepted some sort of paid trip.

Associate editor John Consoli was promoted to news editor, essentially replacing Walker, but with a different title. John, who would be a great supervisor, is a guy with a working-class background, a gruff persona, a good heart, and a penchant for tailgating at Jets football games.

By the way, the "New York" Jets actually play in New Jersey, thank you very much.

As Halloween approached, *E&P* donned a minor-redesign costume. Brown still wouldn't pay for an art/layout person, but he let the editorial staff tweak *E&P*'s look to allow for things like more white space. There was still little color art, though, meaning the magazine continued to resemble an 8x11-inch piano keyboard.

"What do you think?" I asked a couple of United Feature Syndicate publicity people with whom I was having lunch.

They looked carefully at the Oct. 29 issue. "Um … it looks a little less ugly," said Julia.

High praise, indeed.

Then it was Halloween, when I had my first date with a woman who worked as an editorial-production person at a publishing house. We met in a Greenwich Village restaurant after having connected by mail though a group called Single Booklovers. I do indeed love single (and multi-volume) books — including novels by Margaret Atwood, Balzac, Charlotte Bronte, Willa Cather, Margaret Drabble, Alexandre Dumas, Hawthorne, Barbara Kingsolver, Melville, L.M. Montgomery, Erich Maria Remarque, J.K. Rowling (Harry Potter!), Steinbeck, Twain, Edith Wharton, and Zola. None of whom, alas, created a comic strip with cute talking animals.

Anyway, I was living in Brooklyn, my date was living in Queens, we were dining in Manhattan, and soon I was in … love (or thought so). For an unconfident person like myself, the fact that she seemed interested in me and laughed at my jokes were big things. Plus she was well-read, intelligent, reasonably good-looking, and shared my liberal politics.

"What do you think of Reagan?" she asked over dinner.

"I suppose I'd like him if I was rich. What about you?"

"I *hate* him."

"I can't believe he invaded a tiny country like Grenada," I said. "What a bully."

"Yeah." (Silence for a few moments.) "Isn't the Village Halloween parade great?" she asked.

"Absolutely. I saw one guy dressed as the Chrysler Building!"

So we each liked the Halloween parade and disliked Reagan. How's that for compatibility?

I also liked her great cats: the confident calico Gwyneth and the shy "tortie" Samantha.

And I enjoy crosswords, so it was fun to interview *New York Times* puzzle editor Eugene Maleska in November 1983. I opened the story with Maleska's anecdote about 40 of his puzzles being rejected by the old *New York Herald Tribune*. Finally, a puzzle no better than the first 40 was accepted. Maleska called the paper to find out why, and learned that a new puzzle editor had just been hired. "She told me, 'I think what happened is that the previous editor thought you were so good that you were plagiarizing!'"

As the end of 1983 neared, several newspapers got upset by allegedly controversial comics — a frequent occurrence at American dailies afraid of offending readers even though these readers could see much starker material in other media. For instance, Indiana's *Fort Wayne News-Sentinel* pulled a "Far Side" panel picturing a clown being walked to the electric chair as a cop next to him laments, "I don't think I'll be able to tell the kids about this one." It was just a joke!

In December 1983, I took my first *E&P* vacation after finally collecting a very un-European total of just five days off. I and my cousin Gary Blatt — a smart, sensitive, thoughtful person I liked immensely — headed to Mexico where one of the highlights was clambering up the stunning Mayan pyramid at Chichen Itza. For a journalist accustomed to writing news stories in an "inverted pyramid" format, this monument was stunningly pointy-side-up!

CHAPTER SIX

1984:
From George Orwell
to Richard Nixon

As the year began, many commentators said things weren't as bad in the real 1984 as they were in George Orwell's *1984*. That stunning insight was debunked by humorist Russell Baker.

"Orwell didn't foresee the hot tub. No one dreamed there'd be a day when Californians would boil themselves like so many overcooked cabbages," the syndicated *New York Times* columnist informed attendees at a Jan. 9 dinner in New York City's posh Pierre Hotel.

Earlier that month, I reported that *Today* show co-host Jane Pauley gave birth to twins in late December 1983. What did that have to do with newspaper syndication? Well, Pauley was and is married to Garry Trudeau, whose "Doonesbury" comic was on sabbatical at the time. Strangely enough, the twins' arrival didn't get mentioned on any celebrity Web sites. Was it because Web sites didn't exist yet? Beats me.

Meanwhile, syndicated *Chicago Sun-Times* columnist Mike Royko jumped to the *Chicago Tribune* because his newspaper was being acquired by lowbrow media magnate Rupert Murdoch. Given that the feisty Royko wasn't exactly highbrow himself, this was telling. "A man has a right to work for whom he wants to, and I don't want to work for Mr. Murdoch," he snapped. Luckily for Royko, the Murdoch-owned Fox News wasn't around in 1984 to demonize the columnist in a "fair and balanced" way.

You may have noticed that the three syndicated creators mentioned so far in this chapter are white men. Indeed, *Editor & Publisher*'s 1984 pages were full of white editors, white publishers, white reporters, and white space (under the headlines). So I tried to diversify my piece of E&P real estate by writing about the relatively small number of women and people of color creating syndicated cartoons and opinion columns.

For instance, I did a February piece about the sparse African-American presence in the funny pages. Out of the 200-plus comics with major syndicates, I could find only three black cartoonists: Morrie Turner ("Wee Pals"), Brumsic Brandon Jr. ("Luther"), and Ted Shearer ("Quincy"). Interestingly, all entered syndication between 1965 and 1970 — during and soon after the civil rights era.

"Was it a coincidence that the three of you were signed within those five years?" I asked Turner, pretty sure it wasn't.

"Comics only reflect what's going on around us," replied the 1923-born creator, who worked as a freelance cartoonist (among other jobs) for many years before his "Wee Pals" strip was launched by the Lew Little Syndicate in 1965. "We were there at the right time. I think that period is over."

The civil rights era did make editors more conscious about diversifying their media content, but it took the tragic 1968 assassination of Martin Luther King for "Wee Pals" to get a big increase in newspaper clients. Not a sales technique any sane person would recommend.

Of course, there were many talented black cartoonists in the U.S. at that time, but most didn't get past the syndicate and newspaper gatekeepers. One reason "Wee Pals," "Luther," and "Quincy" *did* was that all starred children.

"Black kids are much less threatening than black adults to white editors and readers," Brandon explained to me. "It's a shame it's that way."

There were also great black cartoonists earlier in the 20th century who worked mostly for the African-American press. They included Jackie Ormes and Oliver Harrington — the second of whom you'll "meet" later in this book.

It should also be noted that, by 1984, some white cartoonists had added black characters less stereotypical than the few non-white characters seen on comic pages decades before.

Black cartoonists were so scarce in newspapers that a reader assumed the Oakland, Calif.-based Turner was white when criticizing him for putting an alleged Confederate-style hat on one of his kid characters. "Get to know black people," urged the critic. Turner replied, "I know two black people: my mother and father!"

Also in 1984, I did stories about a number of female creators, including syndicated *Boston Globe* opinion columnist Ellen Goodman, "Sylvia" cartoonist Nicole Hollander (whose comic stars a feisty 50-something woman), and "For Better or For Worse" creator Lynn Johnston (already well on her way to becoming the mostly widely read female cartoonist ever).

Goodman, a 1980 Pulitzer Prize winner whose column ran in 375 newspapers in '84, was known for her feminist views and for fusing personal commentary with the political. The Radcliffe College graduate started her journalism career at *Newsweek* magazine in 1963, and told me that "women back then were usually put in the research department with the 'girls' while men were given the chance to be reporters."

The 1941-born Goodman did go on to become a reporter at the *Detroit Free Press* in 1965 before moving to the *Globe* in 1967 and starting her column in 1974.

Hollander related her struggle to get male newspaper editors to accept "Sylvia" — a struggle summed up in this anecdote: A syndicate salesman brought "Sylvia" samples to a *Detroit Free Press* editor, who said they weren't funny. Then the salesman begged the editor to show the strips to (female) clerical staffers. They laughed uproariously, which embarrassed the editor into buying "Sylvia." Then he never published it!

Johnston's 1979-launched "For Better or For Worse" was published in nearly 700 newspapers in 1984 and more than 2,000 papers by the time the new millennium rolled around.

Why did the Canadian's comic become so popular? "FBorFW" — via its semi-autobiographical focus on the Patterson family — addressed the universal themes of marriage, parenting, and the work/home juggling act with a realistic approach leavened by expert humor and storytelling.

I asked Johnston during the 1984 interview to expound more on her comic's realism, which was buttressed by art that became increasingly detailed over the years. "Elly and John [Patterson] sometimes yell at each other, and the children don't always say impossibly clever things," she said. "I try to make it believable — showing the bad stuff with the good stuff."

Good stuff? Bad stuff? I bet you're no longer wondering why the comic was named "For Better or For Worse"!

Most cartoonists I interviewed told me they started drawing very young, and Johnston had one of the nicest stories in that realm. When she was three, Lynn complained to her mother that her father didn't buy something she wanted during a trip to the store. Her mother didn't understand what Lynn was talking about until the young artist drew a very realistic picture of a folding comb!

The 1947-born Johnston eventually got more cartooning experience in a Michelangelo sort of way. When pregnant with her first child in 1972, she complained to the obstetrician about having nothing to do while lying on the examining table. Johnston said there should at least be pictures on the ceiling — and the doctor challenged her to draw some. Those sketches led to a book, then two more books, and then an offer from Universal Press Syndicate to create a comic.

One other thing that made "FBorFW" popular: The characters aged, which is rare in comic-land. I'm feeling older myself as I look at the photo of Lynn that ran with my 1984 story, because there's an electric typewriter in the background! Remember those? When it was time to "cut and paste," you actually needed scissors and glue!

I needed a train ticket to visit the Rye Brook, N.Y-based Museum of Cartoon Art in the summer of '84 to do a 10th-anniversary story about the institution "Beetle Bailey" creator Mort Walker founded to help make the public think of comics as the important art form they are.

One thing I remember was seeing interesting things on some of the museum's original art. Mort told me the scorch marks on "Dick Tracy" comics were there because Chester Gould often met his deadlines only by holding the strips over a burner to make the ink dry faster. And Walt Kelly put notes on his "Pogo" comics asking, say, an engraver to pay up a small bet on a baseball game!

But I didn't yet have the knack for small talk. When Walker drove me and his cartoonist/cartoon historian son Brian to lunch, I could barely think of anything to say.

"You do a great job with the syndicate section," said Mort conversationally as he turned to glanced at me in the backseat. "What did you do before *E&P*?"

"Um ... writing and stuff," I replied.

Walker was an extremely friendly guy for someone so famous in the cartoon world. Born in Kansas in 1923, Mort sold his first drawing at age 12 and eventually became a popular magazine cartoonist after serving in World War II and graduating from the University of Missouri. He went on to start "Beetle Bailey" in 1950 and "Hi and Lois" (with Dik Browne) in 1954, create several other strips, and write a number of books about comics.

"Beetle Bailey" was among the strips that topped a "most widely syndicated" survey I did in 1984. "Peanuts" was first with 1,941 newspapers worldwide, "Blondie" second with about 1,900, "Beetle" third with 1,660, "Garfield" fourth with 1,508, and "Hagar the Horrible" fifth with 1,475. (Soon after, "Peanuts" became the first comic to reach 2,000 papers — with "Blondie," "Garfield," "Dilbert," "For Better or For Worse," and "Calvin and Hobbes" also cracking that barrier in subsequent years.)

The most widely syndicated editorial cartoonists were Pat Oliphant (about 500 papers) and Jeff MacNelly (about 400). And the top columnists were advice-givers Abigail Van Buren (1,000-plus papers for "Dear Abby") and Ann Landers (800-plus), investigative journalist Jack Anderson (794 for "Washington Merry-Go-Round"), and humorists Erma Bombeck (700-plus) and Art Buchwald (nearly 600). Yes, if you include Dave Barry and the 500-plus papers he would later amass, a widely syndicated humorist apparently needs a last name that starts with "B"!

I was thrilled when my survey was mentioned in *USA Today*, *The Washington Post*, and other publications.

Meanwhile, my girlfriend and I had been dating since that Halloween dinner the previous fall, and things were getting serious. (I had even discovered that Gwyneth the cat liked to burrow under the bedcovers and Samantha the cat liked to lick just-shampooed hair almost as much as drinking tomato juice!)

But I also had some nagging doubts throughout 1984 about how compatible my girlfriend and I were. For instance, she had a lot of credit-card debt when we met, watched way more TV (I didn't even *own* a TV), and was often abrupt with her mother — a mostly sweet person who, admittedly, was difficult to be around because of her chronic complaining and pessimism. To paraphrase that *Star Trek: Voyager* line about the civilization-gobbling Borg, my girlfriend's mother wouldn't know fun if she assimilated an amusement park.

Mort Walker, Dik Browne (seated), and Dave Astor at a 1984 party celebrating the 30th anniversary of Mort and Dik's "Hi and Lois" comic strip. Photo credit: King Features Syndicate.

But I had never had a very successful dating life, and my girlfriend seemed to love me. So I proposed, and she accepted. That was on March 29, 1984 — the day I turned 30.

Two days later, the 1884-founded *E&P* published a huge 100th-anniversary issue — which had been assembled by some Temple University people with help from non-editorial *E&P*ers. Our newsroom staff was deemed too small to handle the supplement along with our usual duties — a kindness that wouldn't have been extended to the small *E&P* staff of the 2000s.

Another 1984 milestone was the 50th anniversary of the launch of "Terry and the Pirates," which Milton Caniff did from 1934 to 1946. As noted in Chapter 2, Caniff gave up his classic adventure strip because he didn't own the rights to it. But Caniff was so well-regarded for his dramatic storytelling, exotic Asian locales, memorable characters (including the Dragon Lady), detailed yet evocative art, and cinematic techniques (close-ups, long shots, angle shots, etc.) that 125 newspapers bought his 1947-launched "Steve Canyon" comic ... sight unseen!

To give you an idea of Caniff's fame back in the day, he was featured on the cover of *Time* magazine in '47. And among his many admirers were Jimmy Stewart, Lyndon Johnson, John Steinbeck, Clare Boothe Luce, and Edward, Duke of Windsor.

Anyway, I did a 1984 interview with Caniff in his Manhattan workspace at 333 East 45th Street. The large room contained several model airplanes (Steve Canyon was an Air Force pilot and Caniff knew Orville Wright). There were also *tons* of books, many of which the cartoonist used for his obsessive fact-checking in those pre-Google days.

"What do you think of 'Doonesbury' and 'Bloom County'?" I asked, a little provocatively but in a deferential tone. I expected the 77-year-old, conservative-leaning cartoonist not to be a big fan of those contemporary, liberal comics.

"I enjoy them," the open-minded, gentlemanly Caniff replied. "Political strips make waves, which is good for all of us. If people argue about a strip in a bar, at least they're talking about comics."

By the 1980s, Caniff was doing "Steve Canyon" with the assistance of Richard Rockwell (nephew of Norman) and Shel Dorf (founder of San Diego's wildly popular Comic-Con event). Caniff himself helped found the National Cartoonists Society in 1946, when it emerged from the collaboration of Milt and other creators who visited and drew for wounded American soldiers during World War II.

Caniff (1907-1988) was an Ohio native and Ohio State alum who initially wondered whether to pursue acting or cartooning as a career. He moved to New York City in 1932, and became an Associated Press artist working on features such as the "Dickie Dare" comic. After leaving AP, he created the "Terry and the Pirates" strip that would rocket him to fame.

Remember my Chapter 4 mention of eight newspapers dropping columnist George Will after he helped Ronald Reagan prep for the 1980 presidential debate and then praised the future president's performance? In 1984, the New York *Daily News* reinstated Will. "I missed the column," one of the paper's editors, James Wieghart, told me.

Yup, the "liberal media."

I also phoned Will for a reaction. Given that I'm no fan of his, I should have been relaxed. But Will is such a big pooh-bah that my voice quavered anyway.

"Um ... this is Dave Astor of *E&P* ... of *Editor & Publisher*. I cover syndication for *Editor & Publisher*." [Sheesh, I told myself, have I mentioned the name of my magazine enough?] "Why do you feel the *Daily News* brought your column back?"

"Maybe New Yorkers had suffered enough," smoothly quipped Will, who further joked that *Daily News* readers were forced to "mimeograph my columns at night in dark basements and read them surreptitiously."

Mimeograph? Boy, technology sure has changed since 1984. Back then, *E&P* staffers wrote stories at out-of-town meetings on Radio Shack TRS-80 portable computers (which had tiny eight-line screens) and then transmitted the articles into *E&P*'s publishing system by attaching "couplers" to a phone receiver.

Another conservative — former President Richard Nixon! — wrote a letter to *E&P* that was published in the May 5 issue. Several weeks earlier, an *E&P* editorial took issue with this 1984 Nixon comment about the media: "I never had them with me." The editorial — written, as always, by owner Robert Brown — noted that daily newspapers had overwhelmingly endorsed Nixon for president in 1968 over Hubert Humphrey and in 1972 over George McGovern. That continued a trend of the Republican candidate almost always getting the most newspaper endorsements — even during FDR's four presidential campaigns.

Yup, the "liberal media."

Anyway, Nixon wrote in his letter: "I should have been more precise in my observation about the media. I was not referring to editorial support but primarily to television reporters and a number of newspaper reporters."

If you're waiting for me to joke that Nixon's letter wasn't a "piece with honor," that ain't happening....

Another president — this time a future one — popped up in my syndicate section in August 1984. The *Arkansas Democrat* had a cat named Otus who "wrote" a column, and I ran an item with a photo showing the feline with Arkansas Gov. Bill Clinton. "I didn't inhale," said Otus as he explained a catnip incident to Clinton, or maybe I made that up.

The following month, "Doonesbury" cartoonist Garry Trudeau returned from his 21-month sabbatical. His Universal Press Syndicate comic had originally started in 1970, soon after the 1948-born Trudeau graduated from Yale University — where his "Bull Tales" college strip was a precursor to "Doonesbury."

When the New York native reentered syndication in 1984, several of his 800 papers dropped the often-topical comic because it spoofed the Republican presidential ticket. This happened even though Ronald Reagan and George H.W. Bush held a large lead over Walter Mondale and Geraldine Ferraro as the election neared.

Yup, the "liberal media."

Actually, Trudeau has noted on several occasions that "Doonesbury" is "basically about the characters" — even though his usually liberal commentary gets the most publicity.

Controversy also arose when Trudeau and his syndicate asked newspaper clients to print the returning "Doonesbury" 44 picas wide rather than the 38.6 picas typical at the time. Trudeau argued that all comics used to run at least 44 picas, and added: "It's self-defeating — and not a little ironic — that at a time when newspapers face their greatest threat from television and other visual media, they have moved to reduce the one area of genuine pictorial interest in their pages."

As cartoonist/writer Jules Feiffer once told me, "Strips used to be a glorious size." A size, by the way, that made the comics easier to enjoy for the many older readers of newspapers.

But perhaps most puzzling of all was the conundrum of the universe expanding while the funnies were shrinking.

Were newspapers chastened by Trudeau's 1984 statement? Nope. Some dropped the bigger "Doonesbury," and most papers to this day shrink comics to save on newsprint costs.

Yup, the profit-driven media.

"Doonesbury" returned Sept. 30, the same day E&P moved its Manhattan office from Lexington Avenue at East 51st Street to West 19th Street near Fifth Avenue, where the magazine would remain until 2000. The last profile I wrote at the old office was of Christian Science Monitor columnist Richard Strout, who, at 86, had been around almost as long as E&P. He even covered a 1923 press conference held by President Harding, who tried to speed things up by telling the reporters: "Be nice to me, gentlemen. I want to play golf."

Strout also accompanied Secretary of Commerce Herbert Hoover to a 1927 demonstration of television, and recalled that a New York Times subhead the next day said of TV: "Commercial Use in Doubt."

Two movie reviewers who appeared together on TV — Roger Ebert of the Chicago Sun-Times and Gene Siskel of the Chicago Tribune — spoke and bantered at a fall Newspaper Features Council meeting in the Windy City.

It was the first out-of-town meeting I covered for *E&P*, and I was terrified about having to introduce myself to dozens of attendees connected with the syndication world. I practically hyperventilated in my hotel room before forcing my shy self to go to the first session.

One thing Ebert and Siskel said is that movie stars should be asked tougher questions, and that some of them even enjoy the non-softball approach. "It wakes them up," said Siskel. "They go out of automatic pilot." Not a bad lesson for a newspaper press that would become so corporatized that it didn't ask George W. Bush tough enough questions before he invaded Iraq in 2003 or ask financial bigwigs tough enough questions before they melted down the U.S. economy in 2008.

The 1942-born Ebert is an Illinois native who became a film critic for the *Sun-Times* when he was in his mid-20s — and the first movie reviewer to win a Pulitzer Prize for criticism, in 1975. Ebert, who lost his voice 30 years later because of cancer, has also authored more than 15 books — including a 2011-released memoir.

Siskel (1946-1999) was a Chicago native who joined the *Tribune* in 1969. Six years later, he began the TV partnership with Ebert that would last until Siskel's death.

Getting reimbursed for trips such as my Chicago one was relatively painless in 1984. You could easily get a cash advance for taxis and meals, and — when you returned — the simple expense form took no more than 10 minutes to fill out. Then you were reimbursed quickly by an *E&P* accounting person sitting in an office just yards away. Dealing with expense reports a couple of decades later at a corporate-owned *E&P*? Read about that nightmare later in this book.

It was also simpler getting pens, reporters' pads, etc., in the 1980s and '90s. You just walked into the mailroom and asked Arthur Dale or Mentor Begolli to open the supply cabinet with something we liked to call a key. Getting supplies in the 2000s? You can read about that later, too.

By the time 1984 ended, I had received dozens of letters complimenting my stories — and my favorites included the first two of 11 handwritten notes Milton Caniff would send me before his health declined in early 1988. One of the '84 letters wryly praised a piece I did about the shrinking size of comics: "Thanks for giving such a good play to the SOS from the Titanic! I don't know how many angels can dance on the head of a pin, but it is tough to illustrate it." In the other letter, Caniff said the profile I did of him was "great" and that "I am grateful to you."

Perhaps the greatest continuity-comic cartoonist of all time grateful to *me*? The always-gracious Caniff was being way too kind, but it was another early brick in the foundation of my increasing confidence.

CHAPTER SEVEN

1985:
'Peanuts' is 35
and 'Calvin' is
Born

My *Editor & Publisher* job may have been making me more confident, but not confident enough to seriously consider calling off the wedding my fiancée and I planned for Jan. 12 at the United Nations Chapel in Manhattan.

One episode that upset me the previous month involved a mentally ill male relative of mine who was staying overnight in the Sunnyside, Queens, apartment my fiancée and I now shared. The relative was a difficult person to be with back then, but she treated him so coldly that I ended up taking the subway to Manhattan the following morning with him rather than her. I switched to a different train at Grand Central Station, but kept the same fiancée.

Then there was a cosmic hint that marrying my fiancée might not be the best idea: Our planned reception site — a Ukrainian restaurant in Manhattan's East Village — had a major fire just weeks before the wedding. Fate was trying to "friend" and "tweet" me, long before Facebook and Twitter were invented. But the phonograph in my mind was still playing that '70s song "Too Late to Turn Back Now."

The reception ended up being held in another Ukrainian restaurant a few blocks away. Great food at reasonable prices. Given that my fiancée and I paid for everything, at least our newly joined bank accounts would live in wedded bliss.

Then it was off to Spain for a two-week honeymoon. We essentially ran out of things to talk about after a couple days, but got along okay. One couldn't be unhappy eating delicious but cheap paella (the exchange rate was very favorable for Americans back then) and visiting great places like Granada — with its awesome Alhambra complex on a hill that soared directly above our hotel.

My honeymoon would be the last time I traveled to Europe until 2004, but it wasn't the first time. After never leaving the U.S. before turning 25, I scraped together enough money to visit London, Paris, Rome, Florence, Venice, and other cities for a whirlwind two weeks in 1979 — flying to England on the budget Laker Airways, riding trains from place to place via a Eurail pass, and flying back to the U.S. from Luxembourg on Icelandair. During a brief stop in Reykjavik Airport, I learned the tricky spelling of where I was: a-i-r-p-o-r-t.

The trip was a solo one, and I was nervous as hell when ordering cheap meals and booking a hostel bed or tiny hotel room in countries where I didn't know the language (though the language in England sounded vaguely familiar).

I flew to Europe again in 1980, took the train to Canada in 1981, and then joined a tour group of about a dozen people for a 15-day stay in the Soviet

Union in 1982. (My reason for going was all about the "c" word — curiosity, not communism.) The most memorable moment back in the USSR was seeing the waxen-looking Vladimir in Lenin's Tomb after waiting on line in Moscow's Red Square for five hours — which was about the same amount of time I stood to get a ticket to one of those legendary Clash concerts at Bond's in Manhattan the previous year. Both the Clash and the Soviet Union eventually broke up.

When my new wife and I were in Spain for two weeks, how did my section of *E&P* get filled? The first week, I used a freelancer and the second week, a fellow staffer pitched in. This is hardly worth mentioning except to compare it with the situation at a corporate-owned *E&P* a couple decades later, when I had to scramble to do sections in advance before going on vacations. More about that on the other side of the millennium.

One of the stories I wrote soon after my 1985 honeymoon focused on a sex survey conducted by syndicated *Chicago Sun-Times* columnist Ann Landers. You could tell how widely read the advice maven was, because 100,000 women responded when asked if they would "be content to be held close and treated tenderly, and forget about 'the act.'" More than 70% said yes. This inspired syndicated *Chicago Tribune* columnist Mike Royko to do a poll of his own, with 66% of 10,000 respondents saying they preferred sex over … bowling.

Landers was born in 1918, when surveys about "the act" were not exactly a staple of feature sections. Ann and her also widely read twin sister — "Dear Abby" columnist Abigail Van Buren — were influential in making matters such as sex, homosexuality, and divorce acceptable topics of tolerant discussion in daily newspapers.

"Ann Landers" was a pen name used by *Sun-Times* columnist Ruth Crowley starting in the 1940s. Eppie Lederer — the person we now know as Landers — took over the name and column in 1955. Soon, she achieved wide popularity with her no-nonsense advice.

There was no hanky-panky in "The Family Circus" comic that turned 25 in March 1985. Bil (not Bill) Keane's feature was G-rated, warm, and often sentimental, yet genuinely funny within those confines.

I did a phone interview with Keane to mark his comic's silver anniversary, and also saw him periodically at meetings of the National Cartoonists Society or Newspaper Features Council (an organization of cartoonists, columnists, syndicate executives, and newspaper editors). Bil often spoke at those gatherings, and I remember my initial shock when he made hilariously sarcastic comments one never saw in "The Family Circus." Keane's humor brain definitely had two sides.

For instance, Keane had this to say about a profit-minded syndicate executive: "He came out to visit us one day, and we said 'our house is your house.' So he sold it."

Keane partly based his comic on the large family he raised with Australia native Thelma Carne, who Bil met during his World War II service.

"What did your kids think of being in the comic?" I asked Keane.

"They liked it, and reveled in it," he replied. But Bil did admit that his children were sometimes embarrassed, as when the three-year-old Jeffy character was shown sucking his thumb while the actual Jeff Keane was in college. For some reason, the real-life Keane kids aged even though their cartoon alter egos did not.

And did you know the round-shaped "Family Circus" was originally called "The Family Circle" for six months in 1960? Keane changed the name after *Family Circle* magazine threatened a lawsuit.

Before starting his iconic comic, the 1922-born Keane worked as a staff artist for the old *Philadelphia Bulletin* and created the TV-themed "Channel Chuckles" syndicated cartoon. The Philadelphia native moved to Arizona in 1959 — a year before "The Family Circus" was launched.

Back in 1985, a *very* early example of comics entering the computer age happened in March when Jeff Danziger put Apple Macintosh-generated type in his newspaper-themed "McGonigle of the Chronicle" strip. Danziger, also an editorial cartoonist, printed out the type and pasted it on.

Before the digital age hurt newspaper circulation and ad revenue, papers made tons of money. Also, there were many cities in the mid-'80s that still had two competing dailies. So there were lots of comic and column sales for syndicates, and lots of *E&P* ads purchased by syndicates and newspapers with money to burn. One result was *E&P*'s ad-laden May 4, 1985, issue — which contained a whopping 156 pages.

In that same magazine, I reported on the National Cartoonists Society event that saw the top-cartoonist Reuben Award go to Brant Parker for his work drawing the Johnny Hart-written "Wizard of Id." I brought my camera to that Manhattan dinner in the hopes of giving my "Syndicates" section a livelier look — putting black-and-white film in my Minolta X-700 because *E&P* still wasn't using much color back then even though *USA Today* and various other newspapers were.

I had to really steel my nerves to ask various cartoonists and syndicate executives if it was okay to take their picture. I mean, I was doing them a favor by putting their faces in *E&P*, but my bashfulness — while somewhat less than it was two years before — made me feel like I was imposing on *them*.

One person I approached was Jeff MacNelly, the "Shoe" comic creator and conservative *Chicago Tribune* editorial cartoonist who had won his third Pulitzer Prize just weeks before. Jeff had received the first of those Pulitzers while working for Virginia's *Richmond News-Leader* in 1972, when he was just 24!

"Can I take a photo of you, Mr. MacNelly?" I asked.

He looked at me sardonically, like I was some sort of wimp. "Just shoot the damn picture," said the powerfully-built cartoonist, but he was smiling.

I ended up publishing 20 photos. One pictured a young Jerry Scott, then a little-known cartoonist doing the late Ernie Bushmiller's "Nancy" comic but later the co-creator of "Baby Blues" (with Rick Kirkman) and "Zits" (with Jim Borgman). Those last two strips each eventually amassed more than 1,000 newspapers — making Scott one of the few cartoonists to have two four-digit-client features. Others included Johnny Hart ("B.C."/"The Wizard of Id"), Mort Walker ("Beetle Bailey"/"Hi and Lois"), and Dik Browne ("Hi and Lois"/"Hagar the Horrible").

Later in 1985, the American Association of Sunday and Feature Editors (AASFE) met in San Francisco — where "Doonesbury" cartoonist Garry Trudeau made a rare speaking appearance.

Trudeau, who had recently satirized Frank Sinatra's alleged Mafia ties after the singer received the Medal of Freedom from President Reagan, responded to Sinatra's charge that he'd been unfair. "Satirists are supposed to be unfair," said the cartoonist, noting that criticizing them for that is like criticizing "a 260-pound lineman for being physical." More than a quarter-century later, I'm stunned by that statement … linemen used to be only 260 pounds?!

The "Doonesbury" creator also said he didn't enjoy controversy because it's "enormously distracting" to his work. "If I wanted publicity so much, I would have granted more than two interviews in the past 12 years," he added.

"Bloom County" cartoonist Berkeley Breathed also spoke at the San Francisco gathering. Though I didn't see Breathed and Trudeau interact with my own eyes, I was told by several attendees that the usually good-natured Trudeau wasn't that friendly to his fellow cartoonist because he was annoyed that early "Bloom County" strips had a somewhat similar style to "Doonesbury" before Breathed made his comic more unique.

Millions of fans thought "Peanuts" was unique, and I got to meet its creator for the first time during the Newspaper Features Council meeting that immediately preceded the AASFE confab. I interviewed Charles Schulz in the lobby of San Francisco's Mark Hopkins Hotel (with my wife taking photos), so I was nervous not only to be talking with the cartooning legend but to be doing it in a public place as gawkers gawked on by. If I hadn't gained a little confidence during my two-plus years at *E&P*, my anxiety would have required much more expensive therapy than what Lucy offered in her five-cent psychiatric booth.

Schulz was a long way from San Francisco when he was born in Minneapolis in 1922 (the year Bil Keane, "Spider-Man" legend Stan Lee, and the Joker creator Jerry Robinson also came into the world). The only child of a barber dad, Schulz wanted to be a cartoonist from a very young age.

After serving in World War II, the future superstar drew a weekly comic for the *St. Paul Pioneer Press* and also contributed to the *Saturday Evening*

Post magazine. Finally, after many rejections, Schulz signed with United Feature Syndicate and saw "Peanuts" launch in a mere seven newspapers in 1950. But before the decade ended, Schulz was a *very* widely read cartoonist.

As I sat down to interview Schulz in 1985, I observed that he wore his trademark patterned sweater under his trademark sport jacket while also "wearing" his trademark humility — though I would learn over the years that there was lots of pride, self-assurance, and competitiveness behind the insecure persona. After all, "Peanuts" was the most famous and successful comic of all time — breaking new ground with its uncluttered look and sophisticated content that expertly mixed humor and pathos. Then there were all those TV specials and licensed products such as greeting cards for almost every event except the word "trademark" appearing three times at the start of this paragraph.

One self-deprecating anecdote Schulz told me involved him sketching Snoopy on the blackboard for a kindergarten class in Las Vegas. One tot responded: "Can't you draw a better one than that?"

The 1950-launched "Peanuts" was turning 35 that October, and I asked Schulz why his comic had been successful for so long. One reason: "Pacing is very important," said the cartoonist, explaining that he used lots of dialogue in some episodes and very little in others, highlighted different characters on different days, etc.

"Why doesn't 'Peanuts' have any adult characters?"

"They would bang their heads against the top of the comic."

"Why do you do all your own drawing, inking, and lettering when some other famous cartoonists have assistants?"

"I'm a purist."

"Do you ever use anyone else's ideas?"

"Almost never," replied Schulz, though he did recall putting the words of one of his five children in the mouth of Linus when the blanket-clutching character asked: "If you hold your hands upside down, do you get the opposite of what you pray for?"

Schulz also told me he disliked the "Peanuts" name that United gave his formerly titled "Li'l Folks" comic. "'Peanuts' sounds too inconsequential," he explained.

I concluded the interview by asking Schulz if his comic would continue after he retired or died. "When I quit, the strip goes," he said emphatically.

As you'll see in this book's 2000 chapter, that didn't quite happen.

Soon after the story ran, I received a letter with a return address of One Snoopy Place in Santa Rosa, Calif. Schulz wrote, in part: "I think you did a beautiful job with the *Editor & Publisher* interview. You got all the quotes right and you blended the little anecdotes in very well."

Well, that made my day. I felt like Charlie Brown would feel if he ever got to kick the football Lucy always yanked away, because "extra points" had been added to my fragile self-esteem.

Looking back, I'm thankful that I was able to polish and fuss over the Schulz story for several days before it was published. In today's Web era, I probably would have run back to my hotel room to get the article online within an hour or two. In that scenario, the story would not have been as good — and the note from Schulz might not have been as complimentary. And if his thank-you note had been emailed rather than postal-mailed, I wouldn't now have Schulz's slightly shaky signature in my possession.

Also, if I had written the story in San Francisco during that pre-Web era, one of the few ways to get it back to New York would've been to fold it into a paper airplane and hurl it east out the hotel window. I doubt it would've made it past Kansas.

Schulz's letter was one of more than 40 very positive mailings I received that year from creators, syndicate executives, and others. Forty doesn't seem like a huge number, but it obviously takes longer to write and send postal letters than emails that can be dashed off as fast as Rickey Henderson stole bases back then.

Also in 1985, News America Syndicate launched a weekly column by ... Pope John Paul II! When I first heard this, I had visions of a pontiff pundit tapping on a video display terminal with a press pass rakishly pinned to his skullcap. But, alas, things were more prosaic. The NAS-distributed "column" consisted of the pope's writings edited into newspaper-sized chunks by a Roman Catholic scholar.

Soon after the feature began in more than 200 newspapers worldwide, the Vatican press office condemned it for using John Paul II's name as a "journalistic byline" for "commercial purposes." Had the pope not approved the feature? Did he have second thoughts? No one would say. But the problem was resolved when the title was changed from "Observations by Pope John Paul II" to "Selected Observations of Pope John Paul II" to reflect the fact that the pontiff was not actually writing the column each week. And NAS President Rick Newcombe visited the Vatican to meet the pope, but left without signing Michelangelo to a cartooning contract.

Coretta Scott King and former UN ambassador Jeane Kirkpatrick also started much-hyped features around that time. Despite my misgivings about big-name columnists who hadn't paid their journalistic dues, I interviewed Kirkpatrick that summer. The neoconservative neo-pundit told me that many syndicates had sought to sign her after she left the Reagan administration several months before. Nice reward for someone who was way too easy on right-wing dictatorships.

That December, I also interviewed Ms. King — whose martyred husband would be honored with the federal government's inaugural Martin

Luther King holiday the next month. The first thing I noticed when I reached her by phone was how bone-tired she sounded — not surprising considering that she headed the Martin Luther King Jr. Center for Nonviolent Social Change, served on the boards of many other organizations, traveled all over the country and world giving speeches and participating in protests, and was now writing the weekly New York Times Syndicate column.

"Does everything you do get to feel like a little too much sometimes?" I asked awkwardly.

King paused a few seconds before replying. "There are a lot of people who don't have a voice," she finally said, explaining that she had an obligation to keep busy and help speak for those people.

The new columnist added that doing a syndicated feature enabled her to offer her views without them being filtered through a journalist's words. "I've learned to be wary," King observed, recalling that after being interviewed by someone for an hour, the article ended up including "two muddled sentences that somehow managed to convey the opposite of what I said."

Martha Stewart would eventually become very famous, too, but she wasn't that well-known in 1985 when I did a story about her new weekly syndicated feature titled "Entertaining." In one column, Stewart wrote: "Holidays and entertaining go together, for a holiday is by its nature a communal celebration." This amazing insight changed my life, because I had previously thought holidays were only for people in solitary confinement.

I met Stewart at a syndicate party more than a decade later, and you might be surprised to hear what she was wearing. To be revealed in a future chapter.

Another late-1985 story I wrote was about the November 1985 launch of "Calvin and Hobbes," which would become one of the top comics of all time.

Bill Watterson's strip about a hyperactive, imaginative boy and his tiger friend (a stuffed animal to everyone but Calvin) started with a good but not spectacular 60 or so newspapers. But by the time I snagged a very rare interview with the reclusive Watterson in early 1986, the strip was starting to explode in popularity (it would eventually have about 2,400 clients). More on that interview — and a strange tussle over a Watterson photo — in the next chapter.

Yet another early *E&P* mention of a future famous person came when I ran a freelancer's story about a new small syndicate whose features included the weekly "Life in Hell" comic by Matt Groening, who would later create *The Simpsons*. As alternative-cartoon fans know, the "Life in Hell" characters look sort of like rabbits and sort of like the cast members of Groening's 1989-launched TV show — which spawned a short-lived "Simpsons" newspaper comic that began in 1999.

My last feature story of 1985 profiled sex/relationship counselor Dr. Ruth Westheimer — who was about to add a syndicated column to a multimedia menu that already included a TV program, radio show, books, board game, and more. "I'm personally *verrry* excited about this new venture," she told me in a distinctive German accent that was as entertaining as the humor with which she laced her serious advice.

The 57-year-old Westheimer did say she would tone things down a bit in her column — noting, for instance, that the phrase "get it up" might be used on her radio show but "erection" would substitute for that in the more staid world of daily newspapers.

Two of Dr. Ruth's favorite phrases: "Have good sex!" and "Are you using contraceptives?"

Meanwhile, my wife was now pregnant.

CHAPTER EIGHT

1986:
Females Make News
at Work and at
Home

A famous cartoonist gets kidnapped by a tobacco-industry guy who forces her to put pro-smoking messages in her comic strip, and the cartoonist tries to get help by putting subliminal "I've been kidnapped" messages in the strip. That was the plot of a novel I came up with in 1986.

It was agent Toni Mendez who suggested I write a book. The 70-something former Rockette and choreographer had clients such as "Steve Canyon" cartoonist Milton Caniff, so she was a regular reader of my *Editor & Publisher* section.

One day, Toni invited me to lunch at Manhattan's Society of Illustrators club. I had no trouble spotting her in the dining room, because she always wore a stylish hat. Then we got some food from the scrumptious buffet before sitting down.

"Day-vid," she said in her patrician, sing-songy voice that fronted a formidable intellect. "You're *the* expert on syndication. You should write a *boook* about the business."

I was flattered, but doing a nonfiction syndication book when I was already covering syndication 40 hours a week didn't sound like fun.

"Maybe a novel with a syndication theme?" I asked hesitantly, not sure I could pull something like that off.

Toni was dubious, too. "Well, Day-vid, if you want to try it...."

I did find time to start writing *The Comic Strip Connection* despite doing my *E&P* work, shopping for the impending baby, and moving to a new Sunnyside, Queens, apartment that had a monthly rent almost twice what my wife and I paid for our previous place. We obviously needed a second bedroom, but I would have been satisfied with a smaller two-bedroom abode. (Perhaps an example of how "men are from Mars and women are from Venus," though I'm not sure those planets can sustain human life.) At least Gwyneth and Samantha the cats would have more room for their longish names.

When longish-last-named cartoonist Bill Watterson agreed to do a phone interview about his 10-week-old "Calvin and Hobbes" comic, Universal Press Syndicate mailed me a picture of him. The media-shy Watterson looked more like the dad of Calvin the boy than of Hobbes the tiger, so that was reassuring.

But I soon received a frantic call from a Universal staffer.

"You can't run that photo!" she exclaimed.

"What photo?"

"The photo of Bill Watterson."

"Why not?"

"Bill doesn't want people to know what he looks like."

"What would I run instead?"

"One of his comics."

"But the story will be a profile of Watterson. It wouldn't look right without a photo of the person being profiled."

"We can get you a caricature Bill did of himself."

Well, being somewhat firm had gotten me a decent alternate option — an accomplishment I might not have pulled off three years earlier. It would have been nice to still run Watterson's photo, but I was never one of those journalists who published a juicy quote from someone if they quickly added that it was "off the record." This photo situation was somewhat analogous.

I guess Universal trusted me, because the syndicate never asked for Watterson's photo back. I still have it filed in my "W" folder of images that thankfully has nothing to do with the president between Clinton and Obama.

"Calvin and Hobbes" was definitely more successful than the second George Bush. The comic's client list more than doubled to 130 newspapers between its November 1985 launch and my February 1986 interview with the 27-year-old Watterson.

I headlined my story "An Overnight Success After Five Years," because Watterson had submitted strips to syndicates since 1980. He said one was an outer-space parody, another was an animal comic, and two starred a young man in his first job and apartment.

"When each was rejected, I would read into any comments the syndicates had written and try to figure out what they were looking for," Watterson told me, adding that he eventually decided this approach was a mistake because that made him try to do something "trendy" rather than what came "most naturally."

Then United Feature Syndicate advised the cartoonist to take two minor characters from one of his comics and have the duo star in a new strip. With Calvin and Hobbes heading the cast, the comic "clicked," said Watterson. But United still rejected the retooled comic, and Universal was happy to sign it.

When I asked Watterson the inevitable question of why "Calvin and Hobbes" was successful, he said one reason was Calvin not being "cutesy" like some other cartoon kids. "There's an undercurrent of nastiness to him," he observed.

Watterson also cited his comic's fantasy elements: Hobbes the tiger being real only to Calvin, the space flights and other adventures Calvin conjured up in his mind, etc. And though Watterson didn't say it, he drew better than 99.9% of his peers.

That self-caricature of Watterson? The drawing showed Watterson slouched at a drawing table with three cats — presumably based on his real-life felines Sprite, Pumpernickel, and Juniper Boots. Watterson did not look like their dad.

Watterson's dad was going to law school when Bill was born in 1958 in Washington, D.C. His parents moved to Ohio when he was in elementary school, and Bill went on to graduate from Kenyon College before becoming a political cartoonist for *The Cincinnati Post* in 1980. That job lasted only a few months.

Soon after speaking with Watterson, I interviewed another artist with a less-than-angelic cartoon kid. That was curmudgeonly Hank Ketcham of "Dennis the Menace" fame.

Actually, Ketcham told me the "menace" description had become a bit overblown. "Maybe Dennis is a pain in the neck, but he's not menacing," he said, while acknowledging that the five-year-old kid was more "antisocial" in the earlier days of the 1951-launched comic.

But, of course, the rhyming title was too good to drop. It had come about when Ketcham's first wife approached him in a state of exasperation with news about their child Dennis: "Henry, your son is a *menace!*"

The rest was cartoon history, with the comic eventually appearing in more than 1,000 newspapers and spawning a live-action TV sitcom that ran from 1959 to 1963. Ironically, Ketcham and his comic-inspiring son Dennis would be estranged for many years.

Near the start of his career, Ketcham was with Walt Disney Productions — and ended up working on classic films such as 1940's *Pinocchio* and *Fantasia*.

"What college did you graduate from?" I asked.

"The University of Walt Disney," quipped Ketcham.

Actually, the Seattle-born Ketcham (1920-2001) attended the University of Washington before working for Disney, and then did a comic called "Half Hitch" while serving in the Navy during World War II.

Ketcham — who lived in Switzerland from 1960 to 1977 — was a Californian when I interviewed him in 1986.

Then I profiled a different kind of humorist: Calvin Trillin — the author, *New Yorker* writer, and *Nation* columnist who did not have a pet tiger named Hobbes Trillin. His "Uncivil Liberties" column was entering syndication in April 1986.

After sitting down in Trillin's Greenwich Village brownstone, I asked why he wanted to write for daily newspapers.

"It's not just the size of the audience, it's the non-select aspect," replied the Kansas City native. "If you live in a town, you read the paper."

Gee, that was so … pre-Internet! Now, if you live in a town, you often get the news via smartphone, tablet, or laptop rather than a printed newspaper. Of course, it can be hard on a laptop when the delivery person tosses it on your lawn each morning.

I had brought my camera, and shot a picture of Trillin wearing a partly buttoned sweater as he leaned against a manual Underwood typewriter that reminded me of the 1920s Remington I have that was first used by my maternal grandparents. I'm also reminded that when they said "the server is down" in pre-Internet days, it meant your waiter had tripped.

Soon after Cowles Syndicate signed Trillin, the Des Moines-based distributor was acquired for a reported $4.2 million by the Hearst Corporation — parent of King Features Syndicate. So Trillin, "The Family Circus" cartoonist Bil Keane, "Spider-Man" writer Stan Lee, humor columnist Lewis Grizzard, and more than 30 other Cowles creators were suddenly switched to a much bigger distributor with a stronger sales force.

But some Cowles creators would eventually be dropped by the New York-based King, and most Cowles staffers immediately lost their jobs. There would also be no more buying of *E&P* ads by the 1922-founded Cowles, which was the Register and Tribune Syndicate for most of its existence. And there would be one less smaller syndicate in an industry where smaller syndicates sometimes offered the most innovative features, as when the just-launched Universal signed "Doonesbury" in 1970.

Indeed, Rosalie Muller Wright — a *San Francisco Chronicle* editor and American Association of Sunday and Feature Editors president — would tell me in 1987 that "mega-syndicates" could lead to more "pablum" and fewer "eccentric" offerings.

So no one can convince me mergers are a good thing — though the low rates newspapers pay for a comic or column (an average of $10-20 a week) make it tempting for syndicates to "double your features without doubling your overhead," as Universal executive Bob Duffy once said.

The merger thing got replicated in a bigger way in late 1986 when King (the biggest syndicate) acquired News America Syndicate (the third largest) for a reported $23 million. NAS employees fearful of losing their jobs were especially furious that Rupert Murdoch did the Scrooge thing by announcing the sale of his syndicate on Christmas Eve.

NAS had 71 full-time employees and a roster of about 85 creators — including Ann Landers, Roger Ebert, "B.C." cartoonist Johnny Hart, editorial cartoonists Herblock and Bill Mauldin, columnist Carl Rowan, and conservative pundit Robert "The Prince of Darkness" Novak, who was then collaborating with Rowland Evans.

The King/NAS deal set off a major chain of events that would shake up the syndicate world in 1987.

A more positive event occurred in 1986 when "For Better or For Worse" creator Lynn Johnston became the first woman to win the annual top-cartoonist Reuben Award from the 1946-founded National Cartoonists Society (she would also become the organization's first female president in 1988). I was there to watch a thrilled Johnston walk to the podium as the crowd at Washington, D.C.'s National Press Club gave her a standing ovation.

I shot photos of Lynn, Charles Schulz ("Peanuts"), Jim Davis ("Garfield"), and other attendees at that '86 NCS dinner. But at all the events I covered during my *E&P* tenure, I never asked anyone to take pictures of *me* with well-known people. That's because I didn't want to impose and because I thought it was unprofessional for journalists to pose with anyone they wrote about.

Luckily, I do have *some* shots of me with syndicated creators that were taken candidly or when a person suggested it. I figured it was okay if it was someone else's idea!

I also never asked cartoonists for originals of their comics, though I would accept a signed strip if it was sent unsolicited to thank me for a story. For instance, after I profiled Pat Brady in 1986, he mailed me a "Rose Is Rose" comic with an accompanying letter saying: "I was extremely happy with your July 19th story. It was entirely accurate and very nicely done.... It would make me very happy if you would accept the enclosed original with my best wishes."

What was I supposed to do? Sending it back would have felt rude.

My "Rose" story, by the way, contained a very funny quote. Brady, who often wrote his comic at the library, said: "I think the librarians are scared of me, because every time I get an idea a light bulb appears above my head!"

Though usually thrilled to meet notable people, I never fawned over them. That was partly because I was a journalist, partly because many of these celebrities had enough self-esteem without me adding to it, and partly because I sensed conversation was preferred over a fawning session.

Indeed, I was slowly getting better at chit-chatting with people at gatherings. In 1983, I mixed stammering and clamming up into a shy-guy stew. By 1986 — after three years of forced practice and experience — I could talk about syndication, the newspaper biz, the weather, or whatever without too many stumbles and pauses. I was finally displaying some adult behavior at age 32.

Pauline Phillips was 37 when she came up with the name Abigail Van Buren for the byline of the "Dear Abby" column she launched in 1956. Some quick math would indicate that her feature turned 30 in 1986, so it was obviously time for an *E&P* interview!

(Speaking of names, I've always wondered why more aspiring cartoonists don't legally become "Charles Schulz." After all, syndicates are always looking for "the next Charles Schulz"!)

Van Buren started "Dear Abby" in quite an interesting way. Then a housewife/volunteer who didn't even have a Social Security number, Phillips phoned *San Francisco Chronicle* editor Stan Arnold to criticize the advice columnist who was appearing in the paper back then. Arnold invited her to stop by "sometime" for an interview, and Phillips showed up the next day. He gave her some letters to answer as a test he thought would occupy her for about a week, but she handed back some snappy replies in 90 minutes.

Phillips was hired, and entered syndication three months later — which reportedly annoyed the heck out of her twin sister Ann Landers, who had been an advice columnist for just a year and didn't want the competition. But, given that they each eventually amassed more than 1,000 newspaper clients, there was room for both Landers and Van Buren to become wildly popular.

"How many letters do you get?" I asked Van Buren on the phone, a little nervous but thinking my mother wasn't going to believe who I was talking to!

"As many as 12,000 a week," she replied. "Do I get mail!"

In fact, Van Buren would receive 210,336 responses when she asked readers in 1987 whether or not they cheated on their mates. Eighty-five percent of the females and 74% of the males said they were faithful — less straying than Kinsey studies had indicated. Were people lying to "Dear Abby"? I shudder at the thought.

Van Buren told me during our 1986 conversation that she employed seven assistants to help with mail and other tasks. Given that only a handful of letters could be published, the columnist wrote or phoned as many other correspondents as possible to give them advice directly.

"When I call, almost everyone reacts the same way," reported Van Buren. "'You're kidding!' they say. They can't believe it's me."

Van Buren was quite friendly, and I soon felt very comfortable talking with her on the phone. After the story ran, she sent me a lovely note saying, in part: "Boyoboy are you ever well read! I have been getting raves about that piece you wrote about me.... It was really a beaut, David, and I can't thank you enough. You were accurate, gentle, kind, and thorough.... If I can ever do something for you, please know that you have a friend right here in sunny California."

So when a traumatic family situation arose the following year, I dropped my journalistic objectivity and picked up the phone to call Abby.

Also in 1986, I did a phone interview with another column legend — Pulitzer Prize-winning political satirist Art Buchwald. This was soon after the 60-year-old writer became only the third humorist since Mark Twain to be inducted into the prestigious American Academy of Arts and Letters, and also soon after he decreased the frequency of his syndicated feature from thrice to twice a week.

"How did readers react to that?" I asked.

"When they meet you, they say 'I read you every day' anyway," Buchwald replied with a chuckle from his Martha's Vineyard summer home. "You don't have to write every day to have people say 'I read you every day'!"

Art had an amazing last act that will be described in my 2006 chapter.

While Buchwald was clearly a "mainstream" creator, "Zippy the Pinhead" cartoonist Bill Griffith was a more "alternative" talent from an "underground comix" background. So Griffith's 1986 signing by the large King Features was a shock. I've heard that Bill might have been signed as sort of a prank by a departing King executive who wanted to get some revenge on the syndicate he was leaving, but I haven't been able to confirm that.

Yet "Zippy" — which inspired "The Coneheads" characters on the early *Saturday Night Live* — was so interesting in its surreal, free-associative, pop-culture-laden way that King managed to sell it to more than 100 newspapers.

Indeed, many readers related to Griffith's dazed, non-sequitur-spouting, clown suit-clad "wise fool" of a title character — who first appeared in 1970 and got his own comic six years later. "The way the world looks to Zippy is the way the world looks to many people of the baby-boom generation," Bill told me. "They are swimming in — they are adrift in — a sea of information."

That comment, I might add, was uttered before the Internet age. Now people are processing so much information that ... that ... I forgot what I was going to write.

Zippy's legendary catch phrase: "Are we having fun yet?"

Ernest Hemingway had fun when he met "The Phantom" and "Mandrake the Magician" creator Lee Falk in 1950s Cuba. Falk — who I interviewed in 1986 to mark the 50th anniversary of "The Phantom" (the first comic with a masked superhero) — told me he had a teacher who claimed he flunked Hemingway a number of years earlier. When the cartoonist asked the author if that was true, all he got was a roar of laughter.

As I wrote about all things syndicated in '86, I had also become the June 10 father of Abigail (a name chosen by my wife; I found it too formal). I enjoyed being a parent despite the exhaustion and the fact that I could do only sporadic work on *The Comic Strip Connection* novel. But I was greatly compensated by my surprise discovery that I had some parenting skills. It was another confidence boost to hold, feed, and do other things in a way that made a helpless baby seem comfortable.

Though the baby stage had its charms, I also looked forward to seeing Abigail walk and talk and caulk (the bathtub needed work). But by the end of 1986, her development didn't seem quite right.

CHAPTER NINE

1987:
A Mouth Needed a
Zipper Near the
Gipper

I mentioned in the previous chapter that the King Features Syndicate/News America Syndicate merger set off a major chain of events. NAS president Rick Newcombe declined to become president of the renamed North America Syndicate, telling me the post would "carry no authority" because NAS was now basically part of King. And Newcombe said syndicates such as King didn't allow many cartoonists ownership of the features these cartoonists dreamed up.

Bil Keane was among the cartoonists in that situation. "The Family Circus" creator recalled seeking ownership when his Register and Tribune Syndicate contract came up for renewal in 1978, but RTS responded by threatening to have another cartoonist take over the 1960-launched, partly autobiographical feature.

"What did you think about *that*?" I asked Keane in early 1987, trying to be objective but undoubtedly letting some indignation creep into my voice.

"It was a point-a-gun-to-the-head approach," declared Keane.

Also in early 1987, "Steve Canyon" cartoonist Milton Caniff mailed me a note recalling the poignant 1968 attempt by "Little Orphan Annie" cartoonist Harold Gray to end his classic strip (which was syndicated by what is now Tribune Media Services). "Gray tried to kill off his feature by drawing a 'final' week of 'Annie,' when Harold knew that he himself was dying," wrote Caniff. "The syndicate simply put two new men on the feature and that was that — after scrapping Gray's final week."

But Newcombe, 36, had different ideas. He launched Creators Syndicate in February 1987, hired some NAS people to staff it, and said the new company would offer all talent ownership rights and shorter contracts. He also soon announced the syndicate's first signing: Ann Landers!

Newcombe had endeared himself to Landers at News America Syndicate by finding more newspapers to run her column, throwing a lavish 1985 party to mark her 30th anniversary of syndication, and giving her the rights to the Ann Landers name that had been used by two other columnists prior to 1955. And the advice titan had a contract that allowed her to move elsewhere if NAS was sold.

So King lost Landers and her 1,100 newspapers — and the *Chicago Sun-Times* lost her, too, when she made the *Chicago Tribune* her home paper. The *Sun-Times* soon launched a Landers-replacement contest that drew 12,000 entries — with one of the two winners 28-year-old *Wall Street Journal* reporter Jeff Zaslow, who entered the contest to give another angle to his *WSJ* coverage of it. Jeff's win was well-deserved — he was a superb writer, and also had a great sense of humor. Zaslow and terminally ill professor Randy Pausch later co-authored *The Last Lecture*, the runaway bestseller of 2008.

"Why did you switch to Creators?" I asked Landers after calling her in Chicago.

"I felt this was an opportunity to help Rick get started," she replied in the nasal, no-nonsense voice that evoked her "wake up and smell the coffee" advice to sometimes-clueless readers. Landers added that it was "high time" a syndicate offered contracts friendlier to talent.

"B.C." cartoonist Johnny Hart soon also moved from NAS/King to Creators, as did legendary *Washington Post* editorial cartoonist Herblock, 77. NAS/King lost Roger Ebert, too, though the renowned film critic gave two thumbs' up to a new contract with Universal Press Syndicate rather than Creators. Ebert said he wanted to be with the syndicate owned by the same company as his Andrews and McMeel book publisher.

The creation of Creators gave the syndication biz — which had been consolidating since before I joined *E&P* — the rarity of a new major player. And it nudged other syndicates to give more of *their* cartoonists and columnists additional rights over the next few years. For instance, the presence of Creators might have indirectly pushed King to grant Bil Keane deserved ownership of "The Family Circus" in early 1989. But it should be noted that several major syndicates had already let at least some of their talent own their work before Creators came along.

Meanwhile, syndicates that offered longer contracts — as much as 10 years, with a 10-year renewal if performance clauses were met — continued to defend them as necessary given the money they spent to introduce, promote, and sell features. Proponents of more creator rights said five years was long enough to potentially recoup an investment.

Eventually, the contracts offered by Creators and its rivals would be pretty similar. This was partly because some of those rivals began allowing friendlier-to-talent pacts and partly because the contracts Creators offered after its 1995 loss of the popular "Baby Blues" comic to King (which reportedly paid the two "BB" cartoonists a large signing bonus) were rumored to be somewhat less talent-friendly than earlier Creators contracts.

Just as Landers helped launch Creators with a bang, political columnist/reporter David Broder was the first person on the Washington Post Writers Group roster when that syndicate began in 1973 — the year Broder won the commentary Pulitzer Prize for his *Washington Post* work.

By the time I interviewed the friendly Broder in early 1987, he was running in more than 300 papers. His centrist (later center-right) column rarely strayed far from the establishment consensus, but the Illinois native did do more "shoe leather" reporting than most op-ed pundits.

Broder (1929-2011) had covered presidential campaigns since the Kennedy-Nixon race in 1960. That was for the *Washington Star*, which would later become one of many American dailies to go out of business.

"Which president was the most interesting to write about?" I asked, reflecting the fascination I've had with Oval Office occupants since reciting all their names to my (eye-rolling) classmates during a third-grade oral report.

"Lyndon Johnson was the most fascinating and multidimensional politician I covered," replied Broder, who appeared on *Meet the Press* more than 400 times.

Broder offered readers political insight and Percy Ross offered readers ... money. Yes, the millionaire former businessman wrote a syndicated column that gave needy people sums that usually ranged from $50 to $300.

Percy got the idea for his "Thanks a Million" feature in 1977 from U.S. senator/former vice president Hubert Humphrey after throwing a $200,000 party in Minneapolis for 1,050 disadvantaged kids, who each received a free bike. The terminally ill Humphrey called his friend Percy the next day to suggest a newspaper column, and ended the conversation this way: "Thanks a million, old buddy, and take care."

Ross now had a column concept and name, but more than a dozen syndicates turned him down over the next few years. He told me in a 1987 interview that syndicates doubted his sincerity, thought he might tire of giving away his $20-million fortune, or felt the 60-something philanthropist was too old to start a column. The Register and Tribune Syndicate finally signed him in 1983, and Ross was soon getting 8,000 letters and 1,000 calls a week from readers of 150 papers.

"Why are you giving your money away?" I asked.

"My family is well provided for and the money won't do me any good when I'm gone," said the warm and convivial Ross. "And it makes me feel good! Most rich people I have absolutely no use for. They don't share."

Percy's recipients included a woman on welfare who needed clothes for her children, a man who wanted a bus ticket to visit his grandmother in a nursing home, and many others.

Among the requests Ross turned down: A woman asked for money to divorce her husband — plus extra money in case she divorced her next husband!

In May 1987, I briefly divorced myself from New Jersey to cover the Association of American Editorial Cartoonists convention in Washington, D.C. I arrived late because of a very serious family situation (explained in the next chapter) and thus missed a meeting between AAECers and President Reagan.

But I heard what happened from those who did attend the White House event, which was covered by the national press. At one point, ABC-TV's Sam Donaldson asked Reagan about the Iran-contra scandal. *Columbus* (Ohio)

Dispatch editorial cartoonist Louis "Doc" Goodwin, in an effort to shield the president from questioning, immediately suggested that the meeting end.

"It was the most embarrassing moment I've ever had in this business," said *Milwaukee Journal* editorial cartoonist Bill Sanders.

Two days later, in a session I *did* cover, the AAEC passed a motion expressing displeasure with Goodwin's action. Cullum Rogers, the organization's secretary-treasurer, would later recall that this was the only time the 1957-founded AAEC ever formally criticized a member. The many people backing the motion said, among other things, that Donaldson was doing his job and that journalists rarely got a chance to question the media-averse Reagan.

Goodwin apologized, but didn't seem too regretful. "It was our party and the TV people were trying to take it over," he declared.

A number of AAEC convention attendees also criticized the previous month's awarding of a Pulitzer to Berkeley Breathed for "Bloom County," arguing that a comic strip shouldn't win an editorial cartooning prize.

I subsequently phoned Breathed — and he responded that while "Bloom County" was often not a political strip, its editorial commentary was sometimes hard-hitting enough "to get me an awful lot of hate letters."

Breathed added that there should be a Pulitzer category for comic strips — something many other cartoonists have suggested (in vain).

The '87 AAEC meeting also saw the first-ever presentation of the John Locher Memorial Award for top college cartoonist. John, who died in 1986 at age 25, was the son of *Chicago Tribune* editorial cartoonist Dick Locher — and worked with his dad on the "Dick Tracy" comic.

This award would continue to be presented every year. Many Locher winners went on to snag full-time editorial cartooning jobs — no mean feat as the number of those positions decreased slowly in the 1990s and then drastically in the 2000s.

Speaking of May prizes, "Calvin and Hobbes" creator Bill Watterson won the peer-voted Reuben Award as top cartoonist at the National Cartoonists Society's annual dinner in New York City. It was an amazing honor considering that Watterson had been in syndication only 18 months, wasn't an NCS member, and didn't even attend the dinner.

I managed to reach Watterson by phone in Ohio.

"Were you surprised to win?"

"It caught me off guard," he admitted. "It was very generous of them to honor a non-member. To be held in esteem by my peers is very gratifying."

Watterson went on to win the Reuben again in 1989 — making him the youngest cartoonist to receive that award twice. But by then he almost never spoke with the media anymore. So 1987 was the last time I ever talked with Watterson, although I did catch a very rare 1989 speech by him at Ohio State University that set off lots of sparks. Look for a description of that in the chapter between 1988 and 1990.

The '87 NCS gathering was also the last time I saw "The Lockhorns" creator Bill Hoest, who died the next year of lymphoma at age 62. In 1993, I would move to the New Jersey town where Hoest lived as a youth — and see the bickering married couple Leroy and Loretta Lockhorn each day in *The Star-Ledger* funny pages. By then, the comic was done by Bunny Hoest (Bill's widow) and artist John Reiner.

While creators like Hoest and Reiner are represented by major syndicates, there have always been many people who self-distribute — either because a major syndicate wouldn't sign them or because they want total control over their features and earnings. Many of these independent creators struggle to build a decent list of newspaper subscribers, but that wasn't the case with James Dulley, who had more than 200 papers running his 1982-launched "Cut Your Utility Bills" column in 1987.

I interviewed the hardworking Dulley in late '87, and he said one of his selling techniques was to not charge for "Cut" if it didn't attract more reader mail than every other syndicated feature in the subscribing newspaper. Given that Dulley received 250,000 or so letters a year, his wallet didn't have a weight-loss problem!

Then there was the team of Franklynn Peterson and Judi K-Turkel, who had a tough time self-syndicating their computer column in the early 1980s because many newspaper editors argued that not enough people were using computers!

After my 1987 story about those columnists ran, Peterson sent one of my favorite thank-you letters. He wrote: "Yours was absolutely the first write-up about Judi and/or me about which we have no quibbles. Everything you said we said we said and everything you said we did we did."

I often wrote about self-syndicated creators because they had compelling stories to tell — plus they needed the "ink" in a magazine read by newspaper editors who often purchased a column or comic after reading about it in *E&P*.

CHAPTER TEN

Still 1987:
The Year of a
Medical Maelstrom

As I mentioned at the end of Chapter 8, my daughter Abigail's development didn't seem right. She was seven months old in January 1987, yet could barely hold up her head and barely roll over — much less sit up or crawl.

"Is there something wrong with her?" my wife and I asked our young pediatrician several times starting in the fall of 1986.

"Some babies develop slower than others," he assured us. "She's fine."

We weren't convinced. But this was our first child, so what did we know?

Then the woman who babysat for Abigail in her Queens apartment insisted in April 1987 that we bring our daughter to a specialist. Linda was a very kind person who knew kids — she took care of her own daughter and son along with Abigail — so we were finally goaded into making an appointment with a pediatric neurologist. It was idiotic not to have made that appointment sooner.

Around that time, I had a dream about Abigail in which her legs made frantic crawling motions but she stayed in one place — as if tethered to a calendar that wouldn't let her turn the pages. I almost never remember dreams, but I remember that one.

My wife and I took the subway from Queens to Manhattan to see the neurologist on May 4, feeling barely suppressed panic during the whole ride.

"What a cute baby!" cooed one subway passenger (surprisingly, a young man) when spotting Abigail.

I could only smile weakly, and my wife stared straight ahead as if she didn't hear him.

We arrived at the doctor's office, and the person at the desk immediately harangued us to pay $300 on the spot — even though we wanted to submit to our insurance first. My furious wife snapped at the woman, but an equally furious me grudgingly paid up. I didn't want to make a scene.

Then we were ushered in, wondering what battery of tests awaited Abigail. But after we described her slow development, the neurologist simply checked our daughter's reflexes before darkening the room to look into her eyes with an ophthalmoscope. Soon, he cleared his throat — twice. "This is very serious," the neurologist said. "I believe this child has Tay-Sachs disease."

"W-what?!" I sputtered.

"I see a 'cherry-red spot' in her eyes — indicating Tay-Sachs."

"But I was tested for that during the pregnancy!" I countered. "They told me I wasn't a carrier."

The doctor looked puzzled. "Both parents have to be carriers for a child to have Tay-Sachs," he said. "Then there's a one in four chance with each pregnancy." The doctor turned toward my wife. "Were *you* tested?"

"No," she choked out. "I was told I couldn't be tested if I was pregnant."

"That's not true," said the doctor.

"But even if my wife was a carrier, I'm not," I rasped, clutching Abigail on my lap. I didn't know much about Tay-Sachs, but I knew it was bad.

The doctor said we should of course have Abigail tested to make sure his diagnosis was correct. He arranged for her blood to be drawn the next day at a Manhattan hospital.

My friend Mark Teich and his wife Pam Weintraub were nice enough to drive us to that hospital (we didn't own a car back then). But the session was horrible. Abigail had to be pricked numerous times to get enough blood, and the poor kid screamed and screamed. But after the needle-jabbing ordeal was over, she actually smiled a little at the adults hovering over her.

We were given the blood (packed in ice) to bring to another hospital about 100 blocks north. Then we were driven home, emotionally exhausted. We would now have to wait several tortuous days for the results.

My wife had been weeping on and off since we saw the neurologist 24 hours earlier, and I burst into tears right after we returned to our apartment.

"I never saw you cry before," my wife later told me.

The apartment was a place we had moved to just six weeks earlier. It was in the same Queens house as our previous place, only we had risen from the first floor to a rental unit that combined the second floor with a mostly finished attic. It was my wife's idea to move again — and the additional rent was more than we could comfortably afford, even on two salaries. But I still didn't have the gumption to say no to things like that.

I paced the apartment endlessly. Then I looked in our bedroom mirror with bleary eyes and spotted the first gray hairs on my 33-year-old head. They had probably been there for months, but I hadn't noticed before.

Later, I turned on the TV and fitfully watched a Yankee game, in no mood to admire Don Mattingly's compact swing. Samantha the cat eyed me Sphinx-like from under a lit lamp on the desk, and Gwyneth the cat perched solemnly in a pear shape on the narrow top of the desk chair's back.

The rest of the week limped along, with my wife and I dragging ourselves to work each day (she was now a copy editor/proofreader at a publishing house). It wasn't until May 11 — seven days after our original May 4 visit — that we got a call from the neurologist asking us to come in. He wouldn't give Abigail's blood results over the phone, which was ominous. So, with our daughter at the babysitter's, we returned to Manhattan on the 7 and 4 trains. May 4 plus 7 equals May 11, and I wondered if our daughter's days were numbered.

We sat in front of the neurologist, and were told that ... Abigail did indeed have Tay-Sachs. Even though our daughter wouldn't have been able to understand what the doctor was saying, I'm glad she wasn't there to hear the words.

But, according to that October 1985 test I had during my wife's pregnancy, I was *not* a carrier! How could this be?

It was in May 1987 that I had that editorial cartoonists' convention I described in the previous chapter, and I decided to attend it for two days rather than four — slicing off the first day (when attendees met President Reagan) and the last. I shouldn't have gone at all, but I selfishly wanted to get the hell out of New York for a little while. Washington, D.C., seemed far enough.

I took the train from Penn Station to Union Station, and what a miserable ride it was. Sitting on the seat in front of me were a mom and dad with their healthy toddler girl. When I saw that, I felt like pushing out a window and dashing my brains against the tracks. I grimly read a book — *The Handmaid's Tale* by Margaret Atwood. I should have chosen a lighter novel.

Somehow, I managed to function during the D.C. meeting — covering sessions and conversing with attendees before going back to my room to wallow in depression.

As you might also recall from the previous chapter, one thing that happened at the convention was the launching of a cartoon award named for John Locher, who had died in 1986 at age 25. His father — cartoonist Dick Locher, who I first interviewed after he won his 1983 Pulitzer — was at the meeting, and I could see this nice man was still visibly hurting a year after John's death. I didn't tell Dick about Abigail in Washington — it wasn't the time — but it was something we later bonded over.

"We both share a pain," Dick would write me in 1991.

Coincidentally, I had run a story about John's death in *E&P*'s June 14, 1986, issue — which came out just four days after Abigail's birth. Heck, I think I penned the piece the day before my wife and I rushed to the hospital when her contractions began.

After returning from D.C., I held Abigail every day and watched closely for signs of tremors. We had been told that her health would nosedive after she began to have seizures, but she was still holding her own.

Later in May, I covered that National Cartoonists Society award dinner I also wrote about in Chapter 9. As attendees danced, I sat at my table in a stupor. Then Milton Caniff approached.

"Looking pensive," he announced.

"Yeah," I replied, and then blurted out the news about Abigail. He was very sympathetic, and I ended up also telling several other attendees that night about my daughter's illness. It wasn't professional, but I wasn't thinking straight.

The people at the NCS gathering told other people, because over the next weeks and months I would get many kind sympathy notes in the mail.

"Terry and the Pirates" cartoonist Milton Caniff, Snoopy, and "Peanuts" cartoonist Charles M. Schulz in 1987. Photo by Dave Astor

Meanwhile, the whole experience was making me more agnostic than ever — which would not be helpful as my wife became more religious in future years.

Then the bombshell hit on June 5. The Manhattan lab that had confirmed Abigail's Tay-Sachs diagnosis called a doctor who headed the lab at a Brooklyn hospital that had been sent my 1985 blood sample for analysis. It turned out that a technician there in '85 had made a simple subtraction error that falsely indicated I was a "non-carrier for the Tay-Sachs gene," as stated in a copy of the lab results we eventually obtained. New York State's Department of Health, in an investigation completed in early 1988, called the boneheaded error "regrettable and preventable."

Indeed, we were told that the Brooklyn lab at the time only spot-checked the math on its Tay-Sachs tests — meaning some calculations never got a second pair of eyes. My sample lost that Russian roulette game.

What would have happened if someone *had* double-checked the math and found I *was* a carrier? My wife would have then been screened for the recessive Tay Sachs gene; testing a pregnant woman is trickier but not impossible. And there are also ways to check if a fetus has Tay-Sachs (via chorionic villus sampling or amniocentesis). Finally, my wife would have had an abortion.

Wherever you stand on the abortion question, you should know that Tay-Sachs babies are terminally ill babies. There was and is no cure. The lack of an enzyme causes a fatty substance to build up in the brain, eventually destroying the central nervous system. The results for the poor kid are brutal.

But Abigail had yet to exhibit any symptoms other than slowly regressing development, and Linda was willing to continue providing day care for her until medical supervision was needed. We were told this would probably be that fall — just a few months away.

Through a doctor serving as an intermediary, my wife and I tried to contact the head of the Brooklyn lab for an apology — and maybe some help paying medical bills. No response, no apology. We were told the hospital's attorneys advised the lab director not to say anything to us.

If the hospital was going to stonewall, well, then we vowed to give them the legal treatment. So we visited one law firm after another — and none would take our case.

"Why not?" I asked one attorney.

He shifted uncomfortably in his large leather chair, framed by dozens of books on the polished-wood shelves behind him. "Well, it's a 'wrongful life' rather than a 'wrongful death' situation," the guy explained.

I wanted to yell: "Oh, so you won't represent us because there's little chance to make a financial killing, you money-grubbing bastard?" Instead, I said politely: "Oh, so it's not a very lucrative case, is it?"

He nodded.

Then we talked to a solo-practicing lawyer who *was* willing to take the case. He was recommended to us by the neurologist who diagnosed Abigail, but we were not impressed with this attorney's knowledge or personality. Still, beggars can't be choosers, so we reluctantly signed with him in July. He went on to represent us as lamely as we expected, and his meandering performance helped cause the case to move so slowly that it got pushed to 1991 — and a surprise conclusion.

In August 1987, I received a letter from National Cartoonists Society treasurer George Wolfe that came with a check for $1,000 from the organization's fund to help needy cartoonists. We definitely could have used that money, but I had to decline it. I just didn't feel comfortable accepting money from an organization I covered.

One reason $1,000 would have come in handy was that our relatively inexpensive babysitter Linda had moved to the Midwest that month. My wife and I were happy for her, but there was now another wrench in our lives.

We scrambled to find another caregiver, because we didn't have the income for one of us to leave our jobs. (My wife would soon get a requested demotion to a production editor position with less stress and $5,000 less pay.) Also, our medical insurers wouldn't even consider paying for a visiting nurse until Abigail showed more overt symptoms. Several babysitters we contacted declined to care for a terminally ill (albeit still relatively healthy) child, and I didn't blame them in the least. We finally found a woman willing to watch Abigail at her nearby apartment, but at a pricey rate.

As we struggled to pay this babysitter, my anger at the Brooklyn lab intensified. Abigail would soon be suffering, and our lives were turned upside down, but this lab was doing nothing to help us. I tried to think of a way to get some payback, and it occurred to me that the press was something I knew about. So, why not a media campaign against the lab? Asking fellow journalists to do stories about my daughter's situation might be a bit unethical, but that was the only advantage I had over a powerful doctor and hospital.

Unfortunately, I didn't seem to have as much "pull" as I hoped — even though I'd been interviewed about syndication by many newspapers and other media outlets since 1984 and was slowly learning to talk in quotable "sound bites." I contacted people at *The New York Times, Wall Street Journal*, and various smaller papers — and none were willing to do a piece about Abigail's case, although some responded kindly. I also struck out with the Associated Press and TV shows such as *60 Minutes*.

Then it hit me: If I contacted Ann Landers or "Dear Abby," I could reach millions of readers in one fell swoop! Not a bad forum to get revenge while also educating parents about the need for both of them to get (accurately) tested.

But Landers and Abigail Van Buren received thousands of letters a week, so I figured this was the longest of long shots. Then I realized I could phone one of them first, and maybe lessen the odds. But which columnist to call?

I admired them both, and each was in 1,200 newspapers. Landers had more readers, but Abby seemed somewhat kinder when giving advice in her column. And I thought we hit it off well during that 1986 interview for the *E&P* story Abby liked so much. So I called California rather than Chicago.

"Ms. Van Buren, this is David Astor from *Editor & Publisher*. I—"

"David, how *are* you? Please call me Abby. How is little Abigail?"

I was shocked she remembered my daughter's name from a year earlier. Perhaps it was because her (pen) name was the same?

Anyway, I proceeded to tell Abby what had happened with Abigail since we last spoke, and then hesitantly asked about possibly submitting a letter to her column. "There's no obligation to run it," I added hastily. "But could you at least take a look?"

"Of course I'll run it," she declared. "Send it to my home address."

I was stunned into silence for a few seconds before blurting out: "Thanks so much, Ms. Van ... uh ... Abby! I *really* appreciate it."

On Oct. 20, 1987, my five-paragraph letter ran in "Dear Abby." It included this statement near the end: "We want to warn other prospective parents so this won't happen to them. No one should have to go through the hell we're presently going through."

Abby even sent me the original column, typed on pink paper. Looking at it today, Abby's stapled pages are an interesting artifact from a time before columns were emailed to syndicates and edited on a computer.

But I was thrilled, in a bittersweet way, with everything else about the letter. It was yet another thing that made me feel I was no longer the nobody of 1983, and maybe it helped spur some couples to both get tested. I sent a heartfelt thank-you note to Abby, who would call and write me many times over the next few years.

Meanwhile, someone at Ann Landers' syndicate told me she was irked I hadn't sent the letter to *her*. Remember, she and her twin Abby could be very competitive (though they wished each other "happy birthday" every July 4th in their columns). And it was true that I had been totally *un*-evenhanded. I'm not sure Landers ever completely warmed up to me until the year before she died; I'll explain how that came about in my 2001 chapter.

Around the time my "Dear Abby" letter ran, I began corresponding with a doctor who was a Tay-Sachs expert. He told me that some other doctors in that specialization were furious at me because I told the world that Tay-Sachs testing was not perfect — blaming the messenger rather than the lab guilty of malpractice. Abby told me one of those doctors sent her a letter, which she declined to run. I had to chuckle at the way these medical bigwigs couldn't win this advice-column battle, though I also felt a little guilty (well, maybe not!) about being the beneficiary of such favoritism from Abby.

Other things were happening — and not happening — that fall. I stopped working on *The Comic Strip Connection* novel to focus more on Abigail, and sometimes found it hard to concentrate at *E&P*. Luckily I still had a freelance budget and several freelancers I occasionally used (an option that would no longer exist in the corporate cost-cutting frenzy of the 2000s). The person who wrote for me the most over the years was Chris Lamb, a great journalist and thoroughly nice guy who eventually became a communication professor at South Carolina's College of Charleston and the author of books such as *Drawn to Extremes: the Use and Abuse of Editorial Cartoons in the United States.*

The abused-by-fate Abigail had her first seizure in late September. It was at the babysitter's apartment, and, after Abigail was hospitalized for three days, it was painfully obvious she now needed a visiting nurse. My wife and I contacted our insurance companies about whether we could get such a nurse, and battled the usual bureaucratic nonsense. But the at-home nursing was finally approved and paid for — at a rate of $200-plus a day. Suzette Lebel, the nurse who came most often, was a wonderful and personable young woman.

So Abigail was watched during the day, and my wife and I took care of her at night and on weekends. In fact, we sort of became nurses ourselves. When Abigail could no longer swallow food, we fed her a special formula through a tube. When Abigail got so congested she almost choked, we cleared her out with a suction machine. When Abigail could no longer move her bowels ... well, I'll spare you the details. By the end of 1987, she had suffered from her first bout of pneumonia — and was paralyzed and blind.

I remember a summer 1987 day when Abigail could still see. I took her for a walk in the neighborhood and watched her slowly swivel her head in the stroller to take in the surroundings. Tears were streaming down my face, because I knew she'd soon be blind and never get to see trees or anything else again.

Abigail also lost most of whatever intelligence and awareness she had. We were thankful for that, because she didn't know she was doomed.

Did Abigail feel *anything*? She couldn't communicate, and almost never made a sound. But one winter day when we took her for a checkup with the expert genetics team at Manhattan's Mount Sinai Hospital, it was so bitterly cold that Abigail let loose an otherworldly yowl as we rushed her inside.

Speaking of other worlds, one way my wife and I kept ourselves sane after we put Abigail to bed was watching the new *Star Trek: the Next Generation* on TV. When you saw an absorbing show set in the future, it made one's present troubles seem a little less significant. But would there be a next generation in my family?

CHAPTER ELEVEN

1988: The Year of Adversity and Diversity

Being a pack rat has its advantages. If I hadn't saved magazines, letters, press kits, and other memory-sparking stuff from my *Editor & Publisher* days, this book might never have happened. But I somehow lost the phone number of Ben Franklin, who did the 1754 "Join, or Die" drawing that showed the colonies as parts of a severed snake. Many people consider it the first political cartoon.

The star of "Hagar the Horrible" had saved pillaged stuff for 15 years by early 1988, so I decided to profile the comic's creator.

"Why is Hagar so popular?" I asked Dik Browne, a gentle man who looked sort of like his plus-sized cartoon Viking. (Also plus-sized was his "Horrible" client list of 1,800 newspapers.)

Dik replied that many men seem to identify with Hagar — a good-hearted guy who also happens to be unkempt and sexist. "But he's not an 'everyman' character," Browne added. "Every man doesn't loot England for a living!"

Then the big question: "Why did you take the 'c' out of your first name?" I asked cautiously.

"Juvenile pretensions," Browne replied with a laugh. He then quoted "The Family Circus" cartoonist Bil Keane as once saying of Dik: "He sends me a 'c' for Christmas each year, and I send him an 'l'!"

Browne (1917-1989) also did the 1954-launched "Hi and Lois" with Mort Walker.

Soon after my interview with Dik, a longtime cartoonist with an *extra* letter in his name became the latest person to jump to the year-old Creators Syndicate. That was Mell Lazarus of "Momma" and "Miss Peach" reknowwn. Actually, I think "reknowwn" has only one "w."

I also enjoyed writing about talented new cartoonists and columnists — some of whom later hit it big. For instance, I did 1987 pieces about editorial cartoonists Michael Ramirez and Walt Handelsman being signed by Copley News Service and Tribune Media Services, respectively. Each man went on to win two Pulitzer Prizes apiece at four newspapers — Ramirez for the Memphis *Commercial Appeal* in 1994 and *Investor's Business Daily* in 2008, and Handelsman for the New Orleans *Times-Picayune* in 1997 and Long Island, N.Y., *Newsday* in 2007.

In 1988, *Detroit Free Press* columnist Mitch Albom was "honored" with a bucket of ice water dumped on his head by Detroit Tigers pitcher Willie Hernandez, who alleged that the future *Tuesdays With Morrie* author turned fans against him. The spring-training incident inspired Albom to write

Wednesdays Without Willie, or maybe I made that up. But I didn't make up the column kerfluffle Albom would experience in 2005.

Back in '88 — on March 31, to be exact — Abigail left my wife and I. We and the nurses had cared for her for five months when my wife decided that a terminally ill child was too much to handle at home.

"It's time for a hospice," she said emphatically, noting that an advocate connected with her medical insurer had mentioned St. Mary's Hospital for Children in Bayside, Queens.

"I'm not sure I want to do that," I replied.

Although I was as exhausted as my wife, I didn't feel comfortable letting Abigail go. Parents weren't supposed to become "empty nesters" until their child left for college — not that Abigail would ever come anywhere near age 18. And although Abigail was in her own world by that spring, her companionship was comforting. One of my fond memories was watching the 1988 Super Bowl with her lying on my lap atop a soft blanket. She was "there" when Doug Williams of the Washington Redskins became the first African-American quarterback to win pro football's biggest game.

But again I gave in. We brought our 21-month-old daughter to St. Mary's "palliative care unit," where nine other dying kids also lived — including Abigail's new roommate, little Danielle de Jong. We kissed Abigail goodbye — she hardly noticed, now that she was in a vegetative state — and left the top-floor hospice to begin the 90-minute trip back to our apartment via foot, bus, and subway.

"How are you feeling?" my wife asked when we had walked about a block away from the hospital.

"Rotten. How am I supposed to feel?"

When I got home and sat down, Gwyneth the cat leaped to her accustomed lap spot as I agonizingly wondered: Would St. Mary's be the right decision?

Not long before Abigail entered the hospice, my wife was invited to testify at a U.S. Senate subcommittee hearing on "the quality of medical laboratory testing." I accompanied her to Washington, D.C., for a hurried day-and-a-half while Suzette the nurse took care of Abigail.

The March 23 hearing began with statements from Senators Carl Levin (D-Mich.) and William Cohen (R-Maine) — the future Secretary of Defense under President Clinton. Levin said one goal of the hearing was "to educate us as consumers, so that we do not blindly accept what we are told about our laboratory results."

In her testimony, my wife stated: "We feel that all lab tests, especially ... for a condition which is life-threatening, should be double-checked. Also, in Tay-Sachs screening in particular, both parents should be tested because both parents have to be carriers.... We also feel that laboratories should be rewarded for high accuracy rates and not for doing as many tests as they possibly can."

Given America's for-profit medical system, that last suggestion had as much chance of passing through a legislative body as a football-sized kidney stone.

States News Service did a nice story covering the hearing, and even contacted the guilty Brooklyn lab for a response. An official there said he couldn't comment because the hospital was negotiating an out-of-court settlement with us. This was news to us and our attorney, who said the hospital and its big-shot law firm wanted to stall as much as possible in the hope that we would become discouraged enough to drop the case.

It was also in 1988 that my wife and I joined the National Tay-Sachs & Allied Diseases Association, which put us in phone contact with other Tay-Sachs parents throughout the U.S. This was helpful, and less expensive than going into therapy to rid ourselves of the delusion that our insurance would pay for therapy.

Unfortunately, the Tay-Sachs organization's Scientific Advisory Committee included the head of the lab that made the error! We reluctantly accepted this, but you'll see in the 1989 chapter how strained it became for us and this non-apologizer to be connected with the same organization.

In addition, I joined a patient rights group called Stop Hospital and Medical Errors. Somehow, I could relate more to the people slammed by malpractice than to Tay-Sachs parents slammed by genetic bad luck, and I soon got elected to the SHAME board of directors and began working on the organization's newsletter. Among SHAME's goals were to comfort families victimized by medical errors, push for more public exposure of the doctors who commit malpractice multiple times, and lobby for stronger disciplinary action against negligent medical practitioners. The 1988 *Medicine on Trial* book noted that for every 252 times a patient is injured or killed by doctor negligence, only once is a serious disciplinary action taken against a doctor.

And I continued my publicity efforts. Stories about Abigail were done by publications such as *Ladies' Home Journal* and *New York Newsday*. Also, my wife and I appeared on the TV shows *New York Views* and *People Are Talking*. The former program taped us in advance at home, so that wasn't too nerve-wracking. But the latter appearance was live in front of a studio audience, and my voice was shaking during my first few comments. Fortunately, I managed to pull myself together and do better as the segment went on.

But though we were getting luckier with media coverage, our luck was rotten in a more important area — trying to have a healthy child. By the spring of 1988, my wife had gone through the ordeal of three miscarriages that might have been caused by stress. Then she managed to have two non-miscarrying pregnancies later in the year, but the fetus had Tay-Sachs each time! So there were two emotionally devastating abortions — and the sick realization that three consecutive "successful" pregnancies (including the one that produced Abigail) had a bad result when the average odds were one Tay-

Sachs pregnancy in four for couples carrying the disastrous gene. Fate was slamming our heads with empty baby bottles, and my agnosticism was solidifying.

(What's an agnostic? A person who's not sure atheism exists....)

The sorrow we were going through would put a strain on even the most compatible of marriages, and my wife and I were not compatible in several areas. She had not yet become more religious, but definitely felt differently about God than I did. Also, she got offended when friends, relatives, and others didn't say quite the right thing about Abigail, while I would let it slide. And she wanted to talk a lot about Abigail's situation, while I often preferred to do things like read, play my guitar, or ride my exercise bike to get my mind off the malpractice elephant in the room. I even resumed my *Comic Strip Connection* novel, which wasn't shaping up as well as I had hoped — but it was an escape. Still, my wife and I had a certain feeling of solidarity in facing the terminal illness of our daughter, so the marriage continued to have some life.

And ultimately I couldn't argue with her decision to put Abigail in hospice care. St. Mary's turned out to be a wonderful place where the kids were cared for expertly and kindly. We became friendly with the nurses and other staffers — including the extraordinarily compassionate social worker Paul Alexander Klincewicz (also an excellent guitarist/singer/songwriter who played weekly for the hospice kids and families, and has released some CDs). We got to know the parents of other St. Mary's children, too, and that was quite a solace. I even watched the 1989 Super Bowl between the San Francisco 49ers and Cincinnati Bengals with one of the dads at his Queens apartment. This time, Abigail wasn't there.

Also (mostly) not there were characters of color in syndicated comics. As you might recall from my 1984 chapter, only three of the 200-plus syndicated strips were done by African-American artists — and the situation was no better in 1988. Meanwhile, multicultural casting in comics created by white cartoonists had improved only slightly. Indeed, the *Detroit Free Press* counted the characters in the syndicated comics it published in a given month, and found that 5,250 were white and 31 black. This was at a time when Detroit was 63% black!

So, three Detroit entities sprang into action. First the Detroit City Council's Youth Advisory Committee (YAC) expressed concern about the near-total whiteness of comic pages, and then the *Free Press* and *Detroit News* sent letters to more than 200 cartoonists and syndicates decrying this homogeneity.

News vice president/executive editor Robert Giles provided me with a copy of his March 1988 letter, which included a YAC comment about how African-Americans often "appear in stories related to crime" but seldom "in the kind of humorous day-to-day stories that are featured in the comics."

Syndicates acknowledged the problem, but said it wasn't intentional. For instance, Universal Press vice president/editorial director Lee Salem — perhaps the best-known comics editor in the biz — told me that Universal was looking for more cartoonists of color and more comics with multicultural casts, but said creators submitting strip ideas continued to be mostly white males.

The issue would continue to be discussed over the next few months. And, lo and behold, comics by cartoonists of color started entering syndication. Ray Billingsley's "Curtis" launched in October via King Features, and was running in nearly 100 newspapers by the end of '88. Interestingly, the King person who first saw the comic's potential was Paul Hendricks, one of the very few black syndicate editors back then. In fact, "Curtis" was in development before the Detroit newspapers sent out those letters.

Then, Robb Armstrong's "Jump Start" and Stephen Bentley's "Herb and Jamaal" launched in 1989 via United Feature Syndicate and Tribune Media Services, respectively, and Barbara Brandon's "Where I'm Coming From" arrived in 1991 via Universal. But it would be a number of years before another cluster of nonwhite-created comics (including the 1999-launched "The Boondocks" by Aaron McGruder of Universal) began landing in the funny pages.

Meanwhile, syndicates in the second half of the 1980s slowly began to offer more columnists of color — including Robert Maynard, Les Payne, and (in 1990) Julianne Malveaux and Roger Hernandez — to join longtime op-ed stalwarts such as Carl Rowan and *The Washington Post*'s William Raspberry.

But there was still a quasi-quota system at some newspapers that figured one comic by a black and one by a woman were enough. Stephen Bentley, speaking at Ohio State in 1995, discussed how wrong this approach was: "Editors say 'I got my black cartoon and I got my woman's cartoon so I don't need another.' But we're all tackling different ideas and relationships. 'Jump Start' is about a family, 'Curtis' is about a kid's life, and 'Herb and Jamaal' is about friends."

As you'll see, this quasi-quota issue would come up again in 2008.

Back in 1988, legendary "Terry and the Pirates"/"Steve Canyon" creator Milton Caniff died April 3 at age 81. I attended Milt's April 6 funeral service in Manhattan, and also phoned some people to get comments about the classy cartoonist. Charles Schulz told me that Caniff — whose widow, Esther, would die the next month — "did more for the profession of comics than any other single person." The "Peanuts" creator was referring not only to Milt's two syndicated strips, but to his mentoring of young cartoonists, his involvement in founding the National Cartoonists Society and Newspaper Features Council, and more.

Just after Caniff died, the 1988 Pulitzers were announced — and the commentary winner was syndicated *Miami Herald* humorist Dave Barry. This was a surprise, because that category usually honored serious op-ed columnists. To misquote Barry, "'The Serious Op-Ed Columnists' would make a great name for a rock band!"

The prize helped rocket Barry into more than 500 newspapers and make him famous enough to have a TV sitcom — the 1993-97 *Dave's World* — based on his life. That life included being born in Armonk, N.Y., in 1947 and joining the *Daily Local News* in West Chester, Pa., in 1971 as a reporter. Dave soon began writing a humor column for that newspaper, in addition to writing stories.

Barry is also known for his membership in the amateur Rock Bottom Remainders rock band along with other famous writers such as Stephen King and Amy Tan.

Another 1988 stunner was the devotion to duty of syndicate sales executive Lisa Klem Wilson that April. The composing room of the Albany, N.Y., *Times Union* lost a week's worth of comics, and it frantically phoned syndicates and other newspapers to get copies of the disappeared funnies. Wilson returned the call and offered help *while attending her wedding reception*. In other words, a new bride returned a "ring" from a *Times Union* person during the time of her union to another person. If I can think of another bad pun to belabor this point, I'll let you know.

Then it was off to San Francisco to cover a National Cartoonists Society meeting, and the thing I remember most about that May confab was the 65-year-old Charles Schulz waiting with other attendees in the street for a much-delayed bus that would take everyone from a Cartoon Art Museum reception to a Ghirardelli Square event. When the bus finally came, Schulz let most of the attendees on first and ended up standing with his hand grasping a metal bar, like a rush-hour commuter.

The NCS also paid tribute to Milton Caniff, but its annual *Cartoonist* magazine unfortunately included a Philip Morris ad for Marlboro cigarettes. Milt, a former smoker, died of lung cancer.

"God, I hate tobacco companies," I muttered.

I also covered the 1988 Association of American Editorial Cartoonists meeting in Milwaukee, and former Led Zeppelin singer Robert Plant happened to be staying at the same hotel. I didn't see this encounter (I heard about it later), but several AAECers were having drinks with Plant when *San Diego Tribune* cartoonist J.D. Crowe played a joke on the rock legend. Crowe pretended he thought Plant was singer David Coverdale of Whitesnake — a band considered derivative of Led Zep — and an enraged Plant head-butted Crowe!

Plant didn't have a "Whole Lotta Love" for Crowe at that moment, but the two ended up burying the hatchet and posing with *Pittsburgh Press* cartoonist Rob Rogers for a photo.

Also at that convention, there was some very early talk about computer transmission of editorial cartoons. That would eventually become the delivery norm, but it sounded very exotic in that era of sending cartoons via postal mail.

Of course, transmission was much slower in the primitive days of 1988. AAEC president Ed Stein of the Denver *Rocky Mountain News* said at the '88 meeting that he was "excited" about electronically transmitting a cartoon to his syndicate in six minutes! Today, that would seem like an eternity — and guarantee you a threatening visit from the Fraternal Order of High-Speed-Connection Police.

There was also talk during that '88 session of one day drawing part or all of a cartoon on a computer. Which made me wonder: If the SATs were ever given digitally, would some sleepy student pencil the entire outside of the computer's screen? After all, the screen looks like one big answer box!

If someone wanted to take a No. 2 pencil to a photo of me, there I was in a promotional ad in *E&P*'s 1988 syndicate directory — a 156-page publication filled with ads from feature distributors that still had large marketing budgets. I was asked to provide a quote to go with my photo, and this was my first line: "When I tell people I have to read the comics for my job, I don't get a lot of sympathy."

Sheesh — I hope that jokester never writes a memoir.

Then there was the Sept. 30, 1988, meeting of the Newspaper Features Council (NFC) — whose executive director was Catherine Walker, the smart and kind wife of "Beetle Bailey" creator Mort Walker. One panel at the New York City event included two female humor columnists — and the funny lines were flung fast and furious. For instance, Judy Markey quipped to fellow panelist Alice Kahn: "You have two years off, because your syndicate touts you as a 'columnist for the '90s.'" (By the way, some say Kahn coined the term "yuppie.")

Also on Sept. 30 — a date that would be very significant for my family in 1989 — I had the privilege of seeing Abigail Van Buren in person for the first time.

I took two photos of Abby, ran one in *E&P*, and then mailed both to her in California. "You really know how to take years off a woman," wrote the columnist, who had turned 70 that summer. "Who needs a cosmetic surgeon?"

Actually, I was a *very* amateur photographer who *unintentionally* made the pictures a little blurry.

Abby continued: "I was really tickled to finally see you in the flesh, Dave." The feeling was mutual.

There was more humor at a "How to Become Syndicated Seminar" that followed the NFC meeting. Columnist Heloise offered some anecdotes, including one from a reader whose husband never helped around the house. She finally got some domestic aid from the lazy bum after he died, because his ashes went into an hourglass the woman used to time eggs!

CHAPTER TWELVE

1989:
Two Comics Pass
Like Strips in the
Night

My wife got pregnant yet again — and thankfully she did *not* have another early miscarriage. But there was still the chorionic villus sampling test that would determine if the fetus had Tay-Sachs.

"We need a break for once," I muttered while accompanying my wife to the procedure.

Then we waited for the results.

Another kind of technology — email — would eventually help catapult the 1989-launched "Dilbert" into the syndication stratosphere, but Scott Adams' comic was only a modest success during its first few years.

Here's the conversation I allegedly had with myself in April '89 as I eyed the inaugural "Dilbert" press kit:

"This is about the stiffest art I've ever seen," said I.

"Yeah, but the art's so bad it's almost good," I replied. "And the writing is *hilarious*."

"How popular will 'Dilbert' become?" I asked.

"Middling popular at best," I answered.

"Do you have a track record for accurate predictions?" I queried.

"This book's next sentence," I predicted, "will *not* be 'I rest my case.'"

I rest my case.

Anyway, the 1957-born Adams is a New York State native who moved to California soon after graduating from college. He worked as a teller and in various management positions for a San Francisco bank, earned an MBA from the University of California at Berkeley, and then joined Pacific Bell — while continuing to draw cartoons on the side. Adams definitely has more of a business background than most comic creators, which is obviously reflected in the content of his workplace-based strip.

Soon after "Dilbert" started, cartoonist Berkeley Breathed announced that the 1980-launched "Bloom County" would end.

The Pulitzer Prize-winning comic was as popular as ever; in fact, it added 62 newspapers in 1989 to push its client list past 1,250, and Opus the penguin was a genuine cartoon-character superstar. But Breathed, 31, wanted to pull the plug while "Bloom County" was still near its peak. "The ugly truth is that, in most cases, comics age less gracefully than their creators," he said in a statement.

Breathed also wanted to do children's books, where he would have more space for his art than in comic-shrinking, profit-obsessed newspapers. One wonders how many talented artists never go into syndicated cartooning because of the space restrictions.

The "Bloom County" creator also probably needed some rest, because in those days before cartoonists emailed their comics to syndicates, he worked so close to deadline that he often raced to the airport to put new strips on a plane to the Washington Post Writers Group syndicate. I'm not sure if Opus watched the pre-flight safety demonstration.

Breathed's decision to lower the boom on "Bloom" was an unusual one in the syndication world. Most cartoonists keep doing a comic even when it's well past its prime — with their children or assistants often taking over after they die. The feature then becomes a "legacy comic," and the legacy might be tired gags and less newspaper space for fresher strips. Several profit-conscious syndicates distribute too many over-the-hill comics (a number of which reliably make at least some money) and not enough newer comics that might or might not sell well.

Breathed himself started a new comic called "Outland" later in 1989, and continued that Sunday-only feature until 1995. Then he did the Sunday-only "Opus" from 2003 to 2008. But both would have nowhere near the clientele, impact, or two-words-in-the-title-ness of "Bloom County."

In May '89, the Association of American Editorial Cartoonists met in Newport, R.I., to discuss serious matters such as ethics, libel law, and the influence of Thomas Nast (1840-1902) — the father of modern political cartooning who created the Republican elephant, Democratic donkey, and our modern images of Uncle Sam and Santa Claus. *Detroit News* cartoonist Draper Hill, a Nast expert, spoke about the *Harper's Weekly* satirist who helped bring down Boss Tweed.

But AAEC attendees responded most enthusiastically to a funny panel featuring several *Mad* magazine artists, including Jack Davis and Mort Drucker. Many AAECers had grown up reading *Mad*, and their editorial cartoons often mixed the magazine's zaniness with more sober-minded "Nast"-iness. (By the way, the word "nasty" predated Thomas Nast.)

Amid frequent bursts of audience applause, the *Mad* artists described how they worked while also tossing out one-liners. Drucker recalled receiving free mints after drawing them in a *Mad* spread. "Now I draw Jaguars and Mercedes," he quipped.

Just before I headed home from Newport, I got a call from my wife. Several weeks before, the test results had revealed ... a healthy fetus! We were beyond thrilled. But now my wife was bleeding. Would it be another miscarriage?

The 1989 train ride from Rhode Island was almost as miserable as my 1987 train ride to Washington after Abigail was diagnosed. I wondered if my pregnant wife had traveled too much in '89; she had flown with me to the National Cartoonists Society meeting in Toronto the month before, and also accompanied me on a trip to Cambridge, Mass., where I had spoken on a "How to Get Syndicated" panel.

The talk didn't go too badly — certainly better than it would have gone in my shyer days of 1983. I cracked some regionally appropriate jokes, including a quip about the Boston Red Sox and Fenway Park. But I got my biggest laugh unintentionally when offering my office phone number to the audience in case any of the 200-plus attendees wanted to find out more about syndication when I returned to New York. My dopey generosity caused me hours of advice-giving over the next few months when I could ill afford the time.

But I digress. Despite the bleeding, the pregnancy held — though my wife and I were terrified that the fetus had been harmed.

Meanwhile, we visited Abigail as much as possible at St. Mary's Hospital for Children. It helped greatly that my editor, John Consoli, let me leave the office early to go to the hospital. And since *E&P* had many fewer layers of management than when it later became part of a conglomerate, magazine owner Robert Brown knew me as an individual rather than as a faceless cog in the corporate wheel — and thus graciously accepted my slightly lower rate of productivity.

At the hospital, I held Abigail on my lap and stroked her hair — hoping for some tiny response.

"This is your father," I whispered to her.

She just stared at the ceiling with her blind eyes.

In those moments, I would think bitter thoughts about the Brooklyn lab that made the error and about a certain lab director who wouldn't apologize.

Our lawsuit against the hospital was going nowhere, and our attorney was irking the heck out of us. He wouldn't return calls or reply to letters, even though I was careful not to contact him too often. He "lost" important material we sent him. And he would make typos and other errors in documents, even giving the wrong year for Abigail's birth.

So I summoned my courage and asked an attorney who advised the Stop Hospital and Medical Errors (SHAME) group I was in if he'd take our non-lucrative case. Marty Baron — a competent lawyer and nice man — agreed!

We soon learned, however, that an attorney who recently joined the Baron & Vesel firm had once represented the Brooklyn hospital in a case — so there was a possible conflict-of-interest perception. But Marty couldn't find us a non-B&V attorney to replace him, and we didn't want to go back to our previous lawyer, so we decided to risk remaining with Marty. We kept our fingers crossed that the hospital — which had already treated us badly — wouldn't add insult to injury by allowing its law firm to contest the good legal representation we had finally found.

But, sure enough, the law firm successfully filed a motion to get Marty bounced from the case. That made us lawyer-less, or so we thought.

At least our media campaign was continuing. For instance, we discussed Abigail's case in a *Sally Jesse Raphael* show segment titled "Hospital Horror Stories."

But a write-up in the *Breakthrough* newsletter published by the National Tay-Sachs & Allied Diseases Association infuriated my wife and I (we were NTSAD members, as you might recall). It was a puff piece about a certain Brooklyn lab by a person who worked there — and the error on my blood analysis wasn't mentioned. Also, NTSAD's intro to the piece lavished praise on the lab! We could only conclude that the organization cared more about the non-apologizing lab head on its Scientific Advisory Committee than about us. Sure, publish the piece — but find a way to show the bad with the good. NTSAD ignored our complaints about the write-up, so we resigned.

With all this stuff going on, I somehow managed to keep working on *The Comic Strip Connection* novel — reaching a total of about 120 handwritten pages. I even added a dying-child subplot that, while perhaps therapeutic for me, muddled the book.

Agent Toni Mendez was now willing to show the manuscript to publishers if I keyboarded the thing.

"Do you have a computer, Day-vid?" Toni asked.

"Um ... no," I replied guiltily.

Because of the medical expenses my wife and I were facing, I couldn't afford to buy a computer or even hire someone to keyboard the novel. They probably couldn't have deciphered my messy handwriting, anyway.

Then Ronnie Telzer, my pre-1983 *Marketing Communications* editor and now a friend, told me she'd be away from her Manhattan apartment for two days and that I could use her computer while she was gone. I took advantage of this very kind offer, going to Ronnie's place for two consecutive nights after work and frantically typing up the book in a pair of marathon sessions lasting past midnight before I took the subway back to Queens. My fingers ached so much I could have written a country-and-western song about them.

Toni subsequently sent around the book, and my luck finally changed (not!). It was "the three R's" — rejection, rejection, rejection — although I received more than three R's. Now the question was whether I had the mental energy to do another "R" thing: revise.

Meanwhile, technology was marching on in syndication. I wrote an *E&P* story about columnist Heloise now accepting household hints from readers via ... fax! ("Dear Heloise: The 500 faxed pages that follow this cover sheet contain foolproof tips about using less fax paper.") And widely syndicated Ranan Lurie and the *Chattanooga Times'* Bruce Plante were among the editorial cartoonists faxing their work to newspapers. Faxing seems almost quaint now, but it was cutting edge in the 1980s. After all, syndicated creators had been using postal mail ever since Alexander the Great wrote his "Traveling With Al" column.

But whatever the technology, lawsuits still happen. The *Dallas Times Herald* filed a $33-million suit in August 1989 after Universal Press Syndicate announced it would transfer 26 features — including blockbusters like "Doonesbury," "For Better or For Worse," "The Far Side," and "Dear Abby" — from the *Times Herald* to the bigger *Dallas Morning News*. This transfer was the outgrowth of a joint venture between the syndicate and the A.H. Belo Corporation (which owned the *Morning News* and television stations) to develop TV programming based on Universal features. Universal said the deal would also give its creators more Dallas-area readers. But another reason for the venture, according to a September *Times Herald* story, was that Belo promised Universal about $1 million for current and future features over the next five years.

Despite its lawsuit, the *Times Herald* never got the features back — and it folded in 1991.

This was not the first time something like this happened. Several years earlier, News America Syndicate switched many features from *The Boston Globe* to the smaller *Boston Herald* — which, like NAS, was owned by Rupert Murdoch.

Meanwhile, former Universal columnist Jesse Jackson was returning to newspapers in 1989 via the Los Angeles Times Syndicate after his stirring 1988 Democratic presidential campaign that netted him a number of primary wins and nearly seven million votes. I had voted for Jackson, so I eagerly sought an interview with him about his new LATS column. I managed to set up an in-person talk for August, but the logistics were tricky.

First I went to a New York City press conference focusing on a walkout by Local 1199 of the Drug, Hospital and Health Care Employees Union. Jackson was one of the speakers, and he gave a rousing talk.

The plan was for me to interview Jackson in some quiet corner after his speech. So I nervously approached him after he left the podium.

"Mr. Jackson? I'm Dave Astor from *E&P* ... um, that is, *Editor & Publisher* magazine. We were going to do an interview ... to talk ... to talk about your column."

He looked at me blankly, and I wondered if he forgot or even knew about our appointment. "Who are you again?"

"Uh ... Dave Astor." Boy did I hate my elitist last name at that moment; Jackson would have no clue I had a blue-collar background. "I write about syndication for *Editor & Publisher*, which covers the newspaper business."

"I have to get to my next appointment."

Though nervous, I had enough presence of mind to lobby my case. "The story will be read by many newspaper editors who decide which columns to buy."

That seemed to work. "How about if you drive with me?" Jackson suggested.

I climbed into the backseat while he sat in the front seat next to another person at the wheel. I would have perhaps 15 minutes, at best. This was the only time in my life I longed for one of those teeth-gnashing Manhattan traffic jams!

Already anxious about meeting Jackson, I was now truly flustered — fumbling with my pen and reporter's notebook as the fast-moving vehicle bumped over potholes. I stammered out a few inane questions, and I could almost see Jackson rolling his eyes even though only the back of his head was visible to me. But, after a few minutes, I managed to get a grip and sound like a professional journalist rather than a professional idiot. This was progress — I could now save myself mid-interview!

It helped that I told Jackson about my 1985 interview with Coretta Scott King. And he eagerly welcomed the chance to answer this question of mine: "Why do you spend a lot of time supporting unions?"

"Because I'm a working person's person," Jackson replied. "My mother was an aide at a hospital. She was a cook. She did three jobs but couldn't earn a living wage. My father was a janitor."

The civil rights leader soon arrived at his destination, so I scrambled out of the car and down some subway stairs to return to *E&P*.

There, I would soon cover another contraction in the syndication biz. The 1922-founded McNaught Syndicate folded, with the much larger Tribune Media Services taking over some of its roster. McNaught's most popular feature was George Gately's "Heathcliff" comic about an occasionally combative cat ("Wuthering Fights?"), and the syndicate had formerly distributed the "Dear Abby" column and "Will Rogers Says," which quoted the legendary humorist. McNaught was not that big a syndicate by 1989, but its death meant a little less competition in a consolidating feature field.

Given that the Dallas features transfer had been recently announced, it was a coincidence that Dallas would be the locale of long-scheduled October meetings by the Newspaper Features Council (NFC) and American Association of Sunday and Feature Editors. An AASFE panel discussed the *Times Herald*-to-*Morning News* transfer, with the highlight being this comment by *Washington Post* executive editor Ben Bradlee of Watergate fame: "We're talking about ethics, and I think it sucks."

At the NFC meeting, the best session focused on how the blandness of many daily newspapers made it hard for them to attract younger readers. This blandness, along with recessions and the rise of the Internet, would bite newspapers badly over the next two decades.

"Many readers feel their paper is as interesting as a phone book," observed humor columnist Joe Bob Briggs, who, along with other panelists, suggested that newspapers run more irreverent material, use candid language when appropriate, etc.

Why were dailies so cautious? Speakers said, among other things, that editors don't want to deal with reader complaints (even if they're from only a small percentage of subscribers) and that papers are increasingly owned by chains more interested in profits than editorial excitement. In other words, we're talking about corporatization, and I think it sucks. (I don't usually talk like that, but I couldn't resist riffing on Bradlee's remark!)

The Dallas gathering also included a "Cartoonists for Literacy" event — chaired by "Beetle Bailey" creator Mort Walker — that showed once again how lots of syndicated creators aid good causes. But even that was awkward because the *Times Herald* and *Morning News* had agreed long before the event to co-sponsor it with the Dallas Public Library. Neither paper backed out, but their representatives at the podium weren't singing "Kumbaya."

Speaking of good causes, Dr. Seuss (1904-1991) drew an anti-drug cartoon in 1989 that appeared in the *San Diego Tribune* and was syndicated by Copley News Service. The drawing showed a kid with a hole in his head, with the not-surprising caption: "Dope! You need it like you need a hole in the head." Though Dr. Seuss was of course most famous for his fabulous children's books, he had also been an editorial cartoonist for New York's *PM* paper from 1941 to 1943. Some say the way Seuss drew Uncle Sam for *PM* influenced the look of The Cat in the Hat when that feline was created years later.

Then I was off to Ohio State University to cover the 1989 Festival of Cartoon Art organized by the incredibly nice and hardworking Lucy Shelton Caswell, who founded what's now called the Billy Ireland Cartoon Library & Museum in 1977. The Ohio State-based CLM started with the papers of "Terry and the Pirates"/"Steve Canyon" cartoonist Milton Caniff (an OSU alum) and then expanded to eventually include 450,000-plus original pieces of art by many different creators.

Lucy was one of the few people in the world who could get private "Calvin and Hobbes" cartoonist Bill Watterson to make a public appearance, but his festival talk came with conditions: no photo taking, no taping of his speech, and no autographs for attendees.

Watterson discussed what he viewed as the sorry state of the comics biz — lamenting strip shrinkage ("you can only eliminate so many words and pictures before the cartoon suffers"); the use of assistants ("I want to draw cartoons, not supervise a factory"); replacements for dead cartoonists ("if a cartoonist can't make it with his own work, he doesn't deserve to be in newspapers"); and the licensing of comics for things like greeting cards ("Calvin is the last kid on Earth to wish anyone well").

The speaker did lavishly praise Charles Schulz despite the huge amount of licensing allowed by the "Peanuts" creator. He told the overflow crowd that Schulz "changed comics" with the emotional depth of "Peanuts," his "deceptively simple" art, his "intellectual children" characters, and his innovative treatment of animals such as Snoopy.

"Beetle Bailey" creator Mort Walker rebutted some of Watterson's talk in his own festival speech the next day. "I use assistants because you need someone around to tell you your mistakes," Mort stated. He added that a number of cartoonists who take over comics do "a marvelous job" — citing John Cullen Murphy of the Hal Foster-created "Prince Valiant" as one example. And Walker said licensed products "add color, life, and good humor to the world."

Mort, who agreed with Watterson on the problem of too-small comics, clearly won the friendliness battle at Ohio State. He graciously called Watterson "a brilliant talent," and I watched Walker do many autographed sketches for fans and pose with them for photos.

I met my future good friend Anne Gibbons at the Ohio State event; it was ironic that happened in Columbus given that we both lived in New York at the time (though her husband Ivan Braun had an Ohio background). Anne is a cartoonist known for her greeting cards, for being a "Six Chix" comic contributor, and more.

Then I rushed home from the October festival, because waiting in Queens was ... a seemingly healthy daughter! Maggie had been born on Sept. 30, and I was so full of emotions while watching her emerge that I didn't know whether to laugh or cry. Instead, I stood there looking so dazed that the obstetrician gave me a quizzical glance. But, after the *three* miscarriages and *two* aborted Tay-Sachs-affected pregnancies my wife had endured, Maggie's birth was *one* very welcome event.

The rest of 1989 was an exhausting whir of new parenting, but I didn't mind waking up for middle-of-the-night feedings. It was amazing to see a baby drink from a bottle rather than through a stomach tube.

Maggie (*not* short for Margaret, because I wanted a name as casual as "Abigail" was formal) met her older sister several times that fall at St. Mary's. But neither of them would remember the encounters. Maggie was too young, and poor Abigail was too oblivious.

CHAPTER THIRTEEN

1990:
An April Fools'
Day Like No Other

Even as Universal Press received flak for its Dallas features transfer, the syndicate's creators kept winning major awards. As noted earlier, Bill Watterson received his second top-cartoonist Reuben in 1989 (the year his *Yukon Ho!* book of "Calvin and Hobbes" comics sold a whopping 1,257,000 copies). Tom Toles — the quiet *Buffalo News* staffer who later succeeded Herblock at *The Washington Post* — snagged the 1990 Pulitzer Prize for his quirky, insightful editorial cartoons. And Gary Larson ("The Far Side") won the Reuben in 1991.

Universal turned 20 in 1990 — and King Features turned 75. I jumped King's November birthday gun a bit by writing a retrospective on the syndicate in late September, so I learned a lot about King's history two weeks before the 498th anniversary of when Christopher Columbus sought a direct sailing route to the Cartoon Library & Museum in Columbus, Ohio.

To prepare for the King story, I leafed through *E&P*'s Nov. 20, 1915, issue in the office archives.

"What are you looking for?" asked librarian Shqipe Malushi.

"King's birth certificate," I replied.

I soon found a brief mention, under "new incorporations," of the fledgling King. But I was more fascinated by other items in that 1915 magazine's yellowed pages, including a story about newspaper editors voting whether "'movie' should be recognized as a legitimate English word to be used without quotation marks." That's the kind of serendipitous tidbit I wouldn't find in future years, because those searches for old *E&P* stories would be conducted online. And Shqipe unfortunately lost her job after the magazine's archives were digitized.

Then I perused other sources to see what they had to say about King's history. It was fascinating to read about the syndicate's past columnists such as Damon Runyon (whose writings inspired *Guys and Dolls*) and Jack Dempsey (yes, the boxer penned a syndicated feature). And King's impressive comics stable once included the wonderfully surreal "Krazy Kat" by George Herriman, "Boob McNutt" by Rube Goldberg (inventor of those hilariously useless contraptions), "Buster Brown" by R.F. Outcault (does a brand of shoes come to mind?), and "Thimble Theatre" by Elzie Segar (whose spinach-eating Popeye character in that comic would've led the league in forearms if he ever played baseball).

I also learned that the Hearst Corp.-owned King was not the first syndication venture for William Randolph Hearst (that *Citizen Kane*-ish model for the profit-driven media moguls of today). The company began distributing content to newspapers in the 1890s.

The in-person interviews I did with King's president Joe D'Angelo and vice president Larry Olsen for the anniversary story were a bit awkward, because the two execs felt my coverage of creator-contract issues and Hearst's purchase of Cowles Syndicate and News America Syndicate had an anti-management/anti-conglomerate tone.

"Why can't all your stories about King be positive?" asked D'Angelo.

"They're positive most of the time," I replied. "More than 90% of the time."

Several years earlier, Joe's question might have flustered me. Instead, I sardonically thought to myself that if King wanted all-glowing coverage, it should hire me for its public-relations department. Actually, it was more satisfying to be an independent reporter — and King's dynamic PR pair of Ted Hannah and Claudia Smith were doing a bang-up job.

I didn't blame D'Angelo and Olsen for some of the corporate things King had done, because I assumed they were basically following the dictates of their corporate supervisors. Indeed, the affable D'Angelo might have helped convince Hearst that cartoonists Bil Keane and Mort Walker should get ownership of "The Family Circus" and "Beetle Bailey," respectively.

D'Angelo and Olsen were close enough to King's creators and employees to see them as people. But top executives at most large companies are far enough removed from creators and employees to see them more as numbers. That's a big reason why I dislike the increasing corporatization of American business.

Walker and Keane were among the King stars of a 1990 birthday event in New York City's World Financial Center that marked the round-number anniversaries of "Blondie" (started by Chic Young in 1930 and later continued by his son Dean), "Beetle Bailey" (begun by Walker in 1950), "Dennis the Menace" (created by Hank Ketcham in 1950 though it didn't enter syndication until '51), and "The Family Circus" (launched by Keane in 1960). The four were crowned "Kings of Comics."

That monarchical mash-up was followed by a 75th birthday party for King at NYC's posh Waldorf-Astoria Hotel. The evening gala was attended by about 600 people, including Stan Lee ("Spider-Man") and columnist Dr. Joyce Brothers.

"Are you related to the Astor in Waldorf-Astoria?" Ketcham asked me as he stood next to a costumed Dennis the Menace.

Sheesh, I hate questions about my misleading last name. That man was a menace.

The lavish King events illustrated how some syndicates back then were still making enough money to have occasional blow-out parties that would mostly disappear in the 2000s.

I don't remember if King's evening gala had free drinks or a cash bar, but that wasn't an issue for a teetotaler like me. *E&P*'s publisher would get annoyed if a reporter ordered pricey alcoholic beverages on the company dime, which made me think of the following hypothetical scene:

Publisher to reporter returning from out-of-town convention: "You spent $1,000 for drinks!?"

Thought balloon over reporter's head: "Dang! You have two beers at a hotel bar and they're all over you."

Another 1990 celebration was a Universal Press party marking the 20th anniversary of "Doonesbury." Cartoonist Garry Trudeau and his TV-host wife Jane Pauley, two private people who rarely cruised the celebrity social circuit, both attended the October bash in New York City.

Also, the National Cartoonists Society held a December holiday party at which John Updike spoke. The novelist was there to receive the organization's Amateur Cartoonist Extraordinary (ACE), which went to a person who did cartoons as a youth before finding fame in another profession.

Was drawing a comic harder than writing books such as *Rabbit, Run* and *The Witches of Eastwick*? Updike seemed to think so. "A cartoonist needs seven ideas a week. As a novelist, I only need one idea every two years," he quipped.

Humor and April 1 usually go together, though that wasn't the case for me in 1990. But let me first backtrack to January. As the year began, my daughter Maggie seemed to be developing normally! She looked alert, smiled, focused on the books I constantly read to her, and did other things babies do. It was wonderful! But it didn't mean my wife and I became wonderfully compatible.

For instance, we had very different reactions to Maggie not sleeping well for many months. I would get out of bed without too much grumbling to comfort and feed Maggie — figuring that finally having a healthy child was more than worth the exhaustion I felt. But my wife was very impatient with the sleep interruption long after she had physically recovered from her pregnancy.

My inadequate sleep, visits to Abigail, *E&P* job, and work for the Stop Hospital and Medical Errors group (I was now SHAME's vice president) finally caused me to give up any attempt to rewrite my *Comic Strip Connection* novel. I did this with regret, but knew I should spend more time with Maggie.

Though Abigail's physical and mental abilities were gone, she was still growing to the point where it became difficult to lift and hold her. But despite her increasing height and weight, her health seemed about the same to me. So it was a surprise in March 1990 to hear from the hospice doctor that Abigail was taking a turn for the worse. Soon, I did notice that her breathing sounded more labored than usual.

My wife and I subsequently made sure one of us visited St. Mary's every day, with the other taking care of Maggie at home. I was even at the hospice on March 29, thinking how weird yet normal it felt to spend my 36th birthday with a dying child.

On April 1, my wife and I were spending a short time away from St. Mary's to eat a Sunday dinner at home when we received a call from the hospital to come quickly. A babysitter who lived close by rushed over (we had told her in advance she might be needed at a moment's notice), and we hopped into a cab.

"I don't want her to die, but I want her to die," my anguished wife said in the taxi.

At least that was one thing we could agree on. Abigail had suffered far too long.

Luckily, the weekend traffic wasn't too bad. We urged the driver to go as fast as he could, and he got us to the hospital in about 30 minutes. We impatiently jabbed St. Mary's elevator button, and rushed into the hospice unit. Abigail was still alive, but breathing with difficulty.

Two hospice nurses carefully put Abigail on my lap in the hospice living room, and I dazedly watched her. She was as pale as a bisque doll. My wife sat to my immediate right, and the doctor was in front of me checking Abigail's pulse and other vital signs every few minutes. I was so choked up I didn't say a word. The soundtrack was provided by *America's Funniest Home Videos* on the hospice's living-room TV.

Suddenly, Abigail shuddered and thick whitish stuff spewed out of her mouth. Then the shuddering stopped.

"W-what was *that*?" I asked the doctor.

The doctor examined Abigail for a full minute before replying awkwardly: "This child is no longer alive."

I started crying, as did my wife. A nurse made an attempt at cleaning up the white stuff on Abigail's clothes, and then quietly backed away. The doctor hovered nearby. Abigail was a little over two months from a fourth birthday she would never reach.

My wife held Abigail for a few minutes, and then I held her again. We both kissed our daughter several times — leaving tears that matted her hair — before she was taken away.

In a sense, Abigail had already been taken away three years before.

The next few days were nuts. Fortunately, at the wise urging of hospice social worker Paul Klincewicz, we had made Abigail's funeral arrangements in 1989. Our daughter was buried April 4 in a Queens cemetery, and then everyone gathered in our apartment to morosely eat some food.

My mother had come up from her New Jersey apartment to help out for a few days, which I greatly appreciated. Unfortunately, she and my wife didn't have that good a relationship, so awkwardness was added to tragedy.

But it was comforting to receive many condolence letters from family, friends, and the hospice staff. One compassionate nurse, Mary O'Connell, even sent a lovely poem she wrote about Abigail.

I also received kind letters from *E&P* owner Robert Brown, my co-workers, and various people I covered. "Your ordeal was one that no loving parent should ever have to endure," wrote Abigail Van Buren.

Brown sent a contribution to St. Mary's in Abigail's memory, as did *E&P* staffers in a donation effort organized by my fellow reporter Debra Gersh (later Debra Gersh Hernandez). Even some of the creators and syndicates I covered made contributions, something I didn't know about until after the money was given. This was one of those journalistic conflicts of interest again but, heck, that great hospital needed the money. And I would donate to St. Mary's (which held a nice memorial service for Abigail on May 1) for years to come.

Meanwhile, it was *beyond* comforting to see Maggie continue to develop so well. When she stood up for the first time in the summer of 1990, it was a revelation.

"She's going to walk soon!" my wife shouted as she watched Maggie totter on two legs, arms grasping the sofa for support.

"Unbelievable," I whispered.

After never seeing Abigail stand up, it was almost like watching an alien — but what an alien!

Also that summer, we gave up our lawsuit against the Brooklyn hospital whose lab had fouled up my blood test. We hadn't found anyone else to take the case after the hospital's law firm pushed out our new attorney, and we still didn't want to go back to the pre-Marty Baron lawyer who had made many mistakes and been uncommunicative.

Perhaps I just didn't want to focus on the past any more, because that September I also resigned from SHAME. I had remained active in the group after Abigail died — even going on a grueling all-day trip to New York's capital city of Albany to lobby state legislators on medical-malpractice reform — but a lot of infighting was developing among board members. I watched this with dismay, because it was diverting energy from more important things. And people on both sides of the board divide would come to me to try to mediate their differences.

"You have to talk with 'E'!" said "L," when calling me at work.

"You have to talk with 'L'!" said "E," when calling me at work.

I left their full names out, because they were both still dealing with their own malpractice situations and I couldn't blame them for being stressed about everything. But I was too tired to deal with organizational battles.

In the fall, my wife and I appeared on Joan Rivers' show to discuss Abigail's case. I was now somewhat more comfortable in front of a camera and studio audience, but decided in the "green room" that day that I had reached my limit of TV segments focusing on malpractice. I don't know, maybe I was starting to feel like a circus freak.

But we did agree to a late-1990 interview for a story on medical-test problems that ran in several hundred newspapers as part of *Parade* magazine's Feb. 3, 1991, issue. The article included a photo of my wife and I with Maggie — our surviving daughter's first media appearance.

Just before her first birthday, Maggie began day care at a place called Adventureland that was about a mile from our Queens apartment. We still couldn't afford a car — we would be paying off funeral expenses until the end of 1991 and couldn't even buy a stone for Abigail's grave (thanks, guilty lab in Brooklyn!). But the walk was great exercise. Occasionally, I'd get a ride from Lori or Larry Esteves, whose daughter Katie was also enrolled at Adventureland. It was a strange experience making friends with the parents of a healthy child!

CHAPTER FOURTEEN

1991:
'I'm Going to Graceland, Graceland...'

The attorney my wife and I "fired" from our Abigail lawsuit never took his name off the case. He wasn't doing any work on our behalf, as far as we could tell, but maybe he hoped something would happen.

Amazingly, something *did*. For whatever reason, the Brooklyn hospital and its guilty lab offered in late 1990 to settle the case for $65,000. We accepted the offer.

The attorney got his $20,000-plus, meaning the case ended up being quite lucrative for someone who spent meager hours on it. My wife and I got the rest, and we quickly paid longstanding medical bills and bought a headstone for Abigail's grave. Our only "splurge" was taking a modest 1992 Vermont farm vacation that Maggie loved.

The settlement also made me feel solvent enough in 1991 to get some intestinal bleeding checked; bleeding I had experienced on and off for two years. I stupidly delayed going to the doctor not only because I worried about the costs that wouldn't be covered by miserly private insurance, but because maybe I had a death wish as I watched Abigail's misery.

A colonoscopy turned up a *very* large polyp, which was removed. If I had waited another year or two, maybe I would have developed colon cancer and outdid "publish or perish" professors by writing this memoir *after* I perished!

By the way, companies seeking more ad opportunities should consider airing colonoscopy commercials. As doctors peer at a monitor during a procedure, they could hear: "We will resume viewing Mr. Smith's intestines after these messages."

I was still alive, but my 1917-born dad wasn't. My mother discovered that my father died in 1991 – nearly 20 years since either of us had seen him.

"How do you feel about his death?" asked my wife, who never met my father.

"I don't feel a thing," I replied.

Actually, I experienced a jumble of feelings that had nothing to do with the "Jumble" newspaper puzzle. I felt sad, I resented the way my younger self's confidence had suffered without a good male role model, I remembered him taking me to baseball's 1964 All-Star Game at Shea Stadium, and I wondered if I should have tried to contact him after I became an adult. But — unlike my wife, who loved to discuss what any person was feeling about anything at any time — I didn't want to talk about my father or the broken family of my youth. I figured I'd wait until the year 3000 or when the "Andy Capp" comic stopped being lame, whichever came first.

But my current family did "interact" with a happy cartoon family for one Sunday. Unbeknownst to me, Bil Keane created a Feb. 10, 1991, "Family Circus" episode showing his cartoon mom sitting opposite my wife and a placid baby Maggie. The cartoon mom says to her little son PJ (who's crying because he wants nothing to do with Maggie): "Look at Mrs. Astor's cute little baby girl! Come on, PJ, don't be that way! Just say hello!" Then, in an O. Henry-like ending, the last panel shows PJ and Maggie getting married 25 years later.

One of Keane's favorite phrases was "see you in the funny pages." He was a man of his word.

When I saw the comic in the Sunday paper, I immediately called Bil in Arizona. "That was *so* nice of you to do that. I almost fainted when I saw it!"

"Don't mention it, Dave. Are Thel and I invited to the wedding in 2016?"

Unfortunately, the 1922-born Bil died in 2011 — three years after the passing of his equally likable wife Thelma, the model for "The Family Circus" mother who shared *my* mother's name.

Thel was Bil's business manager — a job several other people performed for *their* cartoonist spouses. One example was the on-the-mark work Lynn Reznick did for "off the mark" creator Mark Parisi.

Fifteen days after Keane's comic ran, Creators Syndicate took over the 1981-founded Heritage Features Syndicate — a medium-sized distributor with a roster that mostly included conservative columnists. This skewed Creators' pundit lineup even more to the right, but the syndicate did try to rectify that somewhat in the next few years by adding progressive voices such as Molly Ivins.

Heritage's absorption into Creators meant that consolidation had once again hit the syndication biz, so I celebrated by not celebrating because there was nothing to celebrate if one celebrates competition.

But at least the medium-sized Sisters Syndicate did well after its 1990 launch with a roster of mostly women columnists. Then again, the syndicate formed by sisters Christine Negroni and Andrea Lee Negroni would last only a few years.

In a possible sign that Bill Watterson might eventually end the labor-intensive "Calvin and Hobbes," he started a nine-month sabbatical in the spring of 1991. This followed a 14-month hiatus in the late 1980s by "The Far Side" creator Gary Larson. Comics might look easy to write and draw, but most cartoonists I've talked to said this is not the case — especially given the need to do seven episodes a week.

"Cartoonists work like dogs," Mike Peters once told me. And given that his "Mother Goose and Grimm" comic stars a dog, Peters oughta know.

I would personally experience how hard cartooning could be starting in 1997.

Back in 1991, an *E&P* feature story occurred to me as I watched an *Ed Sullivan Show* retrospective on TV. Hadn't Sullivan — the man who brought the Beatles into the living rooms of baby boomers and their parents — also been a syndicated newspaper columnist?

Sure enough, the answer was yes. What surprised me was that Sullivan continued writing his New York *Daily News*-based column — which covered the Broadway nightclub scene, Hollywood, sports celebrities, and more — during the whole 1948-1971 run of his popular CBS variety show.

"Why did he keep doing the column?" I asked *Daily News* sports-cartooning legend Bill Gallo, a sweetheart of a man who had worked with Sullivan.

"Ed just loved being a newspaper guy and hanging around with newspaper people."

"Was he a good writer?"

"He was not a fancy-type writer, but he was good enough."

"Anything else you want to add?" (I usually ended my interviews with that question to give people a chance to say something I might not have asked about.)

"He lived a good life," replied Gallo. "It should happen to all of us!"

But it doesn't.

In April 1991, I covered the Association of American Editorial Cartoonists convention at The Peabody Hotel in Memphis. It was a trip that sticks in my mind more than most of the 70 or so others I took for *E&P*.

The keynote speaker was Sen. Al Gore (D-Tenn.), the future vice president and future almost-president denied that latter post by five partisan Supreme Court justices in 2000. Gore told AAECers he worked as a Nashville *Tennessean* reporter before entering politics, and that his cubicle was near where Sandy Campbell did his editorial cartoons. "I know how much torture some of you go through thinking of ideas," he said.

Gore, then 43, also poked fun at his uncharismatic reputation. "How can you tell Al Gore from a roomful of Secret Service agents?" asked the speaker. "He's the stiff one."

As a reporter, I probably should have walked up to Gore after his speech to ask a few questions. But despite my lessening shyness, I didn't quite have the confidence to pull it off. I had reached a point where I could approach almost any famous columnist or cartoonist at a meeting, but I still couldn't easily do that with politicians. Maybe it's because the majority of them are smooth-talking phonies — though Gore might be better than many, especially as an *ex*-politician in the 2000s warning the world about climate change.

I and some other convention-goers did our environmental part in Memphis, walking all over the place rather than using motorized transportation. I saw the Lorraine Motel (just before it became the National Civil Rights Museum) where Martin Luther King was shot, and thought back to my 1985 interview with his widow. Then I and a group that included Nebraska cartoonist Paul Fell and his wife Arlene visited Graceland, the tacky mansion of the late Elvis Presley. The house left this Elvis non-fan unmoved, but seeing a carpeted *ceiling* and three TVs mounted in a row for simultaneous watching did make me muse about ... when the hell the tour would end.

I soon took a long stroll with cartoonist Jerry Robinson (the aforementioned creator of the Joker) and Mark Cohen (a very friendly real-estate guy who collected cartoons and contributed gags to comics such as Morrie Turner's "Wee Pals"). We stopped for lunch at a restaurant where I tried the fried pickles. Yecch!

We finally ended up at an old shop that sold comic books and the like. Robinson, then 69, was like a kid in an "eye candy" store as he leafed through the stacks — even finding a copy of *The Comics: An Illustrated History of Comic Strip Art* he had authored in 1974. Cartoonists love cartoons!

Then it was back to the hotel for the surreal sight of "The Peabody Ducks" waddling across the lobby to the sounds of John Philip Sousa's "King Cotton March." Later, it occurred to me that The Peabody might be the only hotel where guests see numerous bills before checkout.

One AAEC convention session featured a discussion by AAEC president Mike Keefe about doing animated editorial cartoons via computer. The *Denver Post* cartoonist said he and his wife, Anita Austin, created each 30-second spot on a Macintosh for airing on a local TV station.

Last but not least, several AAECers told me in Memphis that they drew anti-Persian Gulf War cartoons in early 1991 that elicited vicious reader reaction. So I wrote a story about that after I returned to New York.

For instance, Dennis Draughon of the *Scranton* (Pa.) *Times* received two phoned death threats after criticizing Operation Desert Storm in a cartoon inspired by Country Joe McDonald's famous Vietnam-era protest song "I-Feel-Like-I'm-Fixin'-to-Die Rag."

I was appalled that some readers couldn't handle the fact that a small minority of cartoonists and columnists opposed "Desert Storm." Why weren't those readers satisfied that the vast majority of newspaper commentary matched their pro-war views?

It's possible I might not have been tipped off to something like the Gulf War-cartoon threats at future meetings. When I covered conventions for *E&P* in pre-online years such as 1991, I had enough free time between sessions to gab with attendees and pick up story ideas. But when I started in the late 1990s to write stories *at* conferences for quick posting on *E&P*'s Web site, I spent most of the time between sessions pounding the keys of a laptop in my hotel room.

I also traveled to Huntington, W.V., in 1991 to attend my first National Society of Newspaper Columnists conference. As I would soon find out, the NSNC's roster of mostly local columnists, self-syndicated writers, and freelancers couldn't be more convivial and interesting.

To "introduce" myself to the group, I interviewed its president by phone before flying to the meeting. That was gracious *Tallahassee Democrat* columnist Mary Ann Lindley, who had succeeded longtime NSNC president Richard Des Ruisseaux of the Louisville *Courier-Journal*. Then, at the meeting, I introduced myself in person to conference host Jim Casto, the brainy and friendly associate editor/columnist at the Huntington *Herald-Dispatch*.

I proceeded to report the heck out of the conference, filling my "Syndicates" section with NSNC stories (and photos I took) for the next three weeks. Stretching out coverage for that long wasn't exactly an ASAP approach, but it looked more impressive in a way than my post-1998 barrages of online stories that would scroll off the home page of *E&P*'s Web site before or soon after a conference ended.

My family accompanied me to Huntington. Twenty-one-month-old Maggie loved pushing the hotel's elevator buttons, and my wife and I unhappily pushed each other's buttons.

I was happy to report in 1991 that a female black artist had finally been signed by a major syndicate. She was Barbara Brandon, whose "Where I'm Coming From" feature was a comic/editorial cartoon hybrid housed in a large "Feiffer"-shaped rectangle with no separate panels. So I eagerly arranged an interview with the new Universal creator.

"Why do you show just the heads of your characters?" I asked the 32-year-old Brandon.

"Because that's where my characters' minds are. I'm a little tired of how women are portrayed in videos, car ads, and elsewhere. We're always summed up by our bodies."

Most of my other questions focused on Brandon's feature and the universal elements in it, but I did ask why there were no other black women cartoonists at a major syndicate.

"There's a double whammy of sexism and racism in American society," replied Barbara. "If you're born a woman or black, you don't exactly think you're going to be elected president one day."

I totally agreed with that statement back in 1991, little imagining that Barack Obama would enter the White House 18 years later. Of course, there's still plenty of racism around, and sexism was one reason the centrist Hillary Clinton just missed defeating the centrist Obama for the Democratic nomination.

Barbara, by the way, is the daughter of "Luther" cartoonist Brumsic Brandon Jr. I would hear Brumsic say at the 1998 Ohio State Festival of Cartoon Art: "People joke with me that 'your daughter's work is better than yours.' I respond, 'She had a better teacher!'"

In 1992, syndication would continue to diversify with the rare signings of two female African-American columnists: Cynthia Tucker of the *Atlanta Constitution* joined Chronicle Features, and Deborah Mathis of the Jackson, Miss., *Clarion-Ledger* joined Tribune Media Services.

Back in 1991, an increasing number of strips in often-bland comics sections were dealing a little more frankly with real-life topics. For instance, drug addiction was addressed in Ray Billingsley's "Curtis," the title character in Greg Evans' "Luann" had her first period, Elly Patterson breastfed her new child April in Lynn Johnston's "For Better or For Worse," and Sally and Ted in Greg Howard's "Sally Forth" discussed how they were too busy and tired to have sex. The title character in the 1930-launched "Blondie" even launched a catering business after decades of being a housewife.

Why did comics sections — long a "sanitized place," in the words of former *Los Angeles Times* editorial projects manager Nancy Tew — see more strips sample real life in 1991 than in earlier years? Maybe it had something to do with fried pickles.

Actually, it had something to do with the fact that daily newspapers faced declining circulation even in those pre-Web days for reasons such as more competition from other media and a rise in working women with less time to read (though many of these women found time for magazines and books rather than newspapers that tended to be male-oriented). So newspapers needed more readers — including younger people who preferred alternative weeklies, MTV, video games, etc. — and relevant comic content was seen as one way to possibly attract them. "They want more of an edge in their humor. They want more risk-taking," said "Dilbert" cartoonist Scott Adams at the 1991 Newspaper Features Council meeting in Charleston, S.C.

The just-turned-two Maggie was also on that Charleston trip, and I remember a waitress at the hotel restaurant being impressed with how much she talked. "I'll have the pisghetti with grated-and-cheese," my daughter said at one meal.

Actually, Maggie at that age pronounced most words correctly. And I found her conversation to be a wondrous thing. Abigail had never been able to say a thing.

I should mention that "Graceland" singer Paul Simon wasn't at the AAEC convention in Memphis, if you're wondering about that after reading this chapter's title.

CHAPTER FIFTEEN

1992:
Longtime Legend Is Seen for a Short Time

There were more than 1,600 U.S. daily newspapers in 1991, vs. 1,422 in 2008. After carefully studying the numbers and consulting with several mystics, I concluded that some dailies may have gone out of business during those 17 years.

Many other papers reduced their payrolls. One was the *Los Angeles Times*, where staffers taking 1993 buyouts would include renowned editorial cartoonist Paul Conrad — who won Pulitzer Prizes in 1964, 1971, and 1984. Most of the newspapers cutting staff were still quite profitable; their owners (often media chains) wanted to keep the money pouring in for top execs and stockholders.

Diminished or defunct dailies meant fewer jobs for journalists (including columnists and editorial cartoonists), fewer newspapers advertising in *E&P*, and fewer papers for syndicates to sell features to — meaning less income for syndicates, which consequently *also* ran fewer ads in *E&P*. This was a win-win situation ... for sadists and masochists.

For instance, New York Times Syndicate president John Brewer told me in 1992 that NYTS had been selling the now-defunct *Dallas Times Herald* about $1,500-a-month worth of material, only some of which was picked up by the surviving *Dallas Morning News*.

But *E&P* would weather newspaper problems fairly well for a few more years, helped by the fact that it already had a small staff — and that owner Robert Brown made so much money on *E&P* in good times that he could afford less profit for a while.

Given the somewhat difficult environment for syndicates in 1992, I wasn't surprised when the E.W. Scripps Co. announced it might sell or "restructure" United Media. When big corporations aren't making quite as much profit as they'd like, change is as predictable as a huge bonus for an underperforming CEO.

United Media — one of the country's two largest syndication companies at the time — was the parent of United Feature Syndicate, Newspaper Enterprise Association, United Media Licensing, Pharos Books, and the TV Data unit that provided television listings to more than 2,000 newspapers. Its features included the blockbuster comics "Peanuts" and "Garfield."

Scripps ended up selling TV Data in October 1992 to CableSouth Inc. What happened to the rest of United Media will be covered in coming chapters.

The New York Times Syndicate was also in the news in '92 when it started distributing a monthly column by Mikhail Gorbachev. More than 100 newspapers snapped up the feature (originating in Italy's *La Stampa* newspaper) during the first three days it was offered.

After learning that the visionary ex-leader of the Soviet Union had become a newspaper pundit, I did a story asking syndicate executives who their "dream" columnists would be. The best suggestion was to have Madonna and Mother Teresa write a point-counterpoint column offering sex advice to teens!

Another dream team, Calvin the boy and Hobbes the tiger, returned to newspapers in February 1992 when Bill Watterson ended his nine-month sabbatical. But some papers weren't pleased with the cartoonist's new requirement that they run "Calvin and Hobbes" a half page on Sundays. (In '92, many papers were already squeezing at least four or five comics onto each Sunday funnies page.) Dozens of Watterson's 1,800-plus clients complained about the requirement — saying it threatened their editorial autonomy, made it harder to save on newsprint costs, forced the dropping of other strips, and set a bad precedent. But only a few canceled Watterson's feature.

Even some of his fellow cartoonists felt Watterson was being a bit high-handed with his size demand. But many newspapers ran Sunday comics a *full* page earlier in the 20th century, before cost-cutting became rampant. And Watterson worked so hard on his striking art that he deserved a half page, which would result in very creative layouts. Meanwhile, "C&H" continued to win more reader surveys than any other comic.

Speaking of wins, Signe Wilkinson in 1992 became the first woman to receive the editorial cartooning Pulitzer since that Pulitzer category started a whopping 70 years earlier. I interviewed Signe when she visited New York later in '92, around the time her *Philadelphia Daily News* work was picked up for distribution by the Manhattan-based Cartoonists & Writers Syndicate.

"How did it feel to win the Pulitzer?" I asked, pulling a question from the obvious file.

Wilkinson, in her usual sardonic tone, downplayed the award a bit. "It was nice, of course, to be honored," she replied. "But the Pulitzer Prize can't think of ideas and draw cartoons for me."

The *Daily News* staffer added that she had been "slightly suspicious of the validity" of Pulitzers because they don't always go to the most deserving candidates. But Signe said the '92 Pulitzer ceremony was still a moving experience for her.

I also asked: "How significant for you is it to become syndicated?"

"Cartoons are supposed to have a short shelf life, but the speed with which they go from the drawing board to fish wrap can be disheartening. Syndication allows one more nanosecond between creation and oblivion!"

Another syndicated creator, Mike Peters, won the top-cartoonist Reuben Award at the National Cartoonists Society's 1992 gathering in Washington, D.C. Mike, who looked two decades younger than his 48 years, was honored for his *Dayton Daily News* editorial cartoons and "Mother Goose and Grimm" comic.

Once again, "The Family Circus" creator Bil Keane emceed an NCS event with some hilarious lines. For instance, the cartoonist noted that when the NCS had a chance to meet with President Bush, he filled out a form that included the boilerplate question about whether he advocated the overthrow of the U.S. government by force or violence. "I put down violence," quipped Keane.

Also at the D.C. confab was Herblock, 82, the legendary editorial cartoonist making a rare appearance at a public gathering. Herblock (full name: Herbert Block) began his career way back in 1929 at the *Chicago Daily News,* and joined *The Washington Post* in 1946. He won three individual Pulitzers (in 1942, 1954, and 1979); received a fourth as part of the *Post's* Watergate coverage; and even coined the term "McCarthyism"!

"That was in 1950, wasn't it?" I asked during a brief chat with the friendly icon after taking two photos of him.

"Yes. Joe McCarthy made a speech about communists in the U.S. government, and I began doing cartoons about him. I had no idea 'McCarthyism' would be picked up like it was," he said, with a self-deprecating shrug.

Herblock (referred to in this chapter's title) also recalled that the *Post* was not the biggest paper in D.C. when he joined it. "I think it was number four," he chuckled.

Four dailies in a city? Today, you're lucky if your city has one daily and a hyperlocal blog that's not too hyper.

Soon, I was off to Columbus to cover the National Society of Newspaper Columnists for the second time. Why that Ohio city in 1992? It was the 500th anniversary of Christopher Columbus' 1492 voyage, which reminded me that the explorer didn't make the 1491 edition of *Who's Who in the New World.*

I was flattered when NSNC president/*Kansas City Star* columnist Bill Tammeus and other attendees praised my coverage of the 1991 conference in West Virginia. Several attendees said they joined the NSNC after reading those '91 stories. I had an atrocious cold in Columbus, so all I could do was wheeze my thanks while waiting for my ears to pop from the flight to Ohio. Was I in the Buckeye State or the Stuck-ear State?

Then I returned to Columbus in November 1992 to cover the triennial Festival of Cartoon Art at Ohio State, and got quite an education. There was an exhibit of Oliver Harrington cartoons that were so good I couldn't believe the guy wasn't better known. But there were reasons for his obscurity.

Harrington was black, and he began his "Bootsie" cartoon panel at a time (1933) when white-owned daily newspapers were basically closed to African-American artists — especially those who focused on the everyday life of blacks without using pernicious stereotypes. Harrington later became an editorial cartoonist who commented on civil rights, the police, homelessness, and other issues from a liberal perspective — which didn't go over well in conservative post-World War II America. So he cartooned mostly for black newspapers and progressive publications.

Then, while serving as the NAACP's public relations director in 1951, Harrington was warned by an Army Intelligence friend to leave the country for his own safety. He had been working on issues such as the abysmal treatment of black World War II vets in the South, and opponents began labeling him a communist. So he moved to Paris to join a community of prominent expatriates and, in 1961, was trapped behind the newly erected Berlin Wall when seeing a publisher in East Berlin.

After festival attendees admired Harrington's cartoons, the 80-year-old creator spoke. He recalled a racist sixth-grade teacher who said black people should be thrown in the trash. "After that, I would draw doodles of this teacher getting into horrible accidents," said the speaker with a wry smile. "I began to realize that each drawing lifted my spirits a little bit, and I began to dream of becoming a cartoonist."

Harrington, who would die in 1995, got a standing ovation from the 150 people in the Ohio State audience. Too little, too late — but I could see he greatly appreciated it.

E&P owner Robert Brown was nearly 80 himself in 1992, so it came as no surprise that he would groom family members to take over the magazine. His two daughters were bypassed (I'm not sure if it was sexism or if they just weren't interested). Instead, Brown's 20-something grandsons joined the magazine in 1990 and 1992, respectively — with one serving as editorial production manager and the other as photocomposition manager as of '92. They had some trouble relating to non-blue-blood staffers who had gotten their jobs without family connections, but everyone knew it wouldn't be long before the heirs would rise to top spots at the magazine.

It was also in 1992 that *E&P* did its first major redesign in ages. The cover was "the color purple" — with *Editor & Publisher*'s name in yellow and the date in red. This riot of hues reminded me of when Dorothy left Kansas, except Toto was nowhere in sight.

For the initial revamped issue, I did a story about why there were no gay/lesbian-themed features offered by major syndicates. The only quasi-exception was Deb Price's recently launched *Detroit News* column distributed as part of the Gannett News Service package, but not syndicated individually.

It wasn't like gay/lesbian-themed features didn't exist. For instance, cartoonist Alison Bechdel had been self-syndicating "Dykes to Watch Out For" to non-daily publications since 1983. When I first saw and wrote about that comic in 1991, I was bowled over by its humor, story lines, and interesting characters. "Dykes" was clearly better than most of the comics offered by the major syndicates.

So, I asked syndicate executives, why not sign comics and columns like that? They answered by saying they received only a few submissions for gay/lesbian-themed features and that these features "weren't mainstream enough" for general audiences.

"Most of the syndicates have never been pacesetters in our industry," *Detroit News* editor/publisher Robert Giles told me. "They want to invest in columns and comics that are 'safe.'"

Given that major syndicates are big companies often owned by even bigger corporations, playing it safe was unfortunately no surprise.

Los Angeles Times Syndicate (LATS) executive editor Steve Christensen added that "syndicates respond to what they perceive to be the desires of newspaper editors who buy features."

In fact, many newspapers weren't even ready for gays and lesbians in comics by straight creators — as "For Better or For Worse" cartoonist Lynn Johnston would discover in 1993. Yet LATS took a chance and began individual syndication of Deb Price that year.

My daughter Maggie turned three in the fall of 1992, and it was now clear that her mother was a fairly strict parent and her father a more easygoing one. Also, my wife didn't have as much patience as I did for interacting with a young child, so I spent much of the evenings and weekends alone with Maggie "playing Barbie," pushing buttons on toys, going to the Manhattan children's museum, doing food shopping, and eating at kid-friendly restaurants. I also brought Maggie to *E&P* periodically, which was allowed in those days before demands to constantly write Web site stories made children less welcome in the office. Maggie was particularly fond of Robert Brown's assistant Beth Hoben, who interacted with my daughter as much as she could. *E&P* sales rep Bob Glassman was also very nice to Maggie.

All the bonding I had with Maggie was wonderfully fun — and the two-way interaction sure beat the alternative I had experienced with poor Abigail. Since Maggie looked a bit like Abigail, I sometimes almost imagined I was interacting with my first daughter.

CHAPTER SIXTEEN

1993: Alternative Cartoons and an Alternate Home

As 1993 began, my wife and I were busily packing. In February, we would move to a Montclair, N.J., house purchased after I tapped my E&P pension.

Like many city couples, we sought the suburbs for better-funded schools, more trees, and the pleasure of getting bitten by mosquitoes the size of cows. We had mixed feelings about leaving New York, but our new 12-miles-west-of-Manhattan town was an unusual suburb with many urban-like plusses — including old houses, six train stations, many ethnic restaurants, and a population more than a third African-American.

Also, Montclair in 1993 was the former home of astronaut Buzz Aldrin (the second man on the moon), the current home of baseball great Yogi Berra (the zillionth person not to visit Jupiter), and the future home of TV's Stephen Colbert (who may or may not have driven a Saturn).

But despite my having lived in a New Jersey suburb (Teaneck) as a youth, ditching city life after 15 years took some getting used to. The very day we moved into our 1925-built house, the sewer pipe backed up and spewed gross stuff into the basement. There was no landlord to deal with this — it was all on us, so to speak.

Then I raised the water level in the furnace, but the dang thing flooded because I didn't quite turn the knob all the way off.

A few days later, a massive snowstorm was in the forecast.

"I better put the car in the garage," I told my wife. She had already gotten into an accident with the Honda Civic we had bought a month earlier, and wiring was exposed near one of the headlights.

The snowstorm dumped well over a foot of icy white stuff that was very difficult to shovel. Given that our driveway was about five car lengths to the detached garage, clearing that sucker would be a Herculean task. Before every future winter storm, I parked at the foot of the driveway!

Maggie, who loved riding the New York subways, was not initially a fan of auto travel — especially the part that involved getting strapped into a children's car seat.

After dropping off Maggie at the Over the Rainbow day-care center, I would take a Boonton Line train from Montclair to Hoboken, N.J., and then the PATH train from Hoboken to Manhattan.

When I arrived at my E&P desk, one early 1993 story involved Mike Peters moving his Pulitzer Prize-winning editorial cartoons from United Media to Tribune Media Services — which already distributed Peters' "Mother Goose and Grimm" comic to 600-plus papers.

"Why are you leaving United?" I asked Mike, an enthusiastic, extraordinarily outgoing guy who could make anyone feel at ease.

Peters was uncharacteristically low-key and serious this time. "I really like the people at United, but it's up for sale and no one knows who's going to take it over," he replied. "I thought it was best to go with people I know for sure I'll be working with in the future."

When a corporation does something in its never-ending quest to maximize profits, the employees and everyone else below the executive suites usually have little control over their own fates. But Peters' United contract was running out, and his work was in demand elsewhere, so he had the option of leaving.

Then Scripps started making moves *it* had control over — selling United's Pharos Books division to the K-III Communications Corp., and letting go David Hendin. David had been president of Pharos, but also did plenty of non-Pharos work as senior vice president/editorial director of United — which he joined in 1970 and even wrote a syndicated column for at one point.

"I've done nothing but make money for them for 23 years," Hendin told me. "No one at Scripps even called to thank me or say good luck."

Hendin, also an author, went on to become a successful syndication and literary agent who represented people such as "Miss Manners" columnist Judith Martin. Corporations went on to miss having manners, but that was nothing new.

Scripps ultimately decided in August 1993 not to sell the rest of United after reports that it might have been close to a deal with Time Warner. One possible reason TW hesitated was that cartoonist Jim Davis wanted ownership of the popular and lucrative "Garfield" property when his contract ran out the following spring (of 1994).

But change was still in the offing at United under new president/CEO Douglas Stern, who succeeded Robert Roy Metz around the time Scripps opted not to sell (Hendin had previously been considered Metz's heir apparent). In November 1993, United laid off nine of its 140 or so employees — partly because it had grown smaller with the sales of Pharos and TV Data.

Meanwhile, many newspapers continued to shrink their Sunday comics sections. This seemed especially foolish after the Metro-Puck Comics Network, which sold national ads for those sections, released a Belden Associates study in early 1993 noting that a Super Bowl-like audience of 86 million adults and 27 million kids read the Sunday funnies.

But newspaper companies wanted short-term savings on comic and newsprint costs, and if they lost some readers, well, they'd still do a great business — right? *Right*? We'll see how that turned out in the 2000s.

Speaking of features that appeal to *younger* readers, an increasing number of syndicated or self-syndicated alternative cartoons were available in 1993. They included editorial cartoons by Ted Rall, "This Modern World" by Tom Tomorrow (aka Dan Perkins), and "Tom the Dancing Bug" by Ruben Bolling (aka Ken Fisher). But the vast majority of daily papers avoided buying alt-cartoons — so they missed out on a new audience and remained stuck with a staid image. And I suspect a big reason is that alt-cartoons not only tend to be edgy but usually have liberal politics.

"The concept of liberal bias in the media is such nonsense," said Tomorrow more than 700 tomorrows later, in 1995. "Newspapers are corporate-owned publications — and they reflect that."

I profiled Tomorrow, Rall, and Bolling in three separate 1993 stories — and all I can say is that many dailies were depriving themselves of excellent work. The cartoons were usually in a multi-panel format, which enabled them to convey more complex thoughts than one-panel editorial cartoons can.

Rall and 1950s-retro-art-stylist Tomorrow were in the hard-hitting camp (leavened with humor), while Bolling's "Tom the Dancing Bug" was often laugh-out-loud funny with characters such as a mercenary attorney who filed lawsuits for kid clients over things like petty playground squabbles. But there was no dancing bug named Tom.

In years to come, the three creators would be joined by other alt-cartoon stalwarts such as Matt Bors, Keith Knight, Stephanie McMillan, Mikhaela Reid, and Jen Sorensen.

Back in early '93, editorial cartoonist Art Wood announced that his collection of more than 40,000 cartoons by various creators would be housed in a Washington, D.C., museum called the National Gallery of Caricature and Cartoon Art.

Wood was quite meticulous in building his collection, which included work dating back to the 1700s. This was illustrated by an anecdote Wood told me that was also part of his 1987 book *Great Cartoonists and Their Art*. In 1940, 13-year-old Art visited the office of famed *Washington Star* editorial cartoonist C.K. Berryman, who graciously told Wood he could choose one of his originals to keep. Art wanted to pick the best cartoon, so he spent three hours going through 20 years of drawings. By the time Wood finished, Berryman had long since gone home!

At my Montclair home, spring arrived and the lawn was getting high. I decided to buy an old-fashioned manual mower, and enjoyed the exercise and lack of pollution. Meanwhile, my wife and I gave Gwyneth (now 16) and Samantha (15) the option of going outside after they had spent their whole lives as indoor apartment cats. The timid Samantha curiously sniffed the air from the open back door, but would not put a paw outside. The more assertive Gwyneth gratefully strolled into the fenced yard and began eating tasty strands of grass. A second manual mower had arrived on the scene.

And when both cats were inside, sleeping in stretched-out positions on the sofa, they were the very embodiment of "suburban sprawl."

In Canadian suburbia, a gay character arrived on the scene — courtesy of Lynn Johnston's "For Better or For Worse." Lawrence came out in a March-April story line, causing about 70 cautious U.S. newspapers to either cancel the comic or request reruns to replace the sequence. Often, papers in locales with many Christian fundamentalists were the ones that got cold feet.

"The series was pretty well done, but I didn't think the comic page was an appropriate forum for it," commented *Las Vegas Review-Journal* editor Thomas Mitchell. What was the appropriate forum? Johnston's wastebasket?

But as is often the case, readers were ahead of their papers. For instance, I reported that more than 60% of the people contacting the *Review-Journal* disagreed with its decision to temporarily pull "FBorFW." It was also heartening to know that more than 1,300 of the comic's 1,400 newspapers published the sequence. And Johnston told me that papers in her native Canada had little problem with a gay cartoon character.

"What do you think of the sequence?" I asked "Peanuts" cartoonist Charles Schulz when calling him about another matter.

"I thought it was quite mild and handled with great taste," he replied. The Pulitzer people agreed, because Lynn would be a finalist in the editorial cartooning category the following April.

The reason I phoned Schulz was to ask about a "Peanuts" strip that had surprised the heck out of me. In that March 30, 1993, comic, perennial loser Charlie Brown hit a home run to win a game! This from a cartoonist who had said comic creators shouldn't tamper with the basic premise of a strip.

"Why did you decide to have Charlie Brown succeed at something?" was my immediate question.

"I had such a good time drawing him doing cartwheels," Schulz replied sheepishly, adding that "we tend to forget that cartooning is still the drawing of funny pictures. Comic strips should be fun to look at."

Another 1993 winner was Hackensack, N.J., *Record* editorial cartoonist Jimmy Margulies, who wrote me in the spring of 1993 to say he had garnered a New York State Bar Association prize in a weird way. In March 1992, I had interviewed Jimmy for a story and ran one of his *Record* cartoons with the article. Since *E&P* was based in New York, the N.J. cartoon became eligible for the N.Y. bar association honor!

Speaking of awards, I was happy to see that *The Miami Herald*'s Liz Balmaseda became the second consecutive woman (after *New York Times* columnist Anna Quindlen) and the first Latina-American writer to win the Pulitzer Prize for commentary.

In preparing to interview the Cuba-born Balmaseda for an *E&P* profile that fall, I was particularly impressed by these words in a column she wrote criticizing proponents of an English-only ordinance in Florida's Dade County: "Their fight, they said, was about the English language. A lie, of course. It sufficed to read their press releases and pamphlets, riddled with grammatical and spelling errors, to realize that English was neither their motivation nor their forte." Ouch — there was more expert skewering there than in *The Three Musketeers*.

Soon after, I wrote a May 1993 story containing more good news for women: The proportion of female executives at the 10 biggest syndicates had risen from 21% in 1982 to 39.4% in 1992. Many of the execs were still in middle- or lower-management slots, but this was progress.

Meanwhile ... a guy named Herb Caen ... who started as a *San Francisco Chronicle* "three dot" gossip columnist way back in 1938 ... became the National Society of Newspaper Columnists' first Lifetime Achievement Award winner ... at the NSNC conference ... in Oregon ... in 1993....

Caen regaled the Portland audience with great anecdotes ... including one about his pre-*Chronicle* stint at the *Sacramento Union* ... where there was a desk ostensibly used by Mark Twain.... When someone expressed interest in buying the desk ... the newspaper parted with it for $200.... "We sold dozens," Caen chuckled....

Well, enough with the "three dot" paragraphs!

Also in 1993, I did my lowest-tech story of the decade about Kevin Williams' small Oasis Newsfeatures syndicate introducing "The Amish Cook" by Elizabeth Coblentz — who handwrote her weekly column! The Indiana grandmother then mailed the feature (which included recipes and insights into Amish life) to Williams in Ohio for typing up. Sometimes the recipes would get edited, as when Coblentz included the step of slaughtering a hog in a recipe for a pork dish!

If Williams had an urgent question about a column, how did he contact the Amish columnist? He would call the phone at a barn a mile from Coblentz's house, or contact her via overnight mail. Williams told me that, more than once, "I've sent her flowers with the question on the card!"

Jud Hurd also had a fairly low-tech operation in Connecticut, where he produced his 1969-founded *CARTOONIST PROfiles* magazine four times a year with the help of wife Claudia. I took the train to Jud's home (walking distance from the Paul Newman/Joanne Woodward abode) in fall 1993 to do a story about his new autobiographical book *To Cartooning: 60 Years of Magic*. It was my idea to write the article; Jud was too modest to have suggested it.

Hurd, 81, was so soft-spoken that he seemed almost boring at first glance. But underneath the bland exterior was a smart, funny man who had lived a fascinating life. He did several syndicated comics during his career — with the first called "Just Hurd in Hollywood." (Jud's given name was Justin.) For this 1930s strip, Hurd interviewed movie stars such as John Barrymore, Joan Crawford, Gary Cooper, Bing Crosby, Cary Grant, Lana Turner, and John Wayne.

"Was it difficult to get Hollywood stars to talk for a comic strip?" I asked.

"It varied," Jud replied. "Cary Grant was easy. He told me if he could get his publicity department to OK it, I could come on the set the next day. That was when he was shooting *Bringing Up Baby*.

"John Barrymore was harder to interview. When I approached him, his wife kept pulling him away. I remember him protesting, 'I've got to set up an appointment with this young man!'"

Hurd also knew Walt Disney, and would watch him participate in Sunday-afternoon polo matches. One day in 1937, Jud hitched a ride back to Hollywood in Disney's Cadillac. "I got in the front seat beside Walt and he talked for a solid 45 minutes," said Hurd, recalling that Disney discussed how some fairy tales couldn't be handled properly by live actors but could be made into great animated films. *Snow White and the Seven Dwarfs* came out that year.

My daughter Maggie saw her first Disney film in 1993. That was *Aladdin*, which included lyrics by the late Howard Ashman — brother of United Media's then-vice president/director of comic art Sarah Ashman Gillespie.

In September '93, Maggie started public pre-K in Montclair despite still being three years old. She made the Oct. 1 cutoff by 42 minutes — being born at 11:18 p.m. on Sept. 30 — and thus was the youngest (and shortest) kid in class. It was a major adjustment for Maggie, but saving on another year of day-care costs turned out to be crucial. That's because my wife would soon be fired from her full-time publishing job — starting a multi-year run of losing a number of full- and part-time positions while only managing to find sporadic freelance work.

I was never clear on the exact details of why each job was lost. In some cases, my wife seemed to work too slowly or have a hard time getting along with her supervisors.

The loss of a second full-time income throughout much of the 1990s would mean taking only modest vacations (if we took them at all) and putting off various house repairs. When shingles began landing in the backyard, it was perhaps a hint we needed a new roof. Given that we couldn't afford one, I reclassified the shingles as UFOs.

One of Maggie's favorite destinations was the New Jersey Children's Museum. The Paramus-based place was paradise for kids with things like a real fire engine, a pretend supermarket, and a pretend doctor's office. Which reminds me: If a doctor syndicated a medical column, would she accept Medicare payments from newspapers more than 65 years old?

I also used vacation days to be among the parent/teacher posse chaperoning Maggie and her fellow Edgemont elementary school students on class trips to the post office, petting zoo, Manhattan's awesome Museum of Natural History, and elsewhere — and would continue this periodic chaperoning into my daughter's middle-school years. It was a far cry from lobbying legislators for the Stop Hospital and Medical Errors group, but school volunteerism was what I wanted to concentrate on — both for Maggie's sake and because I never had a chance to do that with Abigail.

CHAPTER SEVENTEEN

1994:
A Cat Has Another
Life Elsewhere

The syndication world was still mostly "ink on paper" in 1994 — with columnists and cartoonists usually mailing their work to syndicates for editing, and syndicates then mailing those features to newspapers. But one could spot the light of the digital locomotive that would soon barrel down the track.

In 1993, "Dilbert" creator Scott Adams had become the first cartoonist with a major syndicate to put an email address in a comic, and this started to pay off big time by 1994. The email comments Adams received helped convince him to sharply reduce scenes of Dilbert at home and put the nerdy cartoon engineer mostly where most readers wanted him: in the workplace. And the thousands of emails that poured in were used by United Media sales reps to convince newspapers that Adams' 1989-launched comic was worth buying.

"How many papers would 'Dilbert' have if you weren't publishing your email address?" I asked Adams in 1995, when he topped the 400-client mark.

"About 80," he replied.

Adams — not the warmest guy, but definitely a funny and brilliant guy — went on to become one of *People* magazine's "25 most intriguing people" of 1996 along with the likes of George Clooney, Madonna, and Tiger Woods (who later became the most womanizing jerk of 2009). Also in '96, Adams came out with *The Dilbert Principle* bestseller.

In another 1994 digital development, the "Bottom Liners" team of Eric and Bill Teitelbaum began scanning their hand-drawn line art into a Macintosh computer to add shading, patterns, and other effects. The cartoonists then transmitted their business-themed comic via telephone modem to the Tribune Media Services syndicate, which could then edit it on screen.

Soon after, I learned that a computer was saving "Frank and Ernest" cartoonist Bob Thaves lots of time lettering his 1972-launched comic. "I had fonts created for me to replicate my lettering," he said. "There are three versions of each letter of the alphabet, so the letters bounce around a little."

During the next few years, many other cartoonists would start doing at least part of their work with the help of digital tools.

Also, 1994 saw the debut of Reed Brennan Media Associates, which scanned and formatted comics and other features before delivering customized digital pages to newspapers.

One benefit of electronic distribution was shorter lead times for cartoonists who created topical comics. For instance, Garry Trudeau went from doing "Doonesbury" two weeks ahead of publication in the early 1990s to nine days ahead by 2001.

Change was also coming to Sunday comics sections. In 1994, most cartoonists still drew their Sunday strips in black and white, and then wrote in numbers indicating which colors should be inserted via computer by prepress companies such as American Color (home of respected liaison-to-cartoonists Tim Rosenthal). The result was usually bland, cookie-cutter color.

"Sunday comics used to be the only color you would see in newspapers," was what "Non Sequitur" cartoonist Wiley Miller told me in early 1994. "Now it's the worst color you see in newspapers."

Wiley wanted a better look for his Sunday strips, so he started coloring them himself — after which American Color reproduced Wiley's hues via a separation process and line-art overlay. Each resulting "Non Sequitur" comic had enough blending and texture to look like a curator hung an oil painting in the Sunday funnies rather than on a museum wall.

Later on, a number of cartoonists would do their own Sunday coloring using Photoshop software.

Wiley would continue to innovate in 1995 when he began offering "Non Sequitur" in both its original rectangular strip shape and as a square panel. This required some re-inking and rearranging of elements, but the process would soon become easier via computer. And in 2000, Wiley made his Sunday "Non Sequitur" vertical to give newspapers more layout flexibility.

But all these changes paled next to the February 1994 news that Tess Trueheart was filing for divorce from Dick Tracy because the cartoon detective was so busy fighting crime that she rarely saw him. Panicked readers wondered: Who would get custody of the comic's client newspapers?

Tess and Dick hadn't aged much since "Dick Tracy" started in 1931, and it seemed like some real-life columnists weren't getting older, either. That's because their newspaper photos were, shall we say, un-current.

I wrote a fun February 1994 feature about this. In some cases, the fault rested with columnists who were too vain and/or busy to provide photos of their present selves. But in other cases, papers neglected to use newer pix.

For instance, Heloise told me that some of her 500 "Hints" clients were still running photos of her from the late 1970s or early '80s, even though recent shots had been sent out by King Features Syndicate. And several papers in 1994 still used photos of her mother — the original Heloise, who died in 1977!

Heloise the daughter recalled that when she visited Wisconsin several years before, "People kept telling me, 'You don't look like your picture in the paper.' I picked up the paper and it was mother's picture. When I went there for an interview, I told them they were using the wrong photo. An editor said, swear to God, 'Are you sure?'"

Meanwhile, changes continued at the Scripps-owned United Media. Editorial cartoonist Steve Benson, the 1993 Pulitzer Prize winner from *The Arizona Republic*, switched from Tribune Media Services to United in 1994 —

sort of negating the '93 move of editorial cartoonist Mike Peters from United to TMS.

But then cartoonist Jim Davis made the blockbuster April '94 announcement that he was moving his 16-year-old "Garfield" comic from United to Universal Press Syndicate and the "Garfield" licensing to his own company: Paws Inc. Given that the strip was second only to "Peanuts" in newspaper clients (2,400-plus in 83 countries) and second only to "Peanuts" in licensing revenue, this was a huge loss for United. Or was it? Sources I spoke with off the record said Davis had to pay $31.6 million to buy back his creation, so perhaps Scripps had the last laugh — as big corporations often do.

Be that as it may, you could tell Davis' buttons were pushed by the layoffs and other 1990s changes at United — because in the '80s I had heard Jim say publicly he loved being with United and didn't mind it owning his "Garfield" property.

When I reached Davis in Indiana for a phone interview, the cartoonist said he chose Universal for reasons that included his friendship with syndication legend John McMeel (Universal's charming president/co-founder) and his eagerness to join a roster that included superstar comics such as "Calvin and Hobbes," "The Far Side," and "For Better or For Worse."

In 2011, what had become Universal Uclick took over many of United's functions.

Even as Davis departed in 1994, there continued to be other changes at United — making me wonder if columnist Jack Anderson should rename his "Washington Merry-Go-Round" feature "*United* Merry-Go-Round." Several executives were let go and others promoted or hired. Then, in May 1994, United announced that it would lay off an additional 20 or so people and drop more than 5% of its 150 features. This despite one of its execs telling me that United "is a very profitable company but over the years has not been building profitability." Does that sum up corporations or what?

When *E&P* eventually got bought by a media conglomerate, I would experience corporate profit obsession firsthand.

In reporting on the actions of Scripps and United executives, I always gave them the opportunity to defend their decisions. But I'm sure some of my anti-corporate feelings crept into my stories. After all, it's not very humane to lay off talented people at a "very profitable" firm. Sid Goldberg — who had been promoted to a senior vice president post at United after the (perhaps involuntary) resignation of another longtime exec, Brad Bushell — called me one day to complain.

"United doesn't think your coverage has been fair," said Goldberg, 63, a highly respected syndicate exec for decades.

Goldberg's words stung, though the vast majority of non-management United people probably viewed my stories more positively. "I'm sorry you feel that way, Sid," I replied. "I've tried to give both sides."

"It doesn't look that way to us."

"I can't just rewrite United press releases."

"We're not asking you to do that."

Actually, United would have liked nothing better than for me to do that! But though my hand was shaking a bit as it gripped the phone receiver, I had stood my ground with Sid. I wasn't quite the wimp I used to be.

I have to be fair and say that United in coming years would do a pretty good business (helped by the "Dilbert" juggernaut) and sign some great new comics such as Darby Conley's "Get Fuzzy" and Stephan Pastis' "Pearls Before Swine." Also, I liked most of United's execs — including Goldberg.

Sid, by the way, was the husband of conservative firebrand Lucianne Goldberg (who would help expose President Clinton's affair with Monica Lewinsky) and the father of future right-wing columnist Jonah Goldberg. More on life with Lucianne in my 1998 chapter.

At least 1994 was a good year for diversity, as centrist *Washington Post* columnist William Raspberry became the second African-American to win the commentary Pulitzer (five years after the *Chicago Tribune*'s Clarence Page received it) and conservative Memphis *Commercial Appeal* staffer Michael Ramirez won the '94 editorial cartooning Pulitzer. Also, King's "Best and Wittiest" editorial cartoon package added a rare female voice — future Pulitzer winner Ann Telnaes.

Another new King creator was "Mallard Fillmore" cartoonist Bruce Tinsley, an extremely nice guy whose beautifully drawn topical comic stars a right-wing duck. "Mallard" was touted by conservatives as a worthy alternative to liberal "Doonesbury," but the writing in Garry Trudeau's comic is much better.

So I had mixed feelings when I received a gracious May 1994 thank-you note from Bruce saying my *E&P* mention of "Mallard" a couple of years earlier brought the strip to the attention of King comics editor Jay Kennedy.

Tinsley's letter had a postmark from Indiana, a state that would become significant to me in 2001.

Trudeau's distributor, Universal, announced in 1994 that comic creators with the syndicate for at least five years could take up to four weeks annual vacation. Usually, seven-strip-a-week artists have to scramble to get ahead if they want time off. Universal, whose perhaps unprecedented policy took effect in 1995, would distribute reruns while cartoonists were away.

Universal hoped to prevent its cartoonists (some of whom had taken sabbaticals) from suffering burnout. Indeed, the vacation option helped keep Trudeau in the Universal fold, but there were other futures in store for Gary Larson ("The Far Side") and Bill Watterson ("Calvin and Hobbes").

As noted in Chapter 8, Watterson was briefly an editorial cartoonist for the now-defunct *Cincinnati Post* in 1980. His local competition was the *Cincinnati Enquirer*'s Jim Borgman, who won the Reuben Award in 1994 —

three years after receiving a Pulitzer and three years before co-creating "Zits," one of the fastest-growing comics ever.

During his Reuben acceptance speech at the National Cartoonists Society gathering in La Jolla, Calif., the soft-spoken Borgman offered a great anecdote illustrating how little respect many cartoonists get. He recalled seeing a man at the *Enquirer* who appeared lost, so Borgman asked if he needed help. The man looked at the casually dressed cartoonist and queried him about what he did at the newspaper.

"I draw the political cartoons," Borgman answered.

To which the man snorted: "You mean to tell me that Jim Borgman doesn't even draw his own cartoons?!"

During another speech in La Jolla, Charles Schulz was asked how he juggled working on his "Peanuts" comic, licensed products, TV specials, and more. He replied that being interrupted periodically at the drawing board by his five children helped him learn to stop and then resume various tasks. I believe the Latin term is "cartoonus interruptus."

Soon after, I covered the 1994 National Society of Newspaper Columnists conference in Sarasota, Fla., where Molly Ivins received the organization's Lifetime Achievement Award. Ivins' humor-infused, liberal-from-Texas opinion column was great, but a lifetime honor at age 49?

Still, Ivins gave an excellent talk in Sarasota — mentioning, among other things, one of the reasons former reporters make better columnists than former government officials: "You should have the experience of interviewing five people after a car wreck," said the *Fort Worth Star-Telegram* writer. "It gives you an idea of the fluidity of truth."

Speaking of motor vehicles, I was told Ivins watched the slow-motion O.J. Simpson car chase with other columnists in the NSNC hospitality suite, and cracked jokes as that now-iconic 1994 event unfolded. I wasn't in the suite because of my rule against socializing too much with people I covered, so I missed the scene. I assume former football great O.J. didn't have a Garfield suction toy attached to the window of his Ford Bronco.

A prominent columnist seven years younger than Ivins resigned from *The New York Times* in the late summer of 1994. That was 1992 Pulitzer winner Anna Quindlen, who wanted to focus more on fiction writing. Her first novel, *Object Lessons*, had been published in 1991; her second, *One True Thing*, came out around the time of her *Times* exit.

There were more losses for newspaper readers in October, as both the *St. Petersburg Times* and *Seattle Times* fired their talented staff editorial cartoonists — actions that would presage the cartoonist-cutting carnage of the 2000s.

First to go was Clay Bennett, and the 13-year veteran of the *St. Petersburg Times* was stunned. "I've only taken one sick day since 1981, so they couldn't question my work ethic," Clay said in a voice much more subdued than the one I was accustomed to hearing at conventions. "I've won nine awards, and I've had good evaluations over the years."

Next to get canned was Brian Basset, a 16-year *Seattle Times* veteran and former Association of American Editorial Cartoonists (AAEC) president. Despite his long tenure at the paper, Basset was ordered to pack his stuff and leave the *Times* building in 15 minutes! "They handled it terribly," a shell-shocked Brian told me.

As is usually the case in those situations, managers at both dailies were fuzzy when I phoned to ask why the firings happened, though a *Seattle Times* editor did mention that cost-cutting might have been a factor. And Bennett — one of the nicest, most sociable people I had the pleasure of meeting through *E&P* — told me that the *St. Petersburg Times* editorial page had become more conservative.

More than 100 people at each paper bravely signed petitions urging that the men be reinstated. But, as is *also* usually the case in those situations, their pleas were ignored.

Americans may live in a democracy, but there's little democracy in corporatized workplaces.

Fortunately, Basset and Bennett landed on their feet. Brian continued his "Adam@Home" comic and later started the "Red and Rover" strip. And, after three "wilderness years," Clay was hired by the prestigious *Christian Science Monitor* — where he won a Pulitzer in 2002. Bennett, like Basset, also became an AAEC president — and, in that position, would give me one of the biggest surprises of my life in 2006.

In 1994, the similarities between Bennett and Basset's situations were eerie. They were fired just 15 days apart, their last names both began with "B," they both were 36, they both were employed by *Times* papers, and they worked within walking distance of each other (though, admittedly, walking between Florida and Washington state might take a while).

Come to think of it, the *Seattle Times* was lucky to dodge a plagiarism charge. After all, the *St. Petersburg Times* used the exact same words ("you're fired!") first.

And then this huge loss for newspaper readers: In an October press release issued by Universal, 44-year-old Gary Larson said he was ending "The Far Side" on Jan. 1, 1995, because of "simple fatigue and a fear that if I continue for many more years my work will begin to suffer, or at the very least ease into the Graveyard of Mediocre Cartoons."

To say Larson's comic was wildly popular would be an understatement. The 1980-launched feature ran in nearly 1,900 newspapers, and "Far Side" book collections had sold about 28 million copies in the U.S. and Canada by 1994.

"He revolutionized the sensibility that was permissible in newspapers," said National Cartoonists Society president Bruce Beattie, referring to comics sections that had been far too staid before the offbeat "Far Side" arrived.

Beattie, who did the offbeat "Beattie Blvd." comic and *Daytona Beach* (Fla.) *News-Journal* editorial cartoons, was one of many people I interviewed for reaction to Larson's retirement. And I illustrated the story with a classic macabre "Far Side" panel showing a polar bear chewing an inhabited igloo while telling another bear: "Oh hey! I just love these things! Crunchy on the outside and a chewy center!"

Universal soon announced it would sign Dan Piraro's "Bizarro" comic from Chronicle Features to help fill "The Far Side" void. I felt bad for Chronicle's courtly editor/general manager Stuart Dodds because his syndicate had signed "Bizarro" to replace "The Far Side" after Universal took on Larson's comic in 1984. "There's sort of a path between us and Universal, and I'd like the grass to grow for awhile," Dodds told me unhappily.

Then I was off to chronicle the American Association of Sunday and Feature Editors convention in Seattle, where I found myself sitting directly behind Microsoft co-founder Bill Gates as the casually dressed billionaire prepared to give a speech.

If I had dared tap Gates on the shoulder, there was definitely a question I longed to ask. What deep, transcendent, immortal query might that have been? Only this: "Why is your Windows software so damn glitchy?!"

Gates was not speechless in Seattle because he was there to discuss the New York Times Syndicate column he would start in January 1995 to discuss tech issues and other matters.

Near the end of 1994, Ferdinand Teubner announced he would retire from *E&P* in February 1995 after 33 years — the last 17 as publisher. His co-successors would be owner Robert Brown's young grandsons. "Interesting" times were ahead.

CHAPTER EIGHTEEN

1995: Comics Turn 100 and Web Sites Turn On

You may have noticed that the previous chapter had no information about my family life. Perhaps the most memorable personal event of 1994 was Maggie's fifth birthday party, which my wife and I decided to have at home. We invited 30 kids, figuring about 20 would show up. Instead, virtually everyone attended — including several whose parents never RSVPed. We had to order 10 pizzas, and the kids sitting cross-legged on the crammed living-room floor hemmed the talented magician into a corner so tightly that his DNA is probably still on the wall. But everyone had fun.

"This is a great party!" enthused Eddie Kaluski, the second husband of my friendly Aunt Gertie, as he watched the merry mayhem.

I was frantic with hosting duties, but stopped short at his remark. Eddie, who had done brave work for the Polish Underground during World War II and would die of cancer in 1997, usually seemed so low-key. "Thanks!" I replied, before snapping back into reality when a kid knocked into me.

Another birthday — Universal Press Syndicate's 25th — was celebrated with a big February 1995 bash I covered in frigid Kansas City. About 700 people attended, including syndicate co-founder/president John McMeel and dozens of cartoonists and columnists.

"Doonesbury" creator Garry Trudeau recalled in a speech that many older newspaper publishers weren't ready for his brand of topical humor in 1970. "The strip kept being canceled as fast as John could sell it," Trudeau said, adding that McMeel tried to console him by noting that these publishers wouldn't be around forever.

"He was right," Trudeau continued. "In the years that followed, a happy pattern emerged. Publishers who vowed that 'Doonesbury' would appear in their newspapers over their dead bodies got their wish! Our client list floated upward on the tears of widows and children." I should note that Garry said all this in a deadpan tone.

Later in '95, when speaking at Ohio State's Festival of Cartoon Art, Trudeau also got a big laugh with his answer to an audience question about whether he ever received a death threat. "Only when the government tried to draft me," he quipped.

I returned to K.C. in June to cover the National Society of Newspaper Columnists conference hosted by *The Kansas City Star*'s Bill Tammeus — who, along with *Fort Worth Star-Telegram* columnist Dave Lieber, got National Columnists Day established in 1995. Held on April 18 each year, NCD marks the date in 1945 when columnist extraordinaire Ernie Pyle was killed while covering World War II.

Two months before my second Missouri meeting, I made a much-shorter trip to United Media's office just north of Manhattan's Grand Central

Station. But, in a way, it was a long journey to the future because United executives wanted to show me a new Web site — one of the very first from a syndicate.

As execs clicked on various UnitedMedia.com pages, I eyed the screen and nodded sagely. But I'd never seen a Web site before, so my covert thought was: "What the hell *is* this?"

I'm not an "early adopter." Heck, in 1995 I still listened to music on a turntable and wore a three-cornered hat. But I eventually catch on to new trends, as I would with the Web.

The fledgling United site included the work of "Dilbert" creator Scott Adams and other cartoonists, background info on their features, and more. There were even images of rejection letters received by Adams, who was advised by one syndicate to take drawing classes or find an artist collaborator.

I hopped the subway back to *E&P*'s office, little knowing just how big an impact the new World Wide Web would have on my future at the magazine. *E&P* itself launched a site in August 1995.

But in April '95, there was no computer in the newsroom I could use to surf around the United site before writing about it. The grandson co-publishers were gung ho about all things online, but also interested in saving money where they could. So *E&P* reporters still wrote stories on those pre-1983 video display terminals that were little more than word processors.

I soon did other online-related stories for *E&P*, despite the fact that I was writing about what I couldn't see (the Web). For instance, I put together a May 1995 roundup titled "Syndicates Race into Cyberspace" to prove that I could put a stupid rhyming headline above a piece about smart technology. The story included info about syndicates selling features to newspaper Web sites (which back then were often called "electronic newspapers" — creating visions of printed pages strung with lights). Web sales meant more business for syndicates, but also inspired many readers to stop buying a paper now that they could see content for free on the paper's site — a lack-of-revenue model which would eventually bite print papers badly.

Later in the year, I wrote about "On the Fastrack"/"Safe Havens" cartoonist Bill Holbrook starting an online-only strip called "Kevin and Kell." Holbrook's feature was one of the earliest examples of what would become a very large, very creative category known as "webcomics."

Given that "Kevin and Kell" never appeared in print, it was weirdly appropriate that the "K&K" comic I chose to run with my story was inadvertently omitted by *E&P*'s printing plant, leaving only white space. Mortified, I included the strip in the following week's issue — but not before calling Holbrook.

"I'm so sorry, Bill," I said after explaining what happened.

"That's okay," he replied good-naturedly. "After working in newspapers for 15 years, no apology is necessary for printers' errors."

Have I mentioned that 90% of comic creators are really nice people? Maybe it has something to do with working in such a fun profession.

And, starting in 1996, Universal Press Syndicate's print comics and other features would be delivered to Web sites via UPS's new sister division Uclick.

But amid all the online stuff, I still did plenty of old-fashioned stories. One was inspired by a press release saying Jim Davis' "Garfield" might have passed Charles Schulz's United-distributed "Peanuts" as the most widely syndicated comic in the world. Before writing an article about that, I phoned United executive Sid Goldberg.

"Sid, the 'Garfield' people say the comic has added about 100 newspapers since moving to Universal last year, and now has 2,547 clients. They also say this might be more than 'Peanuts.' Is that true?"

"I doubt it," he replied in an exasperated tone.

"How many papers does 'Peanuts' have?"

"I'll get back to you," promised Sid, and then hung up.

Six days later, I received a fax from Goldberg saying "Peanuts" had 2,595 clients. So I called Davis, and he ... graciously congratulated Schulz.

All that went into a May 1995 story. Sometime after that, I was standing in the back of a room between sessions of a meeting when I felt a tap on my shoulder. It was Schulz.

"How are you, David?" he asked in his congenial way.

"I'm fine, Mr. Schulz," I replied, never comfortable calling him by his "Sparky" nickname (after the horse Spark Plug in the "Barney Google" comic) used by people close to the "Peanuts" creator.

Then Schulz's voice turned not quite so congenial. "You know 'Garfield' never had more newspapers, don't you?"

"I wasn't sure. That's why I checked with your syndicate," I replied nervously, sounding like the 1983 me again.

"Are you sure now?" he continued, with a stern expression that contained a hint of a smile.

"I guess I am."

Schulz turned and walked away.

As I analyzed the exchange in my hotel room that night, I realized yet again that behind Schulz's gentle persona was a very competitive man.

But "Peanuts" wasn't one of the strips honored when the U.S. Postal Service — in a May 4 event at Washington, D.C.'s National Press Club — unveiled 20 commemorative cartoon stamps to mark the 100th anniversary of comics. (The first modern comic was Richard Outcault's "Hogan's Alley," the Yellow Kid-starring feature that made its debut on May 5, 1895.)

"Peanuts" missed the cut partly because the postal service didn't want to commemorate strips whose original creators were still alive — though the creator of "Brenda Starr," one of the honored comics, was very much with us in

1995. That was Dale Messick, whose strip about a glamorous reporter was now being written by Mary Schmich. It was Schmich who had Brenda say these immortal words: "Sometimes I think newspapers care more about profits than they do about people." Observant "journo," that Starr.

Besides "Brenda Starr" and "Hogan's Alley," the other 18 comics getting 32-cent stamps were "Alley Oop," "Barney Google," "Blondie," "Bringing Up Father," "Dick Tracy," "Flash Gordon," "Gasoline Alley," "Krazy Kat," "Li'l Abner," "Little Nemo in Slumberland," "Little Orphan Annie," "Nancy," "Popeye" (aka "Thimble Theatre"), "Prince Valiant," "Rube Goldberg's Inventions," "Terry and the Pirates," "The Katzenjammer Kids," and "Toonerville Folks."

Though only Messick was alive among the originators of those famous comics, some of the strips were still in syndication. For instance, the congenial and talented Jim Scancarelli was doing the Frank King-created "Gasoline Alley."

The 20 cartoon images would end up being the third-most-collected stamps (out of about two dozen designs) that year.

I also marked the 100th anniversary of comics by doing a massive survey published that July in the 1995 edition of *E&P*'s syndicate directory. Here, "Peanuts" got its due when Schulz's feature was voted the top comic of all time — with "Calvin and Hobbes" chosen the best current strip. "Peanuts" was also current in 1995, of course, but the consensus was that it was past its peak.

Given that I didn't yet have email at *E&P*, doing the poll was a labor-intensive process that involved contacting more than 100 cartoonists, comic historians, syndicate executives, newspaper editors, and others by phone or postal letter while still doing my weekly magazine section.

Meanwhile, *E&P*'s look improved with the 1995 hiring of Hector Marrero to design our pages each week. That was the first time since I joined the magazine in 1983 that someone other than editors and reporters handled layout. *E&P*'s appearance also improved when the *Seattle Post-Intelligencer*'s Steve Greenberg became our freelance editorial cartoonist that summer.

Back in May 1995, I attended a star-studded gala at Manhattan's *Saturday Night Live* studio marking the 25th anniversary of the Reporters Committee for Freedom of the Press. The event's four honorees were editorial cartoonist Herblock, *New York Times* columnist/former *NYT* executive editor A.M. Rosenthal, former *Washington Post* executive editor Ben Bradlee, and former NBC News anchor John Chancellor. Presenting the awards were former CBS News anchor Walter Cronkite, ABC News anchor Peter Jennings, *60 Minutes* correspondent Mike Wallace, and NBC News anchor Tom Brokaw. And in the audience were the likes of Barbara Walters and Phil Donahue. It seemed like the only high-wattage celebrity *not* there was Moby-Dick, who had retired to an assisted-swimming community in Melville, N.Y.

I particularly remember this Cronkite comment about Herblock: "The most amazing thing about Herb is that this guy is so nice in person, but can be so damn mean in his cartoons!"

Why are some editorial cartoons "so damn mean"? Jeff MacNelly offered *his* excuse in a speech later that year at Ohio State. He recalled appearing as a child on the *Howdy Doody* show and noticing that the snow falling outside a window on the set was fake. When he pointed this out to Clarabell the clown, young Jeff was told: "Shut up, kid!" That, sighed MacNelly, "was the beginning of a life of cynicism."

At the *SNL* studio, Calvin Trillin cracked up the audience with another of his tales about *The Nation* magazine's low pay. The King Features columnist recalled that *Nation* editor Victor Navasky once questioned him about whether he had fabricated a quote attributed to former U.S. Secretary of State John Foster Dulles. "Victor," Trillin replied, "at these rates you can't expect real quotes."

Then I was off to cover the National Cartoonists Society gathering in Boca Raton, Fla., where retired "Far Side" creator Gary Larson received a going-away present in absentia: the Reuben Award as cartoonist of the year.

Former Reuben winner Lynn Johnston was one of the "Boca Bash" speakers, and her remarks included a report on the intense reader reaction to the 1995 death of beloved "For Better or For Worse" dog Farley (after he saved April Patterson from drowning). Lynn received thousands of letters.

"Peanuts" creator Charles Schulz was upset, too. When Johnston told him she was thinking of having Farley die, he threatened to have Snoopy hit by a truck! That's according to David Michaelis' *Schulz and Peanuts* book, which will be discussed in the 2007 chapter of *this* book. But given that "FBorFW" characters aged, death was inevitable for some of them — as it was for our cat Gwyneth.

The charismatic calico was 18 in 1995 when she began to have trouble moving. She struggled to go up and down the stairs, and to jump. So I put a small seat (which Maggie had used to reach the bathroom sink) next to the bed to make it easier for Gwyneth to climb up. After all, she liked to sleep on the bed during the day and snuggle under the covers at night.

And of course we took Gwyneth to the vet, who had tests done that revealed heart trouble and incurable cancer.

We headed to an animal hospital with Gwyneth to see if anything could be done. I opened the carrier on a side table in the waiting room, and Gwyneth slowly and painfully got onto my lap. I stroked her as I choked back tears. Then we were called in.

It turned out that the humane thing to do was to put Gwyneth to sleep, and we said our goodbyes. Maggie was wailing, like any five-year-old kid would. Gwyneth was her favorite cat, because Samantha was too shy to let any child pet her. My wife was wailing even louder. It was almost embarrassing, but I later figured she might've been not only mourning Gwyneth, but thinking about the last time we faced death firsthand — with Abigail in 1990.

Back in Boca, 71-year-old Mort Walker gave a 100th-anniversary-of-comics talk that included his memories of some late, great National Cartoonists Society members. For instance, the "Beetle Bailey" creator recalled a White House meeting between President Johnson and cartoonists. As the session broke up, Milton Caniff extended an impromptu invitation for LBJ to join the cartoonists for lunch at the National Press Club — and the president ditched his frenetic schedule to accept!

My mother Thelma joined me for part of the Boca gathering. She had lived in nearby Delray Beach since 1992, so it was a short trip for her. It was fun introducing her to Walker and many other people I covered.

One person I would cover live in 1997 was Hillary Clinton, but it was in 1995 that Creators Syndicate launched a weekly column by the first lady that was soon bought by 100-plus papers.

To mark Clinton's syndication, *U.S. News & World Report* asked me to name a small number of syndicated columnists who were currently "hot." I resisted the urge to mention writers who didn't have air-conditioning, and quickly came up with Molly Ivins on the left, Cal Thomas on the right, Donna Britt of *The Washington Post*, and Bill Gates of the Washington state. Those names, as well as a credit to me, appeared in the magazine's July 10, 1995, issue — on the page before a piece titled "Wake Up, Mr. Greenspan." Were my picks *that* boring?

"Thanks for mentioning me, Dave," Cal said in a phone call after the magazine hit newsstands. "That was real nice of you."

"Happy to do it," I replied.

"I'll try to get more money out of my syndicate," Cal added jokingly.

My political views are 180 degrees from Cal's, but the guy is an interesting columnist and a heckuva good guy. Accessible, too. If I needed a comment about anything for an *E&P* story, he was easy to reach and quick with a quote.

Thomas' readers (in nearly 400 papers in 1995) include many religious people. I was still not religious myself, but my wife was by then. And she wanted to put Maggie in after-school religious classes starting that September. I would have been willing if Maggie was willing, but she was vehemently opposed — as was I.

Children shouldn't have input into that, you might say. But if a kid's already going to public school much of the day, that's quite enough classroom time. And if Maggie became interested in religion when older, she could pursue it then. In fact, there might be a better chance she'd do that later if she wasn't forced early on. I had been required to go to religious school as a kid, and it helped sour me on the whole thing.

I fought this one long and hard, but my wife ultimately prevailed. "I can't believe Maggie is being forced to do something she hates that I also hated," I said morosely.

"Deal with it," my wife replied.

In late 1995, Abigail Van Buren sent me a letter with this droll postscript: "Mort and I just celebrated our 54th anniversary. I think it's going to last." Could I say the same about my marriage?

While I continued to be very close to Maggie, the religious differences widened the distance between my wife and I. One way I avoided interacting with her was to continue working on a children's book I had started in 1994 called *A Message from Margaret*, about a girl who finds a letter in her attic from a girl who lived in the house a century before. Still willing to represent me was Toni Mendez, the agent who had tried to sell my *Comic Strip Connection* novel several years earlier.

Then, in October, there was a message about Martha. As you might recall from my 1985 chapter, Martha Stewart did a column back then that lasted a short time. Now — much better known for her books, TV show, magazine, etc. — Stewart was returning to newspapers with a New York Times Syndicate column called "askMartha." Which made one wonder: Was the lack of space between "ask" and "Martha" a "good thing"?

Later in the 1990s, I met Stewart at her syndicate's annual holiday party. We were introduced and briefly exchanged pleasantries. But what I recall most was the lifestyle maven going downtown-chic by wearing jeans and a leather jacket!

Then came the bombshell 1995 announcement that Bill Watterson would end his 1985-launched "Calvin and Hobbes" on Dec. 31 at the ripe old age of 37. Watterson's nearly 2,400 clients were mucho unhappy about the impending loss of a reader-magnet comic, and this was another blow for Universal — which had lost "The Far Side" just months earlier.

Watterson, whose book collections had sold more than 23 million copies as of late '95, issued a retirement statement that read, in part: "I believe I've done what I can do within the constraints of daily deadlines and small panels. I am eager to work at a more thoughtful pace, with fewer artistic compromises." That work would include painting, but Watterson ducked so far out of public view in subsequent years that few people knew how else he spent his time. I'm guessing he ate and breathed each day, but what do I know?

While some people got annoyed at Watterson's penchant for privacy, the guy deserves respect for shunning the spotlight — an unusual trait in our celebrity-saturated age. He just wanted the work to speak for itself. But, ironically, Watterson's continued reclusiveness gave him a J.D. Salinger-like fame.

CHAPTER NINETEEN

1996:
A Hot Spelling Bee and Hotter Weather

In early 1996, I wrote a profile of cartoonist Fred Lasswell, who had worked on "Barney Google and Snuffy Smith" since 1934. Despite being 79, the jovial and avuncular "Uncle Fred" used computer-generated fonts in his comic and electronically transmitted the strip to King Features for distribution to 900 newspapers. Lasswell was probably the oldest of a burgeoning number of cartoonists no longer snail-mailing their work to syndicates.

"Barney Google" was created in 1919 by Billy DeBeck (who coined the term "horsefeathers"). Fred began assisting DeBeck when Billy was shifting the focus of the comic from urbanite Barney Google ("with the goo-goo-googly eyes") to hillbilly Snuffy Smith. Given that Lasswell spent part of his childhood on a Florida farm, he knew enough about rural life to ably take over the comic after DeBeck's 1942 death. "I lived on 10 acres with a plow horse and a cow and a dog and a cat and 2,000 white leghorn chickens," Fred told me. "We didn't have a radio or electricity, and we cooked on a wooden stove."

But Lasswell came a long way from the farm after meeting DeBeck, because Billy introduced Fred to his many celebrity pals. One was Babe Ruth — aka the Sultan of Swat, the Duke of Dissipation, and the Oligarch of Overeating.

Fred told me that Ruth hit a golf ball the same way he hit a baseball. "He would lift his right foot off the ground and knock the living hell out of it," Lasswell recalled with a chuckle. And Fred, who once accompanied the Babe's daughter to a dance, was invited to sit in Ruth's box at Yankee Stadium during a World Series game.

Also in early 1996, *E&P*'s co-publishers finally allowed one shared personal computer in the newsroom, so I could now access the Internet after nearly a year of writing about it. I quickly decided to do a story describing various online destinations — including Web sites for syndicates, cartoonists, and columnists. I even had my headline ready: "A Site-Seeing Trip Along the Internet." But first I had to figure out how the wacky World Wide Web worked.

"How do I get to a Web site?" I asked young *E&P* writer Dorothy Giobbe in a tone I hoped didn't sound *too* embarrassed.

She showed me where to type a URL.

"Remind me again how to use this mouse thing?"

Dorothy showed me that, too, and kindly didn't smirk at my pitiful ignorance.

"Thank you," I said gratefully.

Then I gingerly called up sites and clicked around, afraid I would do something un-PC to the PC. I looked at Web pages for hours, filling numerous legal pad pages with notes. I was too dumb to know that I could have printed out the stuff I was seeing.

Soon it was time to do some real rather than virtual traveling. I returned to Boca Raton, Fla., in March for the grand opening of the International Museum of Cartoon Art (formerly the Rye Brook, N.Y.-based Museum of Cartoon Art that I visited in 1984). IMCA founder/chairman Mort Walker and his wife Cathy hosted the Boca event.

IMCA's whimsical new two-story building — it looked like something at Disney World — opened after an initial fundraising campaign brought in $6 million. A sixth of that money came from "Peanuts" cartoonist Charles Schulz, with "Garfield" cartoonist Jim Davis and IMCA president Joe D'Angelo among the people heavily involved in the effort to elicit donations.

"Joe is president of King Features and I'm with King, so he's my boss. At the museum, I'm his boss," quipped "Beetle Bailey" creator Walker. Most corporate employees wouldn't mind that switcheroo!

IMCA in 1996 had a collection of more than 150,000 original cartoons — including drawings by Ben Franklin and Paul Revere, and the earliest known sketches of Mickey Mouse. Those sketches, donated the previous year by Diamond Comic Distributors president Stephen Geppi, were from 1928. "It sends a chill down my spine to see the very first drawings of Mickey Mouse," said Walker. "Who could have predicted then what an empire those simple pencil drawings would inspire?"

And who could have predicted in 1996 the eventual blog stardom of Arianna Huffington? (Especially given that the word "blog," short for "weblog," wasn't coined until later in the decade!) In April '96, I wrote a short item reporting that Creators Syndicate had signed the super-smart Huffington as a twice-weekly opinion columnist offering "wit and hard-hitting conservatism with a social conscience." That description would eventually need a tiny edit: "conservatism" changed to "liberalism."

Originally from Greece, the 1950-born Arianna moved to England when she was 16 and graduated from Cambridge University with a master's in economics. Arianna, who uses the last name of ex-husband/former Republican congressman Michael Huffington, moved to New York in 1980. She would eventually author more than a dozen books in addition to her column and blog work.

In the same E&P issue that mentioned Huffington, I ran a feature story about Marie Woolf — the talented creator who had just joined one of the smallest groups in newspaper-land: syndicated women editorial cartoonists. Woolf felt this group was so small not only because of sexism, but because "little girls are not encouraged to be politically astute. And, if they become artists, they might be channeled to somewhat 'gentler' art forms."

Woolf was a Brigham Young University alum who majored in history, minored in religion, and fenced. "That," she joked, "was the perfect education for a woman editorial cartoonist!"

Later in '96, I wrote a story noting there were many male-created comics with female title characters ("Blondie," "Luann," "Nancy," "Sally Forth," etc.) but virtually no female-created comics with male title characters. J.K. (Joanne Kathleen) Rowling wasn't an inspiration yet because her fabulous *Harry Potter* books were still in the future.

Of course, some male cartoonists do such a good job with female title characters that readers might wonder if these creators are female themselves. "I get a lot of mail asking whether I'm a man or woman," said "Rose is Rose" man Pat Brady of the unisex first name. "It's embarrassing only when I'm asked that in person!"

Brady and others told me that one reason more men than women have title characters of a different sex is because there are relatively few female cartoonists. So the women who *do* become syndicated figure they have to represent their gender on comic pages overflowing with males.

Erma Bombeck, one of the funniest columnists of either gender, died at age 69 in April 1996 after an unsuccessful kidney transplant that followed several years of dialysis — so I quickly called up some of her journalism-world peers for a tribute story. A sampling of their comments: "Erma was a wonderful writer," said advice columnist Abigail Van Buren. "She showed us that everyday family life is worth writing about," noted National Society of Newspaper Columnists president Sheila Stroup of the New Orleans *Times-Picayune*. "She was one of the most gracious people I've ever met in the business," recalled humor columnist Dave Barry.

Van Buren said Bombeck may have been "*too* terrific" a person, refusing to use her celebrity status to try to get a new kidney sooner. "She waited on line like everyone else," noted the "Dear Abby" writer with a touch of wonder in her voice.

Bombeck, a longtime Ohio resident who later moved to Arizona, authored more than a dozen best-selling books. She collaborated with "The Family Circus" cartoonist Bil Keane on 1971's *Just Wait Till You Have Children of Your Own!*, and I later heard Bil joke: "I'm the only person other than Bill Bombeck who's been between the covers with Erma!"

One way Erma's name and her suburban humor live on is via the Erma Bombeck Writers' Workshop associated with the University of Dayton, her alma mater. The biennial workshop was formerly directed by humor columnist Tim Bete, who would undoubtedly confirm that "biennial" means "every two years."

I traveled to Arizona in June 1996 to cover the Association of American Editorial Cartoonists convention. Boy, was Phoenix hot — more than 110 degrees (but it was dry heat, yada, yada, yada). One AAEC speaker was Joe

Garagiola, the baseball broadcaster and former Major League catcher who was then a correspondent-at-large for NBC's *Today* show.

Garagiola cracked some baseball-clubhouse jokes ("in my day, the whirlpool was putting your elbow in the toilet and flushing") before asking AAECers to do anti-chewing tobacco cartoons to help a campaign he headed. Joe also mentioned his close friend Yogi Berra of Montclair, N.J., where I had now lived for three years. My ears perked up when Garagiola mentioned driving along Watchung Avenue on his way to see Yogi, because that street was near my house! In fact, I walked on Watchung every day to take the train to work, and loved passing the beautiful old Marlboro Inn — which I would often write about after I tried another kind of journalism in 2003.

By the way, it's a coincidence that this chapter mentions two Yankee legends (Berra and Babe Ruth). I used to be a fan of the Bronx Bombers, but they outspend every other baseball team by so much that I now root for the 1869 Cincinnati Red Stockings — whose players are all at least 160 years old. But 160 is the new 140.

Also living in Montclair was Mickey Siporin, a cartoonist/filmmaker who taught at Montclair State University. He was 14 years older than I, but we became friends — as did Mickey's bright, engaging daughter Cordelia and my (bright, engaging!) daughter Maggie. The girls, who were just two years apart in age, initially bonded over games of Chinese checkers.

Mickey was a highly original cartoonist with a distinctive art style that looked almost Picasso-like. This offbeat art, and Mickey's progressive politics, made it hard for Chronicle Features to sell his work to many daily papers after he entered syndication in July 1996. But the affable Mickey never compromised on his drawing style or politics to try to get more sales. He had rock-solid integrity, and I've missed him very much since his 2005 death.

Our wonderful cat Samantha died in 1996, partly from old age (she was 18) and perhaps partly because she was lonely for her 1995-deceased buddy Gwyneth. I miss them both, too.

It was around this time that Maggie announced she didn't want to eat meat anymore.

"Why not?" I asked.

"It was alive," she replied.

Well, that made sense to me, and we let Maggie go vegetarian. I started moving in that direction myself, though I didn't become completely vegetarian until about 10 years later. One big reason for that decision was learning how inhumanely corporate-owned factory farms treat animals destined for our dinner plates. I know how to count, but I often think "corporate" is a four-letter word.

I wanted to hear a four-letter word — "sold!" — for my *Message from Margaret* children's book mentioned in the last chapter, but, alas, agent Toni Mendez's best efforts couldn't get a publisher to bite despite several rewrites on my part. My talented cartoonist friend Anne Gibbons was even willing to do the illustrations if a sale had been made. I thought the story I had dreamed up was very touching, but what can you do? I licked my wounds and vowed to come up with some other kind of project.

National Society of Newspaper Columnists member Diane Ketcham's project was having some kind of competition at each year's NSNC conference. In July 1996, the fun and bubbly *New York Times* columnist challenged a group of English professors meeting in the same Snowbird, Utah, hotel to an impromptu spelling bee.

The bee was in the NSNC's hospitality suite at the mountain resort, so, in order to cover it, I broke my rule of not entering such a suite.

With Diane emceeing, three columnists squared off against three English profs. I felt a little bad for the profs, because there were many more writers than teachers in the room — and the columnists were a vocal cheering section. No foam fingers, though; it's hard to type with those things on.

Convention host Dennis Lythgoe of the Salt Lake City *Deseret News* was the first columnist eliminated after misspelling "pusillanimous." Louisville *Courier-Journal* writer Dianne Aprile hung in for a long time — spelling such words as "lecithin" and "pulchritudinous" — before being tripped up. Then columnist Tony Gabriele of the Newport News, Va., *Daily Press* won it all by correctly tackling "idolator" and "contrapuntal."

"How do you feel about winning?" I asked Tony, as if I was holding an ESPN mike.

"In view of my success here, I'm going to turn pro," he quipped.

I would have my own interaction of journalism and academia less than six years later.

There was another stunt at September's Newspaper Features Council meeting in San Antonio, where two Pulitzer Prize-winning editorial cartoonists were challenged to an un-Alamo-like battle by Copley News Service executive vice president Bob Witty. Michael Ramirez of the Memphis *Commercial Appeal* and Ben Sargent of the *Austin American-Statesman* had to draw an editorial cartoon in just 10 minutes on a topic (President Clinton's Mideast peace efforts) the two didn't know about in advance.

Meanwhile, Tribune Media Services began syndicating a *Milwaukee Journal Sentinel* column by Jacquelyn Mitchard, whose *The Deep End of the Ocean* novel had recently become the first title chosen for Oprah Winfrey's new book club. It's interesting that the TV superstar reeled in a newspaper writer as her inaugural choice.

Then New Jersey-based cartoonist Patrick McDonnell crossed the deep end of the Hudson River to visit me at *E&P* for an interview about "Mutts" — his expertly drawn comic starting Earl the dog and Mooch the cat. It's kinder and gentler than many post-1990-launched strips (with a welcome dose of animal-rights fervor), and has brought the soft-spoken McDonnell about 700 newspaper clients and millions of fans.

Three fans were in *E&P*'s office that November 1996 day: me, copy editor Jennifer Waber, and associate editor Laura Reina. Jennifer and Laura were thrilled to have Patrick draw and sign "Mutts" sketches for them before my interview began.

McDonnell, by the way, was a young 20-something in 1978 when he got a huge career break: illustrating Russell Baker's *New York Times Magazine* column.

In December 1996, comedian/actor Denis Leary made a hilariously profane appearance at a National Cartoonists Society holiday party in New York — where he received the Amateur Cartoonist Extraordinary (ACE) honor for doing some drawing in the past.

Before Leary came to the podium, the NCS's Elzie Segar Award (named after the creator of "Popeye") went to "Marvin" cartoonist Tom Armstrong and the organization's Silver T Square honor to "Beetle Bailey" creator Mort Walker assistant Bill Janocha for compiling the NCS's 50th-anniversary directory. Leary received that phone book-sized directory as well as several other gifts for winning the ACE, but he still feigned anger and disappointment at not receiving the prizes handed to Bill and Tom.

"I've been watching all the good shit disappear," faux-ranted the future star of TV's *Rescue Me*. "The Silver T Square. The Popeye thing. I was starting to think of a place in my house for the giant Popeye. Then they give me a fuckin' phone book? ... I'm glad I didn't wear a tie tonight."

E&P staffers would be upset for real in 1997.

CHAPTER TWENTY

1997: 'Zits' and a Firing That's the Pits

All the President's Men: a book and movie many journalists love. "All the Presidents Are No Longer Men": my headline for a January 1997 story I wrote about a major distributor finally getting a woman president — Gloria Brown Anderson at the New York Times Syndication Sales Corp., the lengthily named parent of NYT's syndicate and news service.

Another parent (me) was impressed when my seven-year-old daughter Maggie memorized the intricate lyrics and sang R.E.M.'s "Man on the Moon" to much applause at her elementary school's talent show in April 1997. I accompanied Maggie on guitar, thinking how I wouldn't have been caught dead doing that in front of 300 parents and kids at the time I joined *E&P* 14 years earlier.

Maggie and I also drew together. Those fun doodling sessions reminded me that I had some artistic talent, so I thought: Why not try cartooning? Not for newspapers or syndicates, because that would be a conflict of interest. But I didn't write about magazines, so maybe I could send stuff to them.

I went to a Manhattan art-supply store at an eerily convenient locale (next to the back entrance of *E&P*'s West 19th Street building) and purchased some India-ink pens and other needed items. Then I scoured my brain for ideas, laboriously drew eight cartoons, and sent one each to eight small "niche" magazines.

From covering cartoonists since 1983, I knew how hard they worked and how difficult it was to stare at a blank piece of paper trying to think of a decent idea. But doing this myself made me realize on a gut level that drawing funny pictures was indeed no easy task.

Still, creating cartoons was as absorbing as it was difficult — and this activity filled evening and weekend hours when Maggie was asleep or with friends. As I've mentioned, my wife and I were growing apart.

Amazingly, one of the eight magazines — *College Bound* — wrote back in April to say they would publish my cartoon and pay me the grand total of $20! After having a play, a novel, and a children's book go nowhere, I read and reread the simple acceptance form in ecstatic disbelief. I would finally have something non-*E&P* in print!

The cartoon — slated to be published that fall (long lead time!) — showed *The Scarlet Letter*'s Hester Prynne standing in a high school hallway with this "thought balloon" above her head: "They gave me an 'A,' but are my SAT scores good enough?"

Back at *E&P*, I learned that King Features would be syndicating *CBS Evening News* anchor Dan Rather. Was this yet another weekly column by a celebrity with no newspaper experience? Then I found out that Rather *had* worked in print journalism early in his career, and decided to do a May phone interview with him.

"How do you feel about starting a column?" I asked.

"I'm really looking forward to it," replied Rather, then 65. "This was meant to be. Printer's ink runs in my veins!"

During the 1950s, the Texas native worked at the Associated Press, United Press International, the *Houston Chronicle,* and a radio station affiliated with the *Chronicle.* Then it was on to a CBS television career that included stints as a White House, Vietnam, and *60 Minutes* correspondent before succeeding Walter Cronkite as anchor in 1981.

"How did the column come about?"

"Like all great ideas, it did not originate with the anchor," Rather joked. Instead, his friend Frank Bennack Jr. — president of the Hearst Corp., King's owner — suggested he become a newspaper pundit.

King also made a big splash in July 1997 with its launch of "Zits" in more than 200 papers — one of the biggest debuts in comics history. The strip starring 15-year-old Jeremy Duncan continued to grow in popularity, eventually passing the rarified 1,500-client mark.

Why did the inelegantly named "Zits" do so well? It's funny and expertly drawn (often from unusual angles), it's not too edgy but not too bland, and its co-creators were already well-known before the strip began. "Zits" writer Jerry Scott co-created the "Baby Blues" comic, while "Zits" artist Jim Borgman was the syndicated, Pulitzer Prize-winning editorial cartoonist for *The Cincinnati Enquirer.*

There were no blemishes on the 14-year *E&P* editorship of John Consoli. He was an excellent journalist and good person who consulted with reporters when making changes in their stories, got the magazine out on time each week, and even wrote many editorials as 80-something owner Robert Brown eased into semi-retirement. Also, John was a guy from a working-class background who interacted with the co-publisher grandsons in a business-like rather than fawning way — for which *E&P* staffers greatly respected him.

The blue-blood grandsons might not have liked that, though. They may have also felt John wasn't gung ho enough about new media, even though he did assign stories about the burgeoning online world. (The co-publishers' cyber concerns were ironic given that they *still* hadn't provided the magazine's reporters with individual computers to access the Internet or with individual *E&P* email addresses.)

In addition, the grandsons were reportedly upset about the state of *E&P*'s ad revenue. Of course, that wasn't John's fault; a big reason was the contracting of the newspaper business as some dailies folded, other dailies were bought by chains, etc. Finally, our two leaders apparently listened too much to a high-priced consultant who had recently been brought in.

Anyway, I had taken a vacation day on Aug. 8 — using that time to go to one of Montclair's pools with Maggie (her mother rarely joined our swimming expeditions). When we returned home, my wife said John had phoned me from his apartment. I immediately called back.

"The brothers fired me," he said with a mixture of shock and anger.

"Dammit! No!"

John did express relief that Robert Brown had given him a good severance package. But the longtime *E&P* owner didn't try to prevent the firing — proving once again that blue blood is thicker than water.

Senior editor George Garneau, who also didn't fawn over those in power, was promoted to acting managing editor to succeed John. The "acting" in his title was a strong clue that the grandsons wanted someone else as head editor in the near future.

All in all, it was not the greatest summer. Even a family vacation at a semi-rural Connecticut inn was far from relaxing. My wife and I snapped at each other about everything from parenting approaches to Maggie's continued dislike of the religious school I didn't want her returning to in September.

"She went for a couple of years," I argued. "That's enough."

"Absolutely not. She'll thank me one day."

"Thanks" has yet to be offered as I write this in 2012.

My wife and I also had different approaches to vacation-time relaxing. I took walks or bike rides before Maggie woke up, and then she and I went swimming in the inn's pool. My wife was content to sit around most of the day, eating and reading. We did manage to visit Nathan Hale's house in Coventry, Conn., and I only regret that we had but one side trip to give life to that vacation in the country.

Speaking of getting away, here's what a narcissist might think while on vacation: "Why is my commuter train still running without me?"

Another train left the Universal Press Syndicate station when cartoonist Lynn Johnston moved "For Better or For Worse" and its 1,800-plus papers to United Feature Syndicate. The September 1997 switch sort of evened the score for Jim Davis' 1994 move of "Garfield" from United to Universal — though Lynn would return "FBorFW" to Universal in 2004.

"Why are you going to United?" I asked Lynn via a phone call to her Canadian studio.

"I needed a change," she replied, adding wryly: "I wanted to be new again."

Don't we all!

The very month Lynn left, Universal got some new comics and columns with its purchase of Chronicle Features. That meant even less competition in the syndication biz, three full-time and three part-time Chronicle staffers losing their jobs, and eight of the syndicate's 17 features being dropped by Universal.

Among the Chronicle creators kept by Universal were future Pulitzer-winning opinion columnist Cynthia Tucker, "Latino Spectrum" writers Patrisia Gonzales and Roberto Rodriguez, and cartoonists Gail Machlis ("Quality Time") and Stephanie Piro ("Fair Game").

I asked Chronicle editor/general manager Stuart Dodds — who had been with the syndicate since 1962, eight years before Universal was founded — why the sale had to happen.

"It was becoming more and more clear that we couldn't continue as a smaller syndicate," he told me. "We couldn't provide all the services expected of a syndicate and stay profitable. It's very hard to compete with huge companies."

The native of England added that Chronicle was small enough to have "almost total freedom" to introduce some offbeat features — and said a comic such as "The Far Side" might never have been syndicated if Chronicle hadn't signed it in 1980.

And how's this for a non-corporate touch? "I live four blocks from Stuart," Gail Machlis told me at the time of the sale. "I dropped off my comic on a piano bench on the front porch of his house!"

A White House resident, first lady Hillary Clinton, addressed the Newspaper Features Council in late September — mostly discussing the weekly, not-for-pay column she had been writing for Los Angeles-based Creators Syndicate since 1995.

"I usually finish it late at night," Clinton told NFC attendees in Washington, D.C. "I've filed from Air Force One on occasion, and from different countries. My math has gotten better — I have to calculate the time in Los Angeles from Mongolia!"

Clinton — who wrote about life in the White House, her travels, people she met, and more — added that being forced to miss the occasional deadline made her marvel at the fact that former first lady Eleanor Roosevelt wrote a long-running *daily* column (for United Feature Syndicate).

Critics of Clinton have called her cold, but I saw no signs of that sexist canard. She came off as warm and relaxed, especially during the unscripted Q&A period following her speech. At one point, an audience member asked Clinton to name her favorite comics.

The future secretary of state, perhaps aware that the NFC crowd included cartoonists and competing syndicates, replied with a chuckle: "That's one of those state secrets you'll have to read about in my memoir!"

What's a "memoir"? Can I write one, too?

Clinton, by the way, came to the meeting through the efforts of Creators president Rick Newcombe and NFC executive director Corinta Kotula, a delight of a person who had a former life as a singer in opera houses and other venues. It ain't over 'til the first lady speaks.

But it was over for many passengers on a certain ship, as viewers of the *Titanic* movie were reminded starting in December 1997. My daughter Maggie saw the blockbuster film several times, and its "My Heart Will Go On" theme song undoubtedly comforted cardiology patients everywhere.

Also in late '97, *E&P*'s co-publishers filled a newly created, upper-level position that paid a rumored six-figure salary (and the first figure wasn't zero). This new hire had worked for several daily newspapers and other media organizations, so the grandsons were undoubtedly dazzled by his resume. But his tenure would turn out to be less than dazzling.

CHAPTER TWENTY-ONE

1998:
'I Want Sex Off
the Table'

In early 1998, there was "shrinkage." No, not the kind plaguing George Costanza after he emerged from cold water in that famous 1994 *Seinfeld* episode, but shrinkage in the size of my weekly *E&P* section. Almost always given three pages since my 1983 hiring, I now often made do with two.

One reason for the downsizing was reduced advertising by cost-cutting syndicates — though *E&P* would soon get some ads (until the dot-com bubble burst in 2000) from online aggregators such as iSyndicate and ScreamingMedia that digitally delivered material from content providers to Web sites. But a bigger reason for my print section's shrinkage was *E&P* management's desire to increase Web traffic by having more of my syndicate coverage appear online than in the weekly "dead tree" edition.

There were consequences to this. My Web-based "Syndicate World" could be read for free, while *E&P*'s print magazine cost money to buy. So, many of my readers — especially cartoonists and columnists on tight budgets — canceled their subscriptions while continuing to follow me online. This obviously cost *E&P* some revenue — and was just one small example of how the free Web model would help devastate many print publications.

Also, I had to work extra hours for no extra pay to do the extra online stuff. I often got home well after 6 p.m., even though I had begun skipping my already short lunch break. I snacked as I wrote, and so many crumbs lodged in my keyboard that they got counted in the 2000 Census.

"You're working late *again*?" my exasperated wife would say when I called from the office.

"Sorry. I can't help it."

Actually, I was partly pleased to have less time with her as our marriage deteriorated, but I greatly missed spending early evenings with my daughter Maggie. And the increased workload meant I couldn't bring her into the office as often as before.

The guy telling me to start "Syndicate World" was Hoag Levins, the *E&P* Web editor just given the additional post of executive editor for the print magazine. Hoag was certainly knowledgeable about digital matters.

Meanwhile, I *finally* got an *E&P* email account in early 1998 — oh, just a few thousand years after most other journalists on Earth had one. It was thrilling to look at four or five electronic messages a day, though the number of emails would mushroom out of hand in future years.

One of my first messages was from United Media director of syndicate promotion Mary Anne Grimes, who was prescient when writing: "Welcome to the brave new world of email! Your life will never be the same!"

Also, *E&P* reporters now each had their own Internet-connected computers to replace our nearly 20-year-old video display terminals. When those ancient VDTs were carted away, I felt a mixture of relief and sadness reminiscent of when my parents' 1950 Oldsmobile was towed to the junkyard in 1966 as I watched from the living room window.

Soon, *E&P* writers were introduced to the Quark Publishing System ("Hi, I'm QPS"/"Hi, I'm Dave") — on which we could write stories and see/correct them on screen after they were paginated by the art director.

There was now even the possibility of "computer-assisted reporting," although the idea of having a computer stand next to me scribbling on a reporter's pad gave me the creeps.

Meanwhile, readers could finally email Ann Landers via Creators Syndicate's Web site starting in March 1998. But Landers, who continued to use an electric typewriter at age 80, never saw those messages on screen. Instead, a Creators staffer in Los Angeles printed out the emails and overnighted them once a week to Ann and her staff in Chicago. A story I did later in '98 noted that emails to Landers were arriving at a rate of 200-plus a day as of August — around the time Universal Press Syndicate's Web site started to accept emails for "Dear Abby."

"You did a fine job on the piece," Landers wrote me that month. "As you know, I am not on the Internet and have no plans to get on. I'm hoping that people with serious problems will use the established channel and write to me in care of the newspaper in which they read the column." Ann, by the way, had two spare electric typewriters in case the one she was using went kaput.

Gary Larson's brilliant "Far Side" comic had died a voluntary death in early 1995. To find out what the now-47-year-old Larson was up to, I contacted him in March 1998 — and he was nice enough to give a rare interview.

The cartoonist had finished working on the *Tales from the Far Side II* animated film as well as an eco-minded book titled *There's a Hair in My Dirt: A Worm's Story*. He was also spending lots of time playing jazz guitar.

"Do you ever regret ending the comic?" I asked.

"I can't honestly say I miss it, although I do have some wistful feelings," Gary replied. "It was just a wonderful experience for me. It's hard to imagine that happening to anyone — to draw cartoons for a living and have all that success follow. It was surreal.

"But I just kind of sensed that the comic had this lifetime. It was time to move on and try other things. One of those 'been there, done that' feelings came over me."

Gary always did give thoughtful answers.

President Clinton's thoughtless relationship with Monica Lewinsky dominated the news in 1998. One person who helped make that sex scandal public was Lucianne Goldberg — the right-wing literary agent who advised former White House aide Linda Tripp to tape Lewinsky's comments about the affair. As I mentioned in my 1994 chapter, Lucianne was married to syndicate executive Sid Goldberg, so I thought it would be interesting to interview the Manhattan-based Sid about life in the media maelstrom.

"It was a circus," Sid told me. "When the story first broke, there was a mob of reporters and TV cameras parked in front of our apartment building. Lucy wouldn't or couldn't go outside for six or seven days."

Sid was able to enter and exit the building normally, because he made sure the camped-out media didn't know he was Lucianne's husband!

Meanwhile, 28-year-old cartoonist Jeff Shesol announced he was ending his "Thatch" comic to become a speechwriter for Bill Clinton. Jeff got the job after the president read *Mutual Contempt*, Shesol's book describing how Clinton and Lucianne felt about each other. Oops — Shesol's well-reviewed book was actually about the strained relationship between Lyndon Johnson and Robert Kennedy.

The Clinton-Lewinsky brouhaha also stirred plenty of discussion and controversy over what kind of language was permissible in the G-rated world of newspaper comics. For instance, about 10 of 1,400 clients puritanically dropped "Doonesbury" after Garry Trudeau used the term "oral sex" in a strip about the White House scandal.

And the Clinton-Lewinsky affair was alluded to at the National Society of Newspaper Columnists (NSNC) conference in San Diego. Speaker Arianna Huffington, in saying the sex lives of politicians should not be a litmus test determining their fitness for office, quipped: "I want sex off the table!"

The pre-Huffington Post Arianna expanded on that remark — which inspired uproarious audience laughter — by adding that keeping one's libido in check doesn't necessarily make for a good politician. But the columnist/author did emphasize that it's a different story when sexual indiscretions lead to perjury or obstruction of justice — or affect government decisions.

When Huffington stepped off the podium after her talk, she greeted me with an enthusiastic "Hi, Dave!" in her charming Greek accent. I had interviewed Arianna several times over the phone, but this was the first time we met.

Another columnist/author addressing the NSNC was Richard Lederer, who regaled the audience with examples of the English language's crazier aspects. He asked: "If a vegetarian eats vegetables, what does a humanitarian eat? If pro and con are opposites, is Congress the opposite of progress? And why is monosyllabic a five-syllable word?"

I'll try to come up with some answers while driving on a parkway or parking on a driveway.

One other thing I remember clearly about the San Diego conference was *Akron* (Ohio) *Beacon Journal* columnist Regina Brett succeeding Portland *Oregonian* columnist Jonathan Nicholas as NSNC president. Brett, a future

Pulitzer Prize finalist for the Cleveland *Plain Dealer,* was battling cancer in 1998 at age 42 — and eventually beat it.

I soon went west again to cover the Association of American Editorial Cartoonists (AAEC) convention in Las Vegas, but didn't mind all that trekking. Air travel was less arduous before 9/11 (remember when you didn't have to doff your shoes before going through security?), and I spent the long plane rides drawing cartoons as the passengers sitting next to me cast surreptitious glances. It was just like an in-flight movie for them — minus the actors, sound, scenery, special effects, plot, and talent.

My cartoon sales were going okay — I sold eight in 1998, including one that appeared in the California Association of Highway Patrolmen's *APB* magazine! It showed a pulled-over driver telling a police officer: "Yes, I was doing 80. But I did only 30 this morning. Could we average the two?" I also started drawing cartoons for Maggie's elementary school newsletter.

"Viva Las Vegas" wasn't in the cartoon "thought balloon" over my head as I disgustedly viewed numerous slot machines in the airport before checking into the huge Caesars Palace hotel where the AAEC was meeting. Walking from the front desk to my room seemed to take 10 minutes, because you had to go through several betting areas before reaching your bedding area. But the weirdness had only begun.

During one AAEC session, kitschy Vegas crooner Wayne Newton actually shared the stage with former Israeli Prime Minister Shimon Peres, the dour 1994 Nobel Peace Prize winner who had recently started a Los Angeles Times Syndicate column.

Peres expressed the hope that the world would one day be peaceful enough to make editorial cartoonists unnecessary. "You can take up painting," Peres quipped.

What about taking up unemployment? The Hearst-owned King Features Syndicate told the Kingsyn Employees Association in July 1998 that it might lay off many staffers and move several KFS functions from New York City to the Hearst-owned Reed Brennan Media Associates in Orlando, Fla. Three months later, Hearst even discussed moving *all* of King to the Sunshine State. Once again, a corporate entity was trying to keep profits at a certain level.

Naturally, I phoned some people for reaction. "King always had sort of a family feeling," said Chris Browne, the gentle man who took over "Hagar the Horrible" from his late father Dik. "Maybe that's part of a world that's fading fast, but I'm sorry to see it go. There's more to life than just business."

Heading the King "reorganization" negotiations were syndicate president Larry Olsen on the management side and King comic art department staffer/"Mama's Boyz" cartoonist Jerry Craft on the employee side. Ultimately, about 30 people (including Craft) were laid off with severance benefits starting in December 1998. And King, perhaps influenced by the pleas of executives and employees who didn't want to relocate, ended up doing a partial rather than complete move to Florida.

Olsen was a fair and "compassionate" negotiator, Jerry told me, and you'll see in the next chapter how Larry's not-too-corporate attitude might have affected his King career.

Speaking of management-employee relations, the new *E&P* exec I mentioned at the end of the previous chapter gave me the first non-stellar evaluation of my 15-year career at the magazine. This despite the fact that I was writing even more than before (because of my new online duties), still making virtually no errors in stories, and still receiving tons of positive letters from people thanking me for articles or for answering questions. Some of those correspondents had even CCed those letters to the exec during the previous months.

When I saw the evaluation (which was done several months late — making my tiny raise oh-so-conveniently late as well), the former wimp known as me marched into his office.

"I'm very upset with this," I said, pointing to the unfair review clutched in my left hand. "I do great work for this magazine."

"That's your opinion," he squeaked.

Actually, when I had run across him in his pre-*E&P* days, this same exec had told me I did great work for the magazine. Just his opinion, I guess.

I soon learned that at least two other *E&P* veterans also received reviews less positive than their previous ones. It made me wonder if the higher-ups wanted longer-tenured staffers to quit to make up for the company payroll being swollen by the new exec's high salary. Had the immortal *Three Musketeers* phrase "one for all and all for one" turned into a management cry of "less for all and more for us"?

The new exec spent some of his time working on an *E&P* redesign that made its debut in September 1998. The now-"newsier" magazine looked like a tabloid on a supermarket checkout line — with a neon-red *Editor & Publisher* logo on the cover, a deep-black headline font, cluttered layouts, etc. It gave me a headache to look at the thing.

There was one good thing about the redesign (and it was a *very* good thing): ending the 83-year-old practice of allowing a big ad on the cover each week. But this was partly negated by a paid "teaser" ad on the cover's top-right corner.

The first new-look issue was barely off the presses when Hoag Levins quit. The redesign and resignation may or may not have been coincidental, but I do know that Hoag chafed at what he felt was frequent interference from the new exec. "This isn't working," I heard an exasperated Levins mutter.

After Hoag resigned, the shaken, red-eyed new exec called a meeting to tell staffers the magazine would be fine, don't panic, blah, blah, blah. So the future was bright ... so bright, in fact, that the exec was out of a job the following month.

Another high-level exec was quickly hired. Just days after the new guy started, I was scrambling to finish three print stories that broke close to deadline. As I wrote as fast as I could, he actually stood at my shoulder badgering me to finish and making less-than-kind remarks about my journalistic ability and speed. I had been at E&P 15 years and this supervisor barely 15 minutes, but he apparently knew best.

Soon after this new guy started, Steve Yahn was named senior managing editor. Steve, a veteran of publications such as *Advertising Age* and the New York *Daily News*, turned out to be a great editor and an even greater guy. Also, the equally nice and talented Carl Sullivan was promoted to replace Hoag as editor of E&P's Web site, and the eccentric but charming Kimberly Scheck was named news editor of the magazine.

In 1999, the brilliant and congenial J.J. McGrath became copy editor, the skilled and friendly Lucia Moses was hired as an associate editor/reporter, the talented and personable Reiko Matsuo was brought in as art/design director, and no one was brought in to control my overuse of adjectives.

Steve and Kimberly might have been mostly responsible for the above personnel decisions. But, while I had issues with the new exec's personality, I must admit that he hired (or at least signed off on) some good people.

Still, the new exec treated me and other longtime E&Pers with less respect than recent hires. He also periodically assigned last-minute stories so large that it was impossible to research and write them well. And he wasn't that fond of the occasional human-interest stories I mixed in with my newsier articles.

One such piece was about a woman named Rhonda Nabors who used United Media's Web site to help find the parents who gave her up for adoption. Her biological dad and mom turned out to be United-syndicated "Luann" cartoonist Greg Evans and his wife Betty.

Another such piece was about *Arizona Republic* editorial cartoonist Steve Benson moonlighting as a volunteer policeman. That story contained this hilarious bit: Whenever a motorist Benson stopped for a traffic violation plaintively asked, "What did I do?" the "coptoonist" was tempted to answer, "Do I have to draw you a picture?"

In a pathetic reaction to this respect deficit from the new exec, I began tacking the many positive letters I received from E&P readers to my cubicle wall for him to see — and later did the same with dozens of holiday cards sent by cartoonists and others. I was also tempted to hang my 1998 *Who's Who in America* plaque on the wall, but decided to keep that ego display at home. Besides, despite knowing when-when I got in *Who's Who*, I wasn't sure how-how and why-why.

After going "meow meow"-less since 1996, my family and I decided to get two kittens to succeed the late Gwyneth and Samantha as honored members of our household. We visited Montclair's wonderful PAWS animal shelter in November 1998, and first spotted a cat named Lucky who had lost most of one ear on the street. She wasn't a kitten — Lucky was three or four — but what a gentle soul!

"She's *so* sweet!" enthused Maggie, as the black-and-white cat melted into my daughter's arms.

We still wanted *one* kitten — and a shy tortie named Patches was our chosen young'un. But she was in the same cage as her mother Madonna, and we couldn't bear to split them up. So we left PAWS with three felines.

We initially placed the trio in our basement to let them briefly get comfortable in a smaller space before giving them the run of the house. But Madonna would have none of that "Borderline" stuff, quickly making a feline beeline to butt the closed basement door — and earning the new name of Exupery for her adventurous nature. Patches became K.C. (short for Kitty Cat) and Lucky was dubbed Mystic (because of her coloring).

The big-boned Exupery — whose diva qualities explained her former Madonna name — was quite sullen at first, perhaps because of post-traumatic stress from her former street life. She also treated Mystic and her daughter K.C. badly, swatting at them and such. We raised our voices with Exupery over this, and she retreated back to the basement. It was then that I decided to try overcoming her funk by showering her with love. I brought water and food down to her, petted her constantly, cooed into her ear, etc. It took several days, but suddenly a switch flipped in her brain and she became as contented as can be. If only that approach worked with some media execs!

Mystic was angelic from the start, even climbing on top of my chest the first night as I lay in bed. K.C. — after a nasty virus cured by Dr. George Cameron, Montclair's expert and dedicated veterinarian — became a great companion, too.

But K.C. was a little too energetic to keep in our bedroom at night. Once, she leaped down from a tall dresser onto our bed, lost her footing, and slowed her fall to the floor by raking her claws down the side of my right ankle.

It was rather painful, like some events would be in 1999. But the coming year also had some nice surprises in store.

CHAPTER TWENTY-TWO

1999: A Trio of Last Stands Near the Alamo

Syndication doesn't just involve creative things like comics, columns, editorial cartoons, and crossword puzzles. There are also "information products" — including TV listings, weather data, and other content that most newspapers would find too expensive and cumbersome to compile themselves. So they buy them from distributors such as Tribune Media Services and AccuWeather.

After I did some begging, my immediate supervisors gave me three magazine pages one week in 1999 to do an info-products overview that elicited many positive emails from readers and interviewees. But, perhaps miffed about that extra space being granted, a person or persons above those supervisors started slashing my section to *one* page during many subsequent weeks. Would minus-one page be far behind?

Speaking of supervisors, Larry Olsen was let go as King Features president in April '99 and succeeded by longtime Hearst exec T.R. "Rocky" Shepard III. One reason Shepard got the job was his new-media experience. But a source who called me wondered if Olsen was forced out partly because he didn't take a harder line against King employees during the layoff/relocation talks I wrote about in the previous chapter. Compassion is a quality many corporations dislike in a manager because they feel it might clash with maximizing profits.

King and Hearst officials wouldn't discuss Olsen's departure with me beyond sending a press release that contained the usual stuff about Olsen leaving "to pursue new challenges" (like unemployment).

But Universal Press Syndicate was happy to comment on these April developments: Bill Amend's 1988-launched "FoxTrot" joined 16 other comics in the 1,000-newspaper-client club, and Aaron McGruder's "The Boondocks" made its debut with an impressive total of more than 160 papers.

"The Boondocks" was good enough to have started with even more clients, but some older white newspaper editors couldn't handle an edgy humor strip that reflected hip-hop culture and commented candidly on racial matters from an African-American cartoonist's perspective.

Speaking several months later, at the Newspaper Features Council meeting I covered in Vancouver, the 24-year-old McGruder discussed his comic's non-city milieu ("The Boondocks" is slang for suburbia). "When you grow up black in the suburbs, everybody's very kind about their racism, but you know it's there," he observed.

Born in Chicago in 1974, McGruder spent much of his childhood in suburban Columbia, Md., before attending the University of Maryland.

In 1999, there were still only about 10 cartoonists of color among the 220 or so comic creators with major syndicates, but this was certainly an improvement over what I discussed in my 1984 and 1988 chapters. And coming in 2000 would be the Hector Cantu/Carlos Castellanos-created "Baldo" to join Peter Ramirez's already-syndicated "Raising Hector" — followed by Lalo Alcaraz's "La Cucaracha" in 2002.

Things were also slowly improving on newspaper op-ed pages. I wrote a 1999 story noting that columnists of color with major syndicates rose from eight in 1989 to 22 a decade later, and that women pundits increased from 13 to 27.5 (that ".5" refers to a female co-writing a column with a male, not a petite woman). Op-ed pages were still much more white and male-dominated than America as a whole, but the weather had become less cloudy with a chance of diversity.

In the multicultural city of San Antonio, a trio of speakers made the May 1999 National Cartoonists Society (NCS) meeting a memorable and poignant event. Memorable because all three — "Peanuts" creator Charles Schulz, "Shoe" creator/*Chicago Tribune* editorial cartoonist Jeff MacNelly, and retired editorial cartoonist Bill Mauldin — were superstars. Poignant because Schulz and MacNelly would die in 2000 and Mauldin was clearly a sick man at the Alamo-land gathering. Ironically, Mauldin outlived Schulz and MacNelly even though the latter two seemed as healthy as cartoon horses that weekend in Texas.

"Dangerous business, this cartooning thing," beloved 1997-99 NCS president George Breisacher wryly commented in an email he sent me after Mauldin's death in 2003 — a year before George himself died.

Mauldin, whose legendary World War II cartoons starring weary foot soldiers Willie and Joe are engraved in the minds of "The Greatest Generation," was too impaired to get many words out at the podium. (I later learned he had Alzheimer's disease.) But the former *St. Louis Post-Dispatch/Chicago Sun-Times* staffer was so respected by the NCSers in attendance that they prompted his recollections with questions, helped him finish his sentences, and responded to his halting words with applause.

When reading my notes of Mauldin's talk before writing an *E&P* story, I found only one quote coherent enough to use. Even that quote required "polishing" to make it sound okay, because I didn't want to embarrass this iconic cartoonist while he was still alive. Mauldin, 77, basically said: "I decided after being in the Army for a short while that it needed reforming, so I set about reforming it. I was largely successful, I think. At least I got all the right people mad. General Patton wanted me thrown in jail, but I had too many low-ranking friends!"

MacNelly, 51, told attendees he now did all his cartooning digitally via a Wacom drawing tablet and Macintosh computer. "I don't smear ink anymore," he announced with a smile.

Schulz, 76, spoke about how the 1990s weren't a golden age for comics. "Television just seems to dominate everything," he said. "And newspapers are shrinking our strips and jamming too many on a page."

The cartoonist also bristled at the way many people said "Peanuts" wasn't as good as it used to be. He compared himself to an opera singer who's described as "pretty good but needs more maturing" in the first part of her career, then lauded for a week, and then described as "not as good as she used to be" for the rest of her career.

Despite his somewhat downbeat talk, Schulz was in a great mood during the NCS meeting's informal moments. At one event, the "Peanuts" creator asked several of the NCS's small (but growing) group of female cartoonists to dance. I still have a strong mental image of Schulz's vigorous hoofing that contrasts sharply with the way his health declined precipitously several months later.

After returning from Texas, I covered the editorial cartoonists' convention in Chattanooga, Tenn., and the columnists' conference in Louisville, Ky. These meetings were brought to life by host cartoonist Bruce Plante of the *Chattanooga Times Free Press*, host columnist Bob Hill of the Louisville *Courier-Journal*, and ... a laptop! For the first time, I sent stories from the road for immediate posting on *E&P*'s Web site. Eighteen-hour days ensued, after which my head felt like it was run over by a Kentucky Derby horse pulling the Chattanooga Choo Choo.

My wife called at around 11 p.m. during one marathon writing session in my hotel room. "I saw this really interesting article," she said. "Can I read it to you?"

"Sorry. I don't have the time. I have to write three more stories before I go to bed."

I even had to skip some sessions to write up the ones I *did* attend. The World Wide Web had made me a harried hotel hermit.

Soon after Louisville, I learned that the 115-year-old *E&P* was being sold after its long history of family ownership! The buyer was BPI Communications, a subsidiary of huge Dutch media conglomerate VNU. The sale was finalized in September, and things quickly became very different.

E&P now had prestigious sister magazines such as *Billboard* and *The Hollywood Reporter*. And we learned that the grandson co-publishers would be gone — undoubtedly sharing in some of the sale's proceeds even as they said the magazine *had* to be dealt because it couldn't adequately compete without a large "corporate infrastructure" in "the new 24/7 news environment." Longtime owner Robert Brown would depart the scene as well.

Brown's father James acquired *E&P* in 1912 and Robert joined the magazine as a reporter way back in 1936. So it was no surprise that Brown cried when announcing the sale to staffers crowding around him near the reception desk. "I'm a little emotional about this," he apologized.

But I doubt any staffers wept after hearing this: The second high-ranking exec the grandsons had hired to replace the first high-ranking exec was let go.

The new *E&P* editor was also the editor of BPI's *Mediaweek* magazine, and his name was ... Bill Gloede! Yes, the man who got me my *E&P* job in 1983! Bill had left the magazine in 1984, and helped found *Mediaweek* in 1991. Now he was back, as friendly and competent as ever. I thought I had died and gone to Veggie Heaven (one of my favorite Montclair restaurants).

In a classy gesture of respect, Bill kept Robert Brown (who would die in 2008 at age 95) on *E&P*'s masthead as editor emeritus.

Meanwhile, a horde of BPI designers descended on *E&P*'s office to quickly scrap the first ex-exec's design in favor of a more pleasing, less-cluttered look.

Despite all this good news, I had some misgivings about *E&P* being owned by a huge corporation — and there would indeed be some troubling times ahead. But things were mostly better in 1999, helped by an economy that was skating nicely atop the dot-com bubble.

In November, I phoned Charles Schulz to ask about the "Peanuts" museum his wife Jeannie and others were planning in Santa Rosa, Calif., where the couple lived.

Schulz was a bit reluctant to discuss the museum, sounding almost embarrassed by the idea. But he did tell me: "We've accumulated thousands of drawings and other things for almost 50 years. We want to put them where people can see them."

Other things were also on Schulz's mind. "I'm not feeling well, David," he said.

"Oh," I replied. "Sorry about that. Should I call back another time?"

The "Peanuts" creator said he could talk for a few more minutes, and that he'd be seeing a doctor. Then Schulz turned the conversation in my direction in a way that made *me* feel embarrassed.

"You should do a book, David. You write well, and you've covered the business for a long time."

"Oh, I don't know," I replied, very flattered at that suggestion from avid-book-reader Schulz. "But thank you."

The story about the incipient Charles M. Schulz Museum appeared in *E&P*'s Nov. 6 issue. Two weeks later, my coverage of Schulz's devastating health problems — which would include colon cancer and a series of strokes — unfortunately began.

Because of those medical issues, Schulz reluctantly ended "Peanuts" in December — not long after his 77th birthday on Nov. 26. But the comics he completed before becoming ill meant his 355 million readers in 75 countries would see new daily strips until Jan. 3, 2000, and new Sunday strips until Feb. 13 of that year.

I hesitantly called Schulz on Dec. 14, 1999, and he had trouble speaking because of his strokes. "Nothing lasts forever," he said haltingly and miserably, adding that he was very disappointed "Peanuts" wouldn't reach its 50th anniversary in October 2000.

As I heard Schulz's words, I glanced at the red invitation on my desk for a 50th-anniversary "Peanuts" cruise to Alaska that had been scheduled for Aug. 14-21, 2000. It would never happen.

It was also in the fall of 1999 that my wife and finally decided to divorce. We had stayed together too long, mostly to keep the family intact for our daughter Maggie and partly because of a fear that we couldn't afford two separate households — especially with my wife still working only sporadically. But she had inherited some money after her mother died in 1998.

The reasons for our breakup — previously alluded to in this book — were many. Among them: She was an often-impatient parent, I a more easy-going one; she didn't mind spending more money than we had, I did; she became religious, I didn't.

We did make a last-ditch attempt to save the relationship with marriage counseling. After several sessions, I thought we had hashed out a rough agreement: I would be less critical of her (though I didn't feel I was that critical) if she would be more patient with Maggie. I thought I kept my promise, I thought she didn't keep hers, and I thought — the heck with this.

Still, we weren't at each other's throats, so we decided to use an arbitrator to make the divorce proceedings as amicable as possible. But this arbitrator charged us more than $400 a session to tell us things we already knew (such as — duh — you have to figure out how to divide your assets). Plus, we would still each have to hire never-cheap lawyers in addition to the arbitrator. So we dropped her.

"What a bloodsucker," I said.

"That's for sure," agreed my wife.

If we had only agreed on more things.

I shouldn't end this chapter without telling you about the ultimate example of celebrity punditry: Universal introduced a pre-Christmas column by ... Santa Claus!

I was skeptical that the North Pole guy was actually putting his own words into (extremely) cold type, and my doubts only increased when I couldn't reach him for comment. Could the column be — gasp! — ghostwritten?

Universal director of communications Kathie Kerr admitted it was, citing St. Nick's busy December schedule. I could only conclude that Santa's reindeer were penning the column.

In another Christmas-time development, *E&P* marked the millennium's end by reprinting several pages from its Dec. 28, 1899, issue in its Dec. 25, 1999, issue. One ad from the 1899 magazine quoted a newspaper executive going gaga over a brand of ink. "Please send me by boat one barrel News Ink, same quality as that you sent me Oct. 5th," he said. "It is the most satisfactory I ever had."

Wow! I want some of that, too!

CHAPTER TWENTY-THREE

2000:
'Guns and Moses'
on the Soundtrack

Green Day would release a 2009 CD called *21st Century Breakdown* nine years after I had a "21st Century Breakup." My wife and I agreed in January 2000 that she'd move out in the early spring, after which we'd have 18 months of living apart before getting a "no fault" New Jersey divorce. (Is it "no fault" because N.J. isn't earthquake-prone?)

Why not the more traditional scenario of Mr. Male packing his bags? We couldn't have bought the Montclair house in 1993 without tapping nearly all my pension — the one *E&P* soon turned into a 401(k). Plus it was mostly my salary that paid the mortgage each month after my wife didn't always keep jobs or earn much as a freelancer from the mid-'90s on. Finally, she wanted to use the 1998 inheritance from her late mother to buy and decorate her own house.

We agreed on joint custody, with Maggie at my house during alternate weeks. But how was I to be there right after school? How would Maggie get to her piano lessons, gymnastics classes, and other activities?

My new editor Bill Gloede was a family-first guy, but I was still nervous when I asked him if I could work 25 hours the weeks I was with Maggie and make up the time by working at least 55 hours the weeks she was with her mother.

"No problem, Dave!" he responded immediately in his booming voice.

People don't get supervisors like that enough.

It was lucky that I needed to start the 25/55 schedule in 2000 rather than later in the decade. That's because the increasing demands of *E&P*'s Web site, especially from 2004 on, would have made this kind of flextime *very* difficult. Even in 2000, writing enough print and Web pieces in a 25-hour week was a challenge that often required me to work at home after Maggie went to bed.

With my schedule and living arrangements in place, it was time to tell Maggie about the impending separation. I dreaded this moment, almost wishing I could say something quick like: "We're getting divorced. For more information, go to our separation Web site at www...."

Maggie took the news hard, like any child in that situation would, and I felt terrible. But, as is often the case with kids in faltering marriages, she was not totally surprised.

This was on Sunday, Feb. 13, and I resolved to spend a lot of time with Maggie during the next few days. But then I learned that "Peanuts" creator Charles Schulz had died in his sleep the night before — forcing me to work until midnight Monday and Tuesday to frantically put together a huge obituary package for the next *E&P* magazine. When published, this five-page spread would bring me dozens of congratulatory emails and phone calls, but I was too exhausted — and feeling too guilty about Maggie — to enjoy the praise.

My package's main article noted the irony of Schulz dying the night before his farewell "Peanuts" strip appeared. But Schulz did get to see his final strip published in a newspaper! That's because cartoonist Paige Braddock, a staffer at Charles M. Schulz Creative Associates, showed the ailing "Peanuts" creator *The Atlanta Journal-Constitution*'s preprinted Feb. 13 comic section on Feb. 9. Paige, a former *AJC* graphics editor, told me Schulz looked at the Sunday section and said in his modest but proud way: "I drew some funny things."

Indeed, the final comic pictured many iconic "Peanuts" images — including Snoopy on his doghouse as the World War I flying ace, Lucy pulling the football away from Charlie Brown, and Linus holding his security blanket. Schulz's retirement note in the comic concluded: "Charlie Brown, Snoopy, Linus, Lucy … how can I ever forget them…."

In my main story, I summed up the multidimensional "Peanuts" this way: "It was simply drawn but psychologically complex, funny but melancholy, secular yet religious, and grounded in reality while capable of soaring flights of Snoopyesque fantasy."

One of the sidebars I wrote contained my personal memories of Schulz (some of which you've read in this book). I also compiled an extensive timeline of Schulz's life and quoted various cartoonists paying tribute to the "Peanuts" creator. For instance, "Mother Goose and Grimm" cartoonist Mike Peters told me Schulz "wasn't a star, he was a supernova. This guy is going to leave a huge black hole on the comics page."

But "Peanuts" wasn't leaving the comics page, because United Media had begun in January 2000 to distribute reruns. About 2,460 of the strip's 2,600-plus newspapers signed on, and while some later dropped the reruns, many papers continue to publish Schulz's old strips even as I write this sentence.

I was appalled at the profit-driven, corporate move to keep the comic going. "Peanuts" reruns took newspaper space away from living cartoonists (some of whom Schulz had helped with advice and encouragement). Not having all those open funnies slots would be especially hard on cartoonists trying to build client lists with post-2000-launched comics — such as "Café Con Leche" (Charlos Gary), "Cul de Sac" (Richard Thompson), "Frazz" (Jef Mallett), "Girls & Sports" (Justin Borus/Andrew Feinstein), "The Flying McCoys" (Glenn and Gary McCoy), "The Other Coast" (Adrian Raeside), "Tina's Groove" (Rina Piccolo), etc. Some of these comics did well, but they could have done better if "Peanuts" slots were available. How would Schulz have felt if 2,460 papers were publishing, say, "Krazy Kat" repeats when he was desperate for clients in 1950?

Besides, fans could always read "Peanuts" in book collections. "There's a reason why 'new' is in 'newspaper,'" Washington Post Writers Group syndicate exec Alan Shearer told me when Tribune Media Services offered Dave Barry column reruns about five years after United did so with "Peanuts."

In early 2000, new titles were bestowed on several staffers who were with E&P for two years or less. Yet I and my friendly, hardworking colleague Jim Rosenberg were not promoted — even though we had been associate editors since joining the magazine in 1983 and 1987, respectively.

When I was a less-confident person in the 1980s, I probably would have just bit my tongue at an injustice like that. But in 2000, I approached Bill Gloede.

"Bill, why didn't Jim and I get promoted when so many other people did?"

"You both do a bang-up job. But I don't have the budget for extra raises."

I thought about this for a few seconds. As a single dad, I could certainly use more money (heck, I would keep my home thermostat at around 60 degrees during the next few winters — and my friendly, expert accountant Al Neiman could only raise his eyebrows at the state of my finances). But I was most irked by the unfairness of newer people getting higher posts when veteran staffers didn't. "I'll just take the promotion," I said, and Jim agreed to do the same.

Parent company VNU did spend a lot of money that year on consolidating E&P and many of its other media properties in a huge East Village Manhattan building that formerly housed the Wanamaker's department store. VNU also allowed some new hires at its magazines, with E&P's editorial staff peaking at 21 full-timers in 2000.

Yet the company could be so slow to reimburse staffers covering out-of-town meetings that we sometimes had to use our own money to pay the balance on our company credit cards before getting reimbursed. And there were no more travel advances for things like taxis to the airport; you had to use your own cash upfront, and the dang cabbies wouldn't accept Monopoly money. All this nonsense was hell on my bank account — and allowed VNU to keep money longer in *its* bank account, earning interest.

Yet all this was trivial compared to the cost-cutting to come.

Other things stressing my bank account included now paying the mortgage on my own and (because my wife didn't have a steady income) paying much more than 50% of Maggie's expenses. Still, I was glad the marriage was moving toward its eventual conclusion — and extraordinarily impressed with how Maggie was handling it. I know she was hurting inside, but that kid kept up her grades and — just prior to the weekend her mother moved out — gave a flawless performance singing "The Sound of Silence" at her school talent show. Maggie displayed discipline, grace under pressure, and a shorter name than Simon & Garfunkel.

As I adjusted to single parenthood and tried to "be there" for Maggie, I initially had no interest in dating. My main weeknight recreation was watching *Star Trek: Voyager* reruns (I was thrilled to spot actress Kate Mulgrew, the show's Capt. Janeway, in a Manhattan restaurant two years later). On weekends, I often saw friends. Given that most were couples, it was nice of them to include an uncoupled person in their lives.

Meanwhile, widely syndicated humorist Dave Barry put a mock White House run in *his* life, as reported in an *E&P* story I wrote about faux-candidate columnists — most of whom used their campaigns to raise money for charity. Barry told me his qualifications for the presidency included being born in the same log cabin as Abraham Lincoln and John F. Kennedy, winning 175 varsity letters in high school, and founding General Motors. His religion? "Same as yours."

There would be more faux-campaigning in future years, as when syndicated editorial cartoonist Khalil Bendib threw his "fez in the ring" for the 2008 presidential race won by Barack Obama. Khalil said the goal of his seriocomic effort was to "debunk the Islamophobic hysteria."

Back in March 2000, the Tribune Co. announced it was buying the Times Mirror Co. As a result of this blockbuster deal, the 1918-founded Tribune Media Services soon absorbed the 1949-launched Los Angeles Times Syndicate — reducing competition in the features world once again. (The Los Angeles Times-Washington Post News Service, headed by the personable Al Leeds, wasn't significantly affected.) I covered 12 major syndicates when I joined *E&P* in 1983; now it would be eight. TMS announced later in 2000 that 34 of the 77 LATS staffers would lose their jobs (some of the 43 survivors were let go in subsequent years), and 19 of the 240 TMS/LATS features were dropped in February 2001.

TMS (a major provider of television listings) would also buy TV Data (the other major provider) in 2001. So, competition plunged in that syndication segment, too — as did jobs, with 52 of 462 people at the combined company soon getting sacked.

But there was *some* new competition in 2000 when the fledgling DBR Media took on the established King Features Weekly Service. Each distributor sold a package of features mostly to America's weekly papers (of which there were more than 11,000 in 2000). DBR — whose roster included columns by syndicate co-founder Diane Eckert and comics such as Mark Szorady's "George" and Polly Keener's "Hamster Alley" — managed to last until 2008.

Other smaller syndicates included the Rita Henley Jensen-run Women's eNews and the Lisa Vives-run Global Information Network. I wrote about the nonprofit Global in May 2000, soon after it received a $100,000 MacArthur Foundation grant for its work distributing stories from developing countries to North American media outlets. And I profiled the June 2000-launched Women's eNews in 2002, the same year editorial cartoonist Ann Telnaes became a contributor. Ann told me she admired the service for offering "real news about women's issues without pieces on dieting and fashion."

There was also the 2001-founded Content That Works — which had a sales exec, Dan Dalton, who uses the middle name of "Patio" because he often works from his ... patio. CTW offered material on autos, health, jobs, children (Vicki Whiting's "Kid Scoop"), and more. Inspired by that syndicate's name, I almost titled this book *Memoir That's Written*.

On May 27, 2000, nearly 100 cartoonists paid tribute to "Peanuts" in their comics — and the National Cartoonists Society posthumously gave Charles Schulz its Milton Caniff Lifetime Achievement Award during its meeting in New York's ill-fated World Trade Center. "The Family Circus" cartoonist Bil Keane said of Schulz that weekend: "'Sparky' and I had a lot in common. We both did comics about kids and family values. He had five kids; I had five kids. He was born in 1922; I was born in 1922. He made a million dollars a week; I ... was born in 1922."

Bil was also the subject of a comedy "roast" during the Reuben weekend, and the funniest line came from his son and comic collaborator. Jeff Keane said some cartoonists get ideas from observing their families, "but our family was based on the comic. If something got a laugh in the newspaper, Bil tried to work it into our family the next week."

Jeff MacNelly left the cartooning family on June 8, when he died of lymphoma at age 52. The three-time Pulitzer Prize winner's detailed but loose drawing style was so imitated that the term "MacNelly clones" became well-known in the biz, and the unpretentious workaholic also did the "Shoe" comic and illustrations for Dave Barry's column. Believe it or not, the *Chicago Tribune* didn't fill the conservative MacNelly's spot until hiring editorial cartoonist Scott Stantis *nine years later*. But that pathetic delay looked good compared to the way dozens of other newspapers in the 2000s *never* replaced editorial cartoonists who left or were laid off.

Cost-cutting was one reason why full-time editorial cartoon positions were decimated, especially when newspapers can buy syndicated cartoons for just a few bucks. But papers that use only outside work lose something. "Local cartoons have more impact," said Rex Babin of the *Sacramento Bee*.

But many corporate-owned papers don't want that impact. Tough local cartoons can make things more interesting for readers, but profit-obsessed owners worry that these drawings might bother the advertisers who provide newspapers with much more revenue than subscribers do. Heck, newspaper owners have been known to play golf with advertisers (and politicians) at posh country clubs, and you don't want to upset your fellow duffers, do you? *Do you*?

MacNelly lived in Virginia despite working for a Chicago paper, and it was in the Old Dominion State that the National Society of Newspaper Columnists met in June 2000. I left for the NSNC conference late because of Maggie's elementary-school graduation. I realize having a convocation for young kids is a bit over the top, but, heck, it was moving. And I would have enjoyed seeing a daughter of mine take part in *any* ceremony after what happened to Abigail.

Then I was off to Minneapolis, where the Association of American Editorial Cartoonists convention's agenda arsenal included a keynote speech by actor/National Rifle Association president Charlton Heston. The "Guns and Moses" guy proceeded to blast the work of many AAECers.

"The 80 million gun owners in this country are portrayed as criminals, kooks, and hicks," he said. "This crosses the line from political cartoons to comic-strip propaganda."

Heston also mentioned that he had fought for civil rights in the 1960s, even marching with Martin Luther King. To which famed caricaturist David Levine, another Minneapolis speaker, responded: "I wonder if it occurred to Mr. Heston how Dr. King was killed and by what?" Whoa — Levine won *that* verbal shootout.

And then there were two "shadow conventions" — co-organized by columnist Arianna Huffington — I didn't attend but wrote about. These summer events were designed to discuss issues, such as campaign-finance reform, that were given short shrift at the scripted Democratic and Republican presidential conventions.

The "shadow conventions" were among the many projects the energetic and ambitious Huffington tried over the years while writing her column (which had moved from Creators Syndicate to the Los Angeles Times Syndicate in 1998). But it wasn't until after she co-launched a certain Web site in 2005 that Arianna would become one of the most famous media people in the world.

Ah, persistence. I needed to have some of that if I was going to possibly meet another woman. So, after six months of post-separation dating hibernation, I started asking friends if they knew anyone around my age who was unattached (from another person, not from reality). I was soon set up with a Manhattan friend's next-door neighbor, who suggested we meet near Lincoln Center. It was my first date with someone other than my wife in nearly 17 years, and I was almost hyperventilating as I climbed the subway stairs at West 66th Street and Broadway. If anyone saw me gasping, they probably wouldn't have guessed that I exercise religiously (well, maybe agnostically).

I managed to pull myself together enough to stumble through the date, but there wasn't much mutual interest. That was also the case with three other women I dated one time apiece in the summer and early fall, after which I started perusing personal ads in the newspaper. It took a couple days to get the hang of the abbreviations — did "DWF" mean "divorced white female" or "driving while farming"?

Soon, I met a New Jersey woman who seemed okay, but she expected me to treat her even though I'm almost certain her salary was higher than mine. I reluctantly went along with this (loneliness, I guess) for a number of dates that took place only on alternate Saturdays because I didn't want to go out during the weeks Maggie lived in my house. Then this woman abruptly broke up with me. Turns out she was using the weeks I was with Maggie to date someone else. She never returned a Brad Anderson "Marmaduke" collection I lent her, so that cartoon book was forced to file a change-of-address form.

My collection of cartoon sales continued to be modest in 2000, when I managed to get just seven published. One drawing, for a parking magazine with the unexpected name of ... *Parking*, showed two tricycles near two kids on a merry-go-round. My caption: "Park and ride."

The American Association of Sunday and Feature Editors parked itself in New York City that September, and keynote speaker Martha Stewart told the 240 editors in attendance that her "askMartha" column had 232 newspaper clients. "What's wrong with the other eight of you?" the lifestyle maven quipped.

Meanwhile, Mort Walker's "Beetle Bailey" reached its 50th anniversary in September, Garry Trudeau's "Doonesbury" turned 30 in October, Scott Adams' "Dilbert" signed its 2,000th newspaper client in October, and Thanksgiving was celebrated in November. I'll leave it to you to decide which of those four events didn't qualify as breaking news.

To mark the "Doonesbury" birthday, I managed to get a rare interview with Trudeau — with the provision that it be done via email. One two-part question I sent: "Should readers trust any comic over 30? Can a cartoonist sustain high quality in a comic for that long and, if so, how?"

Part of Garry's answer: "The only requirement for a long career in satire — besides not losing your mind — is a rolling sense of indignation that the world is so resistant to sanity."

The work of Trudeau and other top cartoonists is well-known, but their faces often are not — meaning comic creators can usually venture out in public without being stared at or asked for autographs.

"Do you like it that Garfield is recognized much more than you?" I asked cartoonist Jim Davis for a December 2000 story about this brand of low-key celebrity.

"Yes," he replied. "It's the best of both worlds. People from TV, movies, and sports get no peace."

Philadelphia Daily News editorial cartoonist Signe Wilkinson agreed. "I like the anonymity. I like the Dear *Mr.* Wilkinson hate mail," *she* told me with a laugh.

And Michael Ramirez recalled that when he arrived at Columbia University to receive the 1994 Pulitzer Prize for his conservative Memphis *Commercial Appeal* cartoons, protesters angry with his AIDS-related commentary didn't realize they were seeing the award winner himself. So they handed Ramirez an anti-Ramirez flyer — and he joined the picketers for a while! Michael said: "I'm protesting myself at the Pulitzers, which is pretty hilarious."

CHAPTER TWENTY-FOUR

2001:
9/11 from 9th
Street, and Home
at 11

My editors wanted a January story about what might happen in syndication during 2001, but the forecast pieces I had written in previous years were always sort of vague. No one can predict the future except groundhog Punxsutawney Phil, who's never available for an interview until Feb. 2. Then I had a goofy idea....

"Could I do a story asking astrology columnists for their 2001 predictions?" I queried Steve Yahn, *E&P*'s executive editor.

"Sure, Dave," replied the always accommodating Steve, whose affirmative answer was in the stars.

One question I asked the horoscopers was whether "Peanuts" reruns would remain popular that year. All said yes — and, by the end of '01, they proved correct. I also sought some non-syndication predictions, such as how George W. Bush would fare as president. Astrologer Linda Black said "the country will prosper" under Bush. Oopsies on that prognostication!

After the story ran, I received an email from astrologer Joyce Jillson asking when my birthday was. She wrote: "You write with the clarity of a Virgo, the wit of a Gemini, the innate kindness of the Cancerian, the business sense of a Capricorn, the crispness of an Aries" ... and Jillson cycled through the other zodiac signs, too.

Obviously, she emailed the wrong journalist — though I once had a case of Aries crispness after neglecting to apply sunscreen.

I didn't know the astrological sign of expert syndication attorney Stu Rees, who I profiled in February 2001. But I did know that the 31-year-old Stu was representing about 120 cartoonists and 20 columnists — far more than any other lawyer. In fact, his client list was bigger than the client lists (i.e. newspaper totals) of many of his clients! That last sentence, by the way, had three clients.

In April, I was pleased when Ann Telnaes won the Pulitzer Prize for editorial cartooning. She was just the second woman (after Signe Wilkinson in 1992) to top that Pulitzer category, and one of the few cartoonists not on a newspaper staff to ever do so. Ann's fluid drawing style (influenced by an earlier career in animation) and use of spot color made her syndicated work a visual treat. Meanwhile, the liberal/feminist Telnaes was more in the hard-hitting than gag-oriented school of editorial cartooning, though she still had a great sense of humor.

Winning the Pulitzer threw the Washington, D.C., resident for a loop. "I was so shocked that I got up and took my dog for a walk," Ann told me the night the prizes were announced.

Clay Bennett — who would receive a Pulitzer 12 months later for his *Christian Science Monitor* cartoons that mixed striking visuals with minimal text

— was in the news for a more personal reason in the spring of 2001. He and another editorial cartoonist, Cindy Procious of the *Huntsville* (Ala.) *Times*, got married — with the officiating done by a third cartoonist, Dennis Draughon of the *Scranton* (Pa.) *Times*! I wasn't at the wedding, so I don't know if it was hard-hitting or gag-oriented, but I'm sure it was wonderful.

The Association of American Editorial Cartoonists met in Toronto in July 2001, and one speaker was Ralph Nader. The consumer advocate/2000 presidential candidate, who was more personable than his dour public image would suggest, urged AAECers to do cartoons about the dangers of globalization. He said multinational corporations can ride roughshod over safety and environmental regulations, and eliminate jobs in one country while hiring lower-wage workers in another. Heck, *E&P*'s ownership would do the outsourcing thing several years later.

Speaking of jobs, AAEC meeting attendees lamented that more than a half-dozen editorial cartoonists had recently lost their positions. Among them were Paul Szep of the *Boston Globe* and Mark Fiore of the *San Jose Mercury News*.

"Never before has our profession been so threatened," said AAEC president David Horsey, the *Seattle Post-Intelligencer* cartoonist who won a Pulitzer in 1999 and would receive another in 2003.

If you ever want to be in a near-empty room, go to a meeting of the Newspaper Owners Fan Club.

The jettisoning of cartoonists, reporters, and other newspaper people was accelerating due to factors such as the dot-com crash and more competition from online media.

VNU-owned *E&P* was also affected, with our editorial staff reduced from 21 in 2000 to 14 by the end of 2001 because of layoffs or departed people not being replaced. (This 33% drop happened during a year when the American Society of Newspaper Editors estimated that about 4% of newsroom positions were eliminated at daily papers.) Among the seven colleagues losing their jobs for cost-cutting rather than competence reasons were Steve Yahn and assistant online editor Karim Mostafa.

E&P's magazine was also getting smaller, because ads decreased as newspapers and dot-com companies sliced their budgets or went out of business. Some of those lost ads were help-wanted classifieds, as papers froze or cut their staffs. And more laid-off journalists meant fewer subscribers for *E&P*.

So I could sort of understand why VNU wanted to reduce costs — though it might have remained profitable (albeit less profitable) without layoffs. And, as is almost always the case with corporations, VNU sacked fewer high-paid upper managers than lower-salaried people who toiled so hard.

E&P staffers certainly were busy. Our Web site still had endless space — meaning 14 people did the work 21 people had done in 2000. And with the freelance budget also reduced, staffers taking time off had to frantically do stuff before and after their vacations to not fall behind.

I wasn't off on Sept. 11, 2001. As usual, I drove my car to the parking lot of Montclair's Walnut Street train station and hopped on board around 8:30. I opened a book and got absorbed in *The Night in Lisbon*, a gripping World War II novel by *All Quiet on the Western Front* author Erich Maria Remarque. Suddenly, cell phones started ringing, and I saw people gesturing towards the train windows. Smoke was pouring from one of the Twin Towers across the Hudson River.

"I wonder if a small plane hit it," said my seatmate, as I vaguely remembered reading about that happening to the Empire State Building in the 1940s (it was in 1945).

As I walked amid the rush-hour crowd in the Hoboken, N.J., train station, everyone was talking about the burning skyscraper. But the PATH train was still running, and I found myself in Manhattan 20 minutes later.

I exited the PATH station on West Ninth Street near Avenue of the Americas, and walked east. When I reached Fifth Avenue, several dozen people were gathered at the intersection gazing southward, where *both* World Trade Center buildings were now billowing dark smoke two miles from where we stood. I joined in the staring for a couple minutes (this was before the structures collapsed), and then hurried on to *E&P*'s office at 770 Broadway.

The phones were out, but my email was working, so I quickly wrote my daughter and (soon-to-be-ex) wife. Then an acrid smell from the towers started seeping into the VNU building, and employees were told they could go home. But no trains or buses were leaving the city, so I stayed at my desk, continuing to send and receive emails. Many messages were from cartoonists and columnists checking on the safety of people they knew in New York; *Hartford* (Conn.) *Courant* editorial cartoonist Bob Englehart's email to me simply said: "Where were you when World War 3 started?"

I couldn't get a train out of the city until after 9 that night, and ended up reaching my car at the Walnut Street lot around 11 p.m. About a dozen cars were still parked there, and I wondered morosely if any of them belonged to people who died in the World Trade Center that day. As it turned out, nine victims were either current or former Montclairites.

The rest of the week, it was "all hands on deck" as *E&P*'s shrunken staff sprang into action to cover how newspapers covered 9/11 and how media people were affected by the disaster.

For instance, I learned that 34-year-old Christopher Hanley — the only child of Crain News Service sales manager Joe Hanley and his wife Marie — died while attending a conference on the 106th floor of one WTC tower. I had met Christopher several years before, when he worked for Bloomberg Business News and Joe was gently trying to convince me to apply for a job there. (I don't "do" financial.)

I also found out that *Kansas City Star* columnist Bill Tammeus' 31-year-old nephew, Karleton Fyfe, died on the first hijacked plane to hit the World Trade Center — two days after Karleton learned his wife was pregnant.

So I decided to write a story about how the syndication world was affected by the attacks — though I felt awful bothering people at a time like that.

"Joe, if you don't want to talk, I totally understand," I said when phoning the Hanley residence in Manhattan.

"It's okay, Dave," the usually upbeat man replied in an exhausted voice.

"I'm not sure what to ask," I continued, knowing full well the feeling of losing a child. "Is there anything you'd like to say?"

"Hopefully he went quickly," Joe replied quietly.

Meanwhile, a Leonard Pitts Jr. column addressed to the attackers was so powerful it elicited more than 30,000 emails. "Did you want us to respect your cause? You just damned your cause," wrote the syndicated *Miami Herald* commentator. "Did you want to make us fear? You just steeled our resolve. Did you want to tear us apart? You just brought us together."

Two months later, Pitts' piece helped make him the columnist winner in *E&P*'s first-ever "Features of the Year" competition.

"What did you do when the number of emails reached 30,000?" I asked Pitts.

"I stopped counting," he replied.

Leonard added that he really appreciated the response ("you write so you can strike a chord") but felt guilty that a disaster brought him so much attention.

"The Boondocks" cartoonist Aaron McGruder also got lots of attention that fall when some of his 250 newspaper clients pulled bitingly humorous strips that ventured from the post-9/11 media love-fest for President Bush and his policies. McGruder compared Bush to 9/11 mastermind Osama bin Laden (each is "from a wealthy oil family" and each "bombs innocents"), noted that the U.S. formerly supported bin Laden (when he fought the Soviet Union in Afghanistan), and generally discussed why America is hated in some parts of the world.

"When you have too much blind patriotism, bad things can happen," Aaron told me.

Other liberal or centrist syndicated creators (with a few exceptions) pulled their punches against Bush at that time because they feared being labeled "unpatriotic" or fired by timid papers. In fact, Tom Gutting of the *Texas City Sun* and Dan Guthrie of the *Daily Courier* in Grants Pass, Ore., were let go after penning columns critical of Bush. Gutting wrote, among other things, that the president on 9/11 "was flying around the country like a scared child."

To its great credit, the National Society of Newspaper Columnists protested the firings. NSNC president Pete Rowe of the *San Diego Union-Tribune* said columnists "must be free to express controversial and unpopular views," and added eloquently: "Freedom of the press is not worth defending if it only means the freedom to avoid offending anyone."

I flew to Chicago in early October — on one of those planes that were mostly empty in the weeks after 9/11 — to cover the American Association of Sunday and Feature Editors convention. At that gathering, 83-year-old advice columnists Ann Landers and Abigail Van Buren became the first non-editors inducted into the AASFE hall of fame.

Landers attended, as did Van Buren's daughter — "Dear Abby" co-writer Jeanne Phillips. Jeanne's mother appeared via video, quipping to the editors: "Since my column is delivered to most of you electronically, why not me, too?"

In her AASFE remarks, Landers recalled having help from high places to win the 1955 *Chicago Sun-Times* contest to replace the previous Ann Landers. After being given 30 test questions, she phoned famous people around the country — including her Supreme Court friend William Douglas!

Landers concluded: "I thank God for the energy to do this work. It's not easy. Sometimes I'm up to 3 or 4 a.m. struggling with the column. But I can't imagine doing anything else that would give me more pleasure or satisfaction."

It was a "last lecture" of sorts, because the healthy Landers of October 2001 would pass away within months.

My *E&P* story about the induction featured a photo of Landers that was bigger than a picture of Van Buren and her daughter. The famed competitiveness of the twin sisters surfaced when Landers sent me a post-AASFE letter that read, in part: "That was an excellent story about the induction of my sister and me.... I have always enjoyed your writing style and accuracy — and, as usual, you produced an even-handed interesting piece. I noticed, however, that you gave me a considerable edge in the photo department. So thanks for that."

Maybe I was subconsciously trying to make amends for choosing Van Buren over Landers to publish that 1987 letter about my daughter Abigail.

The day after the Chicago meeting ended, a legendary editorial cartoonist who started his career at the *Chicago Daily News* in 1929 died at age 91. That was Herblock, who was still cartooning for *The Washington Post* in 2001 — giving him an amazing 72 years in newspapers.

Early in 2002, it would be announced that the late bachelor endowed his new Herb Block Foundation with $50 million — an amount of money that shocked almost everyone. "Herb was kind of rumpled," foundation president Frank Swoboda told me. "You wouldn't think he had two nickels. He broke all the rules of investing, essentially having only one stock — the Washington Post

Co. — and keeping it. When it split, it was like having a rabbit in a safety-deposit box!"

The foundation would give out many grants to organizations such as those fighting poverty, and also start the $10,000 Herblock Prize for editorial cartooning in 2004. The first winner was Matt Davies — the White Plains, N.Y., *Journal News* staffer who would soon also win a 2004 Pulitzer for his work.

On the home front, my daughter Maggie was doing great at Montclair's Renaissance Middle School, smartly getting grades that matched the first letter of my stupid "Astor" name. Maggie's Renaissance era would last until 2003, which puzzled scholars who thought that historical period ended around 1600.

Meanwhile, I continued taking part in the singles scene. I dated a New Jersey art teacher for four months before deciding that if I was really more mature and confident than I was in the 1980s, I better break this off. She was nice, but very much a follower of a certain guru. (I'm an open-minded guy who can find common ground with Caucasian-Americans, African-Americans, Hispanic-Americans, and Asian-Americans — but Guru-Americans are a heavier lift for me.) Then I met a Brooklyn legal-aid attorney who was *extremely* nice, but she also had a religious side — of a liberal Protestant nature. To each their own, but organized spirituality wasn't for me.

I met both women via a great online dating service called Concerned Singles, which matched people who were liberal politically or in other ways.

In October, I received a postal letter via Concerned Singles from an Indiana woman near my age. She sounded very smart and kind and thoughtful and low-key, but — darn! — she lived 700 miles away. Her letter included an email address, so I wrote a reply politely declining the chance to correspond and prepared to hit "send." Then I looked at her letter again and ... deleted my message. There was something about this woman's note that was very compelling.

So we exchanged letters during the rest of 2001. Soon, one or the other was sending an email almost every day. I learned that her name was Laurel Cummins, that she was a French professor at Indiana State in Terre Haute, that she had taught in Rwanda in the 1980s (as a Peace Corps volunteer) and in New Zealand in the 1990s, that her late mother had been a kindergarten teacher when Laurel was growing up in Michigan, and that her late father had worked on newspapers!

There were other little coincidences besides the journalistic one. Her dad was a TV repairman (my father's job) when he was blacklisted in the 1950s (being an Abraham Lincoln Brigade volunteer during the Spanish Civil War didn't endear him to McCarthyites). Also, the Chicago-born Laurel had written her first letter to me on Oct. 5 — while I was covering that meeting in ... Chicago, which I hadn't visited since 1984.

Where would this correspondence take us in 2002?

CHAPTER TWENTY-FIVE

2002: Indiana Becomes My Favorite State

E&P editor Bill Gloede was ideologically conservative, but had little tolerance for corporate stuff such as laying off hardworking employees more than top managers. So, much to his staff's dismay, Bill left in early 2002.

I and most of the other people Gloede supervised thought he'd be replaced by managing editor J.J. McGrath, who was described in my 1999 chapter as "brilliant and collegial." J.J. also had a superb work ethic, awesome editing skills, and a sly sense of humor. Instead, someone else was chosen.

My first major experience with the new, non-J.J. editor involved a Web story I did about "Dear Abby" co-writer Jeanne Phillips alerting the Milwaukee police after she received a letter from a man fantasizing about having sex with young girls. When my article was edited, two passages were changed in a way that made them wrong. The editor eventually fixed it, but didn't seem too concerned. This was around the time he emailed staffers to urge that we "avoid errors."

Meanwhile, I and the Terre Haute, Ind.-based Laurel continued to email each other almost every day — and the subject of meeting was finally broached. I booked a cheap flight, got up at 3 a.m. on Feb. 9, and found myself in the Indianapolis airport not long after I'd normally be getting out of bed on a Saturday.

The sleep deprivation and steep anticipation must have addled my brain, because I waited for Laurel near my arrival gate when of course she couldn't go there. Finally, I came to my senses after about 45 minutes and walked to the center of the airport — and there she was.

"Hi, Dave," she said in a soft voice, giving me a hug even though I could tell there was an air of shyness about her.

"I'm so sorry you had to wait," I replied, hoping I didn't sound as nervous as I felt. "I stupidly stayed near the gate."

We hesitantly conversed as we walked to the baggage-claim area, and I glanced sideways at her several times in secret appreciation. The pretty woman I saw was about 5'4", with brownish-blonde hair and scholarly-looking glasses.

Then we headed to her car — and I was pleased to see it was modest (a 1992 Ford Escort). I guess Laurel was nervous, too, because she took a wrong turn out of the airport, and we ended up briefly on Route 70 going *away* from Terre Haute. But soon we headed southwest toward Greencastle, Ind., for breakfast. We also saw a bit of the DePauw University campus before continuing on to Terre Haute, where Boston Celtics basketball great Larry Bird had starred for Indiana State.

Laurel and I crammed in so much that weekend I'm not sure how we did it. We visited her Indiana State office, met her friend and fellow professor

Ann Rider, toured the Scope Museum and the house of legendary labor leader Eugene Debs, saw *The Count of Monte Cristo* movie, and met her cat Angus — an orange tabby who loved roaming the cornfield next to Laurel's apartment complex. This lovable fellow had followed Laurel on a snowy March 2001 day, perhaps after being cruelly abandoned by his previous "owners."

Laurel also showed me a chapter from a book she was writing about the work of renowned French author Colette, and inscribed a copy of Emile Zola's *Germinal* I had purchased for plane reading on her recommendation. I was so bowled over by *Germinal* that I soon devoured more novels by Zola — and by other French writers such as Balzac, Camus, and the aforementioned Colette. But Proust was a bit much for me.

During my Terre Haute stay, I got a glimpse of Laurel's kindheartedness when a bug showed up in her apartment. Instead of killing it, she captured it in a cup and brought it outside.

I suppose I should give more details about the conversations Laurel and I had that weekend. After all, this is a memoir. But Laurel is a mostly private person, and the deeper conversations one has when falling in love should perhaps be kept … well … private. Suffice to say that the simple act of holding hands was magical — and that I was totally bowled over by Laurel's rare combination of confidence and modesty. On the plane ride home that Sunday afternoon, I marveled at how someone that nice and accomplished could love me — and how that probably wouldn't have happened in my semi-basket-case days before *E&P*.

We agreed that Laurel would visit New Jersey the next month — coincidentally right around the time my divorce would become final. I eagerly looked forward to both events.

Back at the *E&P* ranch, one story I wrote was about "Pearls Before Swine" entering print syndication. Stephan Pastis' hilarious strip — starring an arrogant rat, a sweet but dumb pig, and later a bunch of goofy crocodiles trying to eat their "zeeba" (zebra) neighbor — would become the cartoon hit of the decade.

Then it was March — time for Laurel's arrival! She had never been to New Jersey, and had visited New York City just once to attend a Modern Language Association meeting several years earlier. So I had quite an itinerary planned. We went to the Montclair Art Museum and the Thomas Edison historic site in West Orange (museum visits were a big thing with the two of us) before heading to dinner at a Peruvian restaurant in Paterson with my good friends: the brainy, congenial couple of Ed Levy and Lisa Pearlstein.

The next day, we drove to Manhattan — where we managed in about eight hours to visit the observation deck of the Empire State Building, subway up to the Metropolitan Museum of Art, walk along Central Park, subway down to the Battery Park area to catch a glimpse of the Statue of Liberty, and eat at a Ukrainian restaurant in the East Village. It was cold and windy, but holding hands made me forget about the weather. And Manhattan was certainly warmer than Quebec City, where Laurel would head in a few days to visit her sister Sarah and brother-in-law Bill.

(Laurel also has sisters Sheila in California, Eileen in Michigan, and Rachel in Texas. The five Cummins siblings are all accomplished people who work at universities, libraries, etc. And the geographical distance between them means more frequent-flyer miles than you can shake a stick at — after which the stick gets confiscated by airport security.)

While in New Jersey, Laurel also met my daughter Maggie, which was of course awkward. But they got along okay, helped by the fact that we played a few games of Chinese checkers — which Maggie was still into back then. Both Laurel and I lost badly.

"What do you think of her?" I tentatively asked my daughter a few days later.

"She's nice," Maggie replied, which was about as much as a parent would get from a 12-year-old in that situation.

When I flew to Terre Haute again that summer, one place we visited was Bloomington — where Laurel had earned her doctorate at Indiana University and where National Society of Newspaper Columnists (NSNC) president Mike Leonard worked for *The Herald-Times*. We met Mike and his wife Mardi at the Uptown Café, and I didn't charge *E&P* for the semi-business lunch!

Also, Laurel's past and present universities came up in a weird story I wrote about a new doll of famed journalist Ernie Pyle. Hasbro put on the box that Pyle attended Indiana *State* University, when in fact it was Indiana University. Don't know if the doll was anatomically correct, but it sure wasn't academically correct....

The NSNC's June 2002 conference was in Pittsburgh, and the highlight was Leonard Pitts Jr. getting the organization's first "Columnist of the Year" award for his memorable post-9/11 piece discussed in the last chapter. The NSNC created the honor after Pitts inexplicably didn't win the Pulitzer Prize for commentary two months earlier. Pitts *would* win the Pulitzer in 2004, but many people in 2002 felt he wuz robbed, just like this sentence wuz robbed of the correct spelling of "was."

Pitts, by the way, covered pop music before switching to op-ed writing. "I spent nearly two decades interviewing Rod Stewart in his hotel suite and asking Mariah Carey to please tell me about her latest tour," he said. "I realized I no longer cared that much."

I was at the NSNC meeting June 22 when attendees heard that advice colossus Ann Landers had died of multiple myeloma at age 83. Naturally, I wrote a tribute story with many admiring quotes. For instance, Jeff Zaslow — who succeeded Landers at the *Chicago Sun-Times* in 1987 — told me that Landers' clout, compassion, and "moxie" made her "like Oprah before Oprah."

But Landers, like other syndicated columnists by 2002, no longer had the cultural clout of an Oprah. As I mentioned in Chapter 7, Ann and her "Dear Abby"-writing twin sister Abigail Van Buren had a big impact back in the day (1950s to 1980s) when it came to things like making people more comfortable with divorce, homosexuality, and public discussion of sex. Meanwhile, political columnists of decades past such as Walter Lippmann, James Reston, and Jack Anderson also had plenty of influence from *their* section of the newspaper pulpit.

By 2002, the impact of political and advice writers was greatly reduced for reasons such as the splintering of media. With the Internet, cable TV, and other outlets competing for people's attention, no newspaper columnists had the potential audience size or intense reader spotlight Landers and Lippmann once had.

Also, 21st-century newspaper readership became disproportionately older — meaning syndicated columnists no longer had as large a following among the trend-setting younger crowd. Among the reasons many younger people turned to other media is that daily papers can be bland, unexciting, and way too cautious in terms of topics covered, use of frank language, etc.

The clout of editorial cartoonists ebbed, too, so Herblock's 2001 death marked the end of an era for visual satirists as much as Landers' passing symbolized the lesser power of newspaper columnists.

In the 1950s, Herblock was one of the people setting the debate in the fight against McCarthyism (the word he coined). In the 1970s, his syndicated *Washington Post* cartoons skewering President Nixon helped *Post* reporters Bob Woodward and Carl Bernstein bring the Watergate scandal into the public eye. But no cartoonist in the 2000s had that kind of effect. Just look at how Aaron McGruder's masterful satire of President Bush's post-9/11 warmongering made no dent in George W.'s popularity at the time.

And you won't see many comic creators these days be the cover-story subjects of general-interest national magazines, as was "Terry and the Pirates"/"Steve Canyon" cartoonist Milton Caniff in a 1947 issue of *Time*.

Of course, syndicated cartoonists and columnists still entertain and educate their (smaller number of) readers today.

Speaking of a splintered audience, newspapers in 2002 filled many of the late Landers' 1,200 advice-column slots with … many advice columnists. They included the team of Kathy Mitchell and Marcy Sugar (Ann's former assistants), "Dear Abby" writer Jeanne Phillips, Carolyn Hax, Harriette Cole, Amy Alkon, as well as a rare male in the field: Harlan Cohen. And Amy Dickinson (yes, she's related to 19th-century poet Emily Dickinson) would replace Landers at the *Chicago Tribune* in 2003.

You may have noticed that I didn't name Jeanne Phillips' mother Abigail Van Buren in the previous paragraph's mention of "Dear Abby." The wonderfully kind woman who helped me and millions of others had, to my deep dismay, been diagnosed with Alzheimer's disease. She no longer worked on the column she created in 1956.

Just before heading to Pittsburgh, I did a five-page cover story about what the struggling syndication business might be like in 10 years. Interviewees provided me with some on-the-mark predictions, such as more selling of features to wireless devices and the loss of some major syndicates (one of which would be sold in 2008).

I also put some eye-catching numbers in the article. For instance, licensing revenue (much of it fueled by "Peanuts" and "Dilbert") accounted for a whopping $65.9 million of United Media's $88.8 million in 2001 revenue.

Another story I remember well was about multitasker extraordinaire Ray Hanania. The columnist, stand-up comic, and radio host (who would later invite me to appear several times on his Chicago-area *Mornings with Ray Hanania* program) was going to be the opening act for Jewish comedian Jackie Mason at Chicago's Zanies club in 2002, but Mason narrow-mindedly wanted Hanania off the bill after learning he was Palestinian-American. This despite the fact that the congenial Ray was a U.S. Air Force veteran married to a Jewish woman!

Also in 2002, *Chicago Tribune* columnist Bob Greene lost his newspaper job and syndication perch after it was revealed he had sexual relations with a 17-year-old girl who contacted him while working on a school journalism project. That tryst happened in 1988, when Greene (married since 1971) was a 41-year-old father of two. I recalled hearing Greene speak in 1999, when the columnist known for his "family values" persona talked earnestly about the horrors of child abuse.

"What a hypocrite," I said to fellow *E&P* writer Lucia Moses over the cubicle wall that separated our desks. "He deserved to lose his job." I also talked disgustedly about how some (male) journalists were defending Greene — saying the tryst happened 14 years earlier, it was allegedly consensual, blah, blah, blah.

Lucia mentioned my comments to the new editor, who asked if I wanted to write a column about Greene. There was a page to fill in *E&P*'s Sept. 30 issue, and the deadline was just two hours away. I agreed, and frantically started keyboarding.

My conclusion to the partly sarcastic piece: "Greene made his own bed (or beds). Hopefully, he's doing a lot of introspective thinking about his actions rather than wondering if being a notorious ex-columnist is a turn-on to women young enough to be his daughter."

The column appeared both in print and on *E&P*'s Web site, and was then linked on Jim Romenesko's popular media blog. Soon, I got more positive reaction to the piece (mostly from women) than to almost anything else I had ever written. Columnist Penny Hastings emailed: "Gawd, I'm sick of these holier-than-thou types who don't practice what they preach." Amen to that.

After years of being a (mostly) objective reporter, I enjoyed my stab at opinion writing — and was eager to do more.

The Sept. 30 issue came out the same day my daughter turned 13. In recent years, Maggie had celebrated her birthdays by having friends sleep over. I would feed them pizza and cake before making myself scarce. One year after I went to bed, the girls commandeered an empty box and began tobogganing down the (carpeted) attic stairs amid shrieks of laughter! I put my pillow over my head and hoped the girls would have waffles rather than concussions for breakfast.

Later in the fall, I was asked to write *E&P*'s second-annual "Features of the Year" spread. Winning the columnist category was liberal *New York Times* writer Paul Krugman, who often discussed the intersection of politics and economics — and accurately predicted that the U.S. economy was heading for a big fall (which came in 2008, the same year Krugman received the Nobel Prize for economics). Many other commentators were cheerleading for greedy Wall Street in 2002.

When I tried to interview Krugman, the New York Times News Service told me he was on vacation in the Caribbean until after my story deadline. But I got his email address, sent Krugman a note, and hoped for the best. The columnist eventually emailed me his cell-phone number with this joking proviso: "If you tell anyone that number, you have to kill them."

Among the questions I asked the Princeton University faculty member: "How does being a professor impact your *Times* work?" (Yikes — "impact" used as a verb!)

"In effect, I'm moonlighting as a columnist," he replied. "I'm probably willing to say unpopular things more than people for whom journalism is their solo career."

Hmm ... more columnists need to be professors!

Also that fall, *E&P* associate editor Wayne Robins was let go in another VNU cost-cutting move. Given that Wayne ably covered the burgeoning online world, his layoff was puzzling.

Our staff was now unfortunately down to 11, so the workload of surviving people increased yet again. Also, I was now receiving scores of emails a day — many of them welcome (such as story ideas) and some not welcome (such as "corporate-speak" messages from company higher-ups discussing things like "maintaining shareholder value"). Reading all these emails took a big chunk of my time, but I still answered every answerable one.

Some evenings, I was so tired when I got home that I fell asleep reading the newspaper. Maybe I should have told the carrier the following morning: "I haven't finished yesterday's paper! Why are you delivering another?"

CHAPTER TWENTY-SIX

2003:
My Occupation
Covers Iraq's
Occupation

Buoyed by the reaction to my 2002 opinion piece about disgraced columnist Bob Greene, I decided to jump the journalistic rails again with a humorous 2003 forecast story written in a mock question-and-answer format (I made up the questions I answered).

In one Q&A, I had a syndicate ask how it could deal with the difficult selling environment caused by the recession and tighter newspaper feature budgets. My response: "Threaten to invade another syndicate to take your creators' minds off dwindling royalties."

That was a reference to the Bush administration's push for a preemptive war with Iraq. Starting in the fall of 2002, *E&P* did a number of stories about how newspapers were covering the possible invasion of a country that had nothing to do with 9/11.

A January 2003 piece I co-wrote was headlined "On the War Path." One person I interviewed, columnist Richard Reeves, said Iraq-related media coverage had been "generally pro-war" — and not just because newspapers were owned by corporations mostly run by wealthy Republican conservatives who supported Bush. "War is a great story — interesting, challenging, and great for journalists' careers," explained Reeves, who was not fond of the GOP president's saber-rattling. "It's like military leaders whose careers are usually advanced when there's a war."

I also called Arianna Huffington in California (where the columnist finished fifth among 100-plus candidates in the 2003 gubernatorial "recall" election won by Arnold Schwarzenegger). "What do you feel is missing in the Iraq coverage?" I asked.

"The lack of reporting on potential casualties," Arianna replied. "The number of Americans in favor of going to war with Iraq plummets when the prospect of thousands of American casualties is added to the question."

But Bush went ahead with the invasion that eventually killed thousands of Iraqis and Americans, including syndicated columnist Michael Kelly.

Another person I interviewed was columnist Norman Solomon, who said journalists can lose objectivity when they embed with U.S. troops rather than move around Iraq independently.

Back on the home front, Laurel visited me in February 2003 — and I proposed to her on the 22nd after we returned to New Jersey from a wonderful outing in snowy Manhattan. This run-up to marriage felt absolutely right.

February was definitely a watershed month for me every 10 years. In February 1993, I moved to Montclair. In February 1983, I joined *E&P*. In

February 1973, I ... um ... celebrated the one-month anniversary of January 1973.

In 2003, my daughter Maggie was an avid reader of *CosmoGirl* magazine. So when I learned *CG* editor-in-chief Atoosa Rubinstein had started a syndicated column, the wheels started turning in my head. Why not do an *E&P* story about the column, and bring Maggie along to co-interview Rubinstein?

Atoosa quickly won over my daughter by not only being personable, upbeat, brainy, and young (31), but also by pulling up a chair close to us rather than sitting behind her desk.

Maggie and I alternated questions, including one about *CosmoGirl's* stated goal of improving the self-esteem of readers. "Where did that come from?" Maggie asked in a mature-journalist voice.

"When I was a girl, anything that could happen happened to me," Rubinstein replied. "I had bad hair, bad skin, friends dumped me, my father passed away, and we had money problems." Atoosa said she wanted to convey to her readers that life can eventually improve.

Somehow I managed to cram on one *E&P* page a story by me and a separate first-person piece by Maggie, whose opening paragraph read: "I am a 13-year-old who reads newspapers only for school assignments or for articles about subjects that interest me — like Harry Potter or celebrities I admire. But Atoosa Rubinstein's column might make me read a newspaper more...."

I felt guilty about the nepotistic approach I took with the Atoosa coverage, so it would be Maggie's only *E&P* story. But I figured one unpaid piece was okay because *E&P's* 2002-named editor allowed his wife to write a number of articles for the magazine.

Rubenstein wasn't the only syndicated person multitasking in 2003. I wrote a March cover story about syndicated creators who do other things besides their newspaper features. Among the people I focused on were cartoonist/novelist Doug Marlette and "Dilbert" creator/restaurant owner Scott Adams.

Accompanying the story was a sidebar that spotlighted Bill O'Reilly, the Fox News TV host who also wrote a newspaper column that entered syndication in 2001. Boy did that guy sound confident — almost intimidating, in fact.

"What approach do you take with your column?" I asked him during a phone interview.

"I'm *not* trying to show everyone I can write like Norman Mailer," O'Reilly replied. "I get to the point quickly — 600 words, bang, and I'm out."

Out in a different way was editorial cartoonist Kirk Anderson, who was laid off in April by the Knight Ridder-owned *St. Paul Pioneer Press*. But unlike most cost-cutted employees who understandably go quietly to avoid jeopardizing their severance pay, Kirk publicly slammed the corporate mentality of firing people while spending lavishly on executive salaries and other things. "I'd probably cut the private service that comes in to water and dust and turn the plants in the publisher's office before I'd cut a local cartoonist," Anderson observed in a memo posted on Jim Romenesko's media blog.

Then I reached Kirk on the phone. He said Knight Ridder's highly compensated chairman/CEO was "taking great newspapers and draining them like blood sausage. He expects you to throw a shot put after cutting off your thumb."

I left a message with the chairman/CEO's office to get a response to this strong comment, but got no callback for a couple hours. Since E&P's editor often pushed us to get Web stories up quickly to avoid being "scooped" by Romenesko, my incomplete piece was posted.

By the time the article came to the Knight Ridder exec's attention, I had gone home. I was told the media titan called E&P and went ballistic over Anderson's comment. Did he offer a response that could have easily been added to the Web piece? No, he ignored the First Amendment that newspaper owners claim they swear by and demanded that Kirk's quote be yanked from the story. And it was. Knight Ridder had been a big advertiser in E&P.

Anderson's ouster left the Twin Cities with one staff editorial cartoonist: the Minneapolis Star Tribune's Steve Sack.

Soon after, the irreplaceable J.J. McGrath resigned from the managing editor post from which he did the work of several people. There were a couple weeks between J.J.'s departure and the arrival of successor Shawn Moynihan, so E&P's editor told me to compile the weekly "Newspeople in the News" section until Shawn could take it over. This task of listing journalists who were hired, promoted, etc., was always done by someone who hadn't been at E&P for long — and I was the longest-tenured staffer!

On a happier note, it was soon time for my daughter's middle-school graduation. Not long before that ceremony, Maggie was voted "most likely to succeed" by fellow students! I guess getting straight A's for three years didn't hurt. Heck, she was already beating me at Scrabble. I was so proud of Maggie, and thankful that fate gave her a chance to succeed after her late sister Abigail had not been given that opportunity.

Also nice was the National Cartoonists Society's 2003 gathering in magnificent San Francisco. One highlight was seeing The Simpsons creator Matt Groening accept the Reuben Award as cartoonist of the year, though — d'oh! — I didn't get a chance to talk with him. I also heard "Pearls Before Swine" creator Stephan Pastis discuss the circuitous route he took to syndication after working as an attorney in California.

"I hated every moment of being a lawyer," the 1968-born Pastis told the NCS crowd. "I always wanted to be a cartoonist." One way he trained for that was by studying every "Dilbert" comic collection. Then Stephan drew 200

"Pearls" strips, had his law-firm associates pick the best 40, and sent them to syndicates.

United Media was interested, and planned to launch "Pearls" in 2000 before deciding a comic starring a rat and pig had no target demographic. (I guess rats and pigs, like many humans, were canceling their newspaper subscriptions.) So United put the strip on its Comics.com site rather than try to sell it to papers. "Pearls" was getting a modest 2,000 hits a day when Scott Adams gave it a rave review on Dilbert.com. The next day, Stephan got 95,000 hits — and print syndication beckoned in early 2002.

NCS meeting attendees were invited to the Charles M. Schulz Museum by Schulz's widow Jeannie, and several hundred rode chartered buses to Santa Rosa. One great artifact on display was an entire nursery-room wall — transported from a Colorado house where Schulz lived briefly in the early 1950s — covered by art the cartoonist painted for daughter Meredith. And there was a re-creation of Schulz's studio, complete with his drawing board and desk as well as dozens of titles from his extensive library. I spotted books about religion, biographies of Shakespeare and Abraham Lincoln, and novels such as *The Great Gatsby* and *Anna Karenina*.

But the highlight of my Bay Area stay was getting several calls from Laurel while she traveled in France with her sister Sheila. A European trip wasn't in my budget in those single-parent days, but I think Laurel emailed me a croissant.

Back in New York, I learned Walter Cronkite would be writing a weekly column. King Features managing editor Glenn Mott approached him after seeing the legendary CBS anchor's *New York Times* piece about the media's increasing corporatization. (Increasing media corporatization? Gee, I had no idea!)

"They dreamed the column up," Cronkite said of King, when I reached him. "Or maybe it was a wild nightmare they were having!"

"Why did you agree to do it?" I asked.

Cronkite, 86, replied that he was unhappy with the Bush administration. "But I'm not exactly pleased with the Democrats, either," he added, in the mellow voice I had heard so often on TV. "I'm liberally inclined but definitely not partisan."

Then Cronkite asked: "How's Bob Brown doing?"

Of course! Cronkite knew *E&P*'s former owner.

"I think he's okay — still living up in Connecticut," I replied.

"Do you have his phone number?"

I didn't. But I got the number later that day and relayed it to Cronkite's friendly "chief of staff" Marlene Adler.

Well before 2003, my confidence had increased enough to comfortably handle interviews with a big celebrity like Cronkite.

Speaking of big, a 135-by-47-foot comic was created in a 2003 fundraising effort. "Lucky Cow" cartoonist Mark Pett of Indianola, Miss., used his computer to separate the strip into 1,508 rectangles, after which each fragment was enlarged onto poster board. Then, 135 art students at Indianola's Gentry High School taped everything together.

That was reminiscent of what happened during a University of Wisconsin/Green Bay fundraiser in 2000. A 22-acre version of a Joe Heller *Green Bay Press-Gazette* cartoon picturing George W. Bush and Al Gore was carved into a cornfield!

Cartoons were shrinking in newspapers, but not in a cornfield and high school parking lot.

And July 2003 was a big month for reasons relating to my hometown *Montclair Times* newspaper, columnist Robert Novak, and Laurel — as will now all be explained.

In June 2003, I had tried another mock-Q&A humor piece — this time about newspaper coverage of the Iraq War. *E&P*'s editor had suggested that staffers do columns on their own time for *E&P*'s Web site, so I spent about 10 hours writing the Iraq piece one weekend. Then I emailed it to the editor, didn't hear back for several days, politely emailed a reminder note, and still didn't hear back. When I finally asked in person, he remembered the unanswered emails, but didn't want the piece.

I thought I had something publishable with my mock-Q&A format, so I resolved to get a column accepted elsewhere. And one possibility was my hometown weekly.

The Montclair Times is an excellent paper. And, like many other community weeklies, it has weathered bad times better than most dailies because it offers very local coverage and gets very local advertising. So the 1877-founded *Times* had a fairly large "news hole" and editorial/opinion section.

I proceeded to write a piece satirizing things like the parking and pothole problems in my New Jersey town. Then I stared at my home computer for hours, trying to name the column. I brainstormed all kinds of wordplay relating to the name "Montclair" until it finally hit me: "Montclairvoyant"!

One question in the column: "Winter is long gone, but there are still bone-jarring potholes all over the place. When will our streets be repaired?" Montclairvoyant's answer: "When the town finds dentists willing to fill cavities that large." (My expert dentist Dr. David St. Ledger doesn't do that!)

I emailed the piece to *Times* editor Mark Porter, and he replied with a conditional yes! All I had to do was make two of the Q&As more tied to current local news. I quickly did so, and the column ran on July 3, 2003.

Then, in mid-July, Robert Novak wrote his infamous column outing CIA agent Valerie Plame. Her name had been leaked by two Bush administration officials — apparently to retaliate against Plame's husband, ex-ambassador Joseph Wilson, for writing a *New York Times* op-ed piece poking holes in the administration's rationale for invading Iraq.

I of course tried to get a comment from Novak, who had been more than happy to talk with me earlier in the year for that puff piece I did about multitaskers (he appeared on TV a lot). But this allegedly tough columnist, who had written negative things about people for decades, wouldn't say a thing. It's amazing how some journalists dish it out but can't take it.

I did talk to Creators Syndicate, which distributed Novak's column. But CS president Rick Newcombe would not publicly criticize Novak for outing a CIA agent — just as he would not publicly criticize Bill O'Reilly the following year when *that* Creators columnist was accused of sexual harassment by producer Andrea Mackris. The conservative O'Reilly, who had slammed President Clinton and others involved in sex scandals, settled with Mackris for what was reportedly a large sum of money.

Thankfully, some other syndicates know when *not* to support their talent, as you'll see in my 2005 chapter.

Then, in late July '03, Laurel moved to Montclair! The long gaps between our visits would finally be a thing of the past. Laurel obviously had mixed feelings about this huge change in her life. She was excited that we would finally be together, but also sad to leave her Indiana State job and colleagues — and the Midwest in general. If I wasn't the parent of a school-age child, I would have considered moving to Terre Haute, which I really liked. Heck, by the time Laurel's friendly Indiana pals Deb and Merrill hosted a wonderful going-away dinner for us in their shotgun-style Bloomington home, I almost felt more comfortable in the Midwest than in the frenetic New York area.

But I couldn't bring myself to uproot Maggie when divorce and my relationship with Laurel were already changing her life so much. Also, my daughter had developed a nice circle of friends in Montclair.

Though very conscious of Laurel's ambivalence, I was so happy about conjoining our lives I felt I could fly!

I flew to Indianapolis (on a plane) to help my fiancée pack. Most of her stuff would be transported by a moving company, but we also crammed Laurel's tiny Ford Escort with lots of stuff — and Angus the cat.

We felt so bad for Angus, who was shivering with fear. We knew he'd enjoy being in a house rather than an apartment, but he of course had no idea where he was going. Halfway to New Jersey, we stopped for the night at the Pittsburgh abode of Laurel's cousins Jean and Mike, and let Angus out of his carrier. Perhaps he thought that was his new home, but there was one more day to "go east, young cat."

Also during that frenetic July, I visited Chicago to do a "day in the life of a salesperson" story with Margo Sugrue of Creators Syndicate. I flew out in the *very* early morning (*E&P* wouldn't spring for a hotel); tagged along with

Margo when she visited the *Chicago Tribune, Chicago Sun-Times,* and *Waukegan News-Sun*; and flew back the same day. A highlight was meeting *Tribune* associate managing editor/features Geoff Brown, an extremely nice and cerebral guy who I had interviewed several times about comics.

I liked the "day in the life" format so much I did the same thing that fall with excellent editorial cartoonist Walt Handelsman of Long Island, N.Y., *Newsday*.

Handelsman would one day also create animated political cartoons — and, as you'll see, was amply rewarded for that in 2007. Among the online political artists predating Walt was Mark Fiore, who went multimedia after the *San Jose Mercury News* laid him off in 2001.

I profiled Mark in October 2003, and learned he spent more than 35 hours preparing each 45-to-60-second Flash animation — which included words, pictures, motion, voices, sound effects, and music. But he did his drawings the old-fashioned way (ink on paper) before scanning them into his computer.

"How come?" I asked.

"I want to have a 'line' so it doesn't look too 'computery,'" replied the San Francisco creator, whose clients included newspaper Web sites. In 2010, Fiore would become the first person to win the editorial cartooning Pulitzer for animated-only work.

Back in my home state, Laurel found adjunct jobs for the 2003-4 academic year teaching French at Montclair State University and the Madison, N.J.-based Drew University. Meanwhile, she sought a scarce full-time French professor position for 2004-5 and beyond.

Laurel and I also started making plans for a 2004 wedding. We wanted Maggie to play the piano at the start of the ceremony, and were thrilled when she agreed. Of the two songs, one would be an award-winning composition Maggie had written for the piano class she took in Montclair with talented teacher Judy de Wette.

Like most teens, Maggie often preferred to be with friends. But she, Laurel, and I did enjoy doing some things together, such as going to the Sushi Hana restaurant in Montclair that Maggie loved. We sort of resembled the "blended" family that populates Jan Eliot's superb "Stone Soup" strip — except our house was slightly bigger than a newspaper comic.

And, when Maggie was with her mother, among the things Laurel and I did in 2003 was join about 175 others in Connecticut for "Beetle Bailey" cartoonist Mort Walker's 80th birthday party. We also continued our exploration of museums by visiting the fascinating FDR library in Hyde Park, N.Y.

Back in North Jersey, longtime midwesterner Laurel was struck by how close many of the towns were. For instance, our personable and compassionate doctor Peter Dabrowski worked two towns away in Bloomfield back then. Walking time to his office from our house: nine minutes.

Meanwhile, the 119-year-old *E&P* was struggling so much that big changes were in the offing.

CHAPTER TWENTY-SEVEN

2004: Almost All Web Almost All the Time

When I was with New Jersey's *Passaic Herald News* in 1978, I sometimes wrote four or five stories day. You can't do many in-depth articles under those circumstances, so I was happy to write longer features for the monthly *Marketing Communications* magazine between late 1978 and early 1983. But working for a monthly was a little *too* leisurely, so I subsequently found *E&P*'s weekly schedule to be just right.

Then the Internet forced me full circle. *E&P*'s print magazine switched from weekly to monthly publication in January 2004, but the requirement that everyone now write *many* more Web stories made me feel like I was again working for a daily — on steroids. More work for no extra pay was something also being faced by countless other journalists and non-journalists.

E&P's redesigned site had six new sections, including one on syndication for which I was soon writing three or four pieces a day — a total that would only rise. I was also doing stories for other parts of the site and for the print magazine, as well as reading 1,000 or so emails a week (resolutely still answering all the answerable ones).

Yet staffers were pushed to produce even more. I was putting in plenty of unpaid overtime, but vowed to myself to reserve some evening hours for my family. After all, I had a fiancée and daughter I wanted to be with after going through a difficult marriage and watching my first child die. I would have been nuts, now that things were better at home, to allow work to become the be-all and end-all of my life. Of course, I realized this might put my employment at risk.

On the other hand, it was a pleasure working for excellent *Montclair Times* editor Mark Porter, who had published a number of my "Montclairvoyant" columns by early 2004. Mark was friendly, modest, treated people with respect, edited copy carefully, and consulted writers when he wanted to change something.

But I no longer answered to any cartoon editor, because I had dropped my drawing efforts in 2003. The *E&P* job and *Times* column took up many hours, and I couldn't justify using more family time to also keep doing cartoons. Besides, the tough economy had lowered the revenues of the niche magazines that published me, so my sales went from modest in the late 1990s to pathetic by '03. But I was grateful that my six-year drawing "career" gave me more insight into the cartoon field I covered for *E&P*, just like "Montclairvoyant" helped me understand the column field I also covered in my day job. (Given that I often worked into the evening at *E&P*, "day job" isn't quite the right term!)

One thing I often satirized in my early *Times* pieces was a greedy local developer's ultimately successful effort to knock down Montclair's beautiful Marlboro Inn (which partly dated back to the 1840s) in order to cram the property with 10 tacky but pricey McMansions. The subdivision originally had the snooty name of "Hempstead at Montclair," which I shortened to HAM in my columns so I could call its future rich residents HAMsters and HAMburghers. But the darn developer changed the name to the less-mock-able Christopher Court.

I'm a great believer in historic preservation and a big foe of overdevelopment — and also had some personal interest in the Marlboro Inn's survival. I lived three blocks from it, and Laurel and I had been considering it for our wedding site. But with the inn's future looking bleak, we instead chose the Montclair Women's Club for the ceremony and reception that would take place on May 15.

With the demanding *E&P* job and the scramble to find an affordable caterer, officiant, photographer, and DJ, could life become any crazier? Well … yes.

"I'm heading to *The Montclair Times* office," I told Laurel on March 2. "They want to take a photo to run with the column."

"That's wonderful, Dave!"

"If it comes out well," I replied. Photogenic wasn't my middle name.

After the picture session, I began driving home to make a quick pit stop before heading to the train station and Manhattan for a "day in the life" story about the New York Times News Service (NYTNS). Then another car ran a stop sign and plowed into my Honda Civic — sending it spinning, I kid you not, onto the lawn of the high school my daughter was inside of at that very moment. During the crash, my left hand smashed into something, and it was already swelling up by the time I stumbled out of my totaled vehicle. I was lucky not to get hurt worse, because the damn airbag never deployed in the aging 1993 car.

Laurel took me to the emergency room, and X-rays found a major fracture at the bottom of my left ring finger that would require an operation two weeks later. I also had chest pain and other aches that eventually went away on their own.

I was in a daze, but managed to call NYTNS executive editor Laurence Paul to cancel after I got home from the emergency room. Then I talked to *E&P*'s editor, who told me about various things I needed to do, asked me when I would come in, and generally hinted that the staff was now so small that I needed to keep up with my work.

The new confident me should have told the editor that I'd resume working when I was ready. I had been at *E&P* for 21 years (16 more than my supervisor), and took fewer than 10 sick days that whole time. But I went back to work the next day. I guess I wanted to be a "trouper" — especially with our much more demanding Web site — and I knew that *E&P*'s small, overburdened staff would have to do my work if I didn't do it. Profit-obsessed corporations depend on that camaraderie; it's cheaper than hiring a temp for an injured employee.

So, for the next six weeks — with only a little time off here and there for the operation and orthopedist appointments — I typed away despite my left hand being in a bulky cast. My left thumb and index finger stuck out of the cast, allowing me to keyboard with both hands by holding a pencil upside down with those two fingers so that the eraser hit the keys. I felt a jolt of pain creating every letter that appeared on my computer screen, but it was doable.

The result? My repeatedly-jarred fracture didn't heal properly, and my left hand and ring finger remain permanently stiffer than before. Doing yard work is more difficult, and I can no longer comfortably bend my fingers to the frets of my guitar — causing me to give up an instrument I had loved playing since college. Also, I still can't get my wedding ring over my injured finger.

But 2004 was wonderful in other ways. On May 15, about 80 guests watched as Laurel walked down the aisle of the Montclair Women's Club — which mostly consists of one big room that's nice but not ornate. I waited in front, gazing at Laurel in her lovely ivory-colored silk blouse and floor-length brown skirt. She looked infinitely more beautiful than if she had been wearing a fancy wedding dress. I was wearing a gray suit (Montclair has a Tuxedo Road, but my road to "I do" was happily tuxedo-free).

Maggie played her two piano pieces flawlessly, and I stumbled over only one line during the vows — causing attendees to chuckle and me to smile. A similar stumble would have shattered the younger me — as when flubbing a line in a junior-high oral report would depress me for days.

Laurel and I had a weekend mini-honeymoon at a Princeton, N.J., inn — delaying a decision on a longer, more expensive trip to see if she could find a full-time teaching job.

She could! Laurel landed a tenure-track position as an assistant professor of French starting that fall at Bronx Community College, part of the not-puny CUNY (City University of New York). So we decided to honeymoon in Europe, which I hadn't visited since 1985.

We spent a week (I couldn't get away from *E&P* longer) in Tours, Paris, and Venice — staying in modest hotels and walking ourselves silly. We walked ourselves especially silly one afternoon to escape the packed tourist areas of Venice, reaching a quiet neighborhood where we ate a long, leisurely lunch at an outdoor table next to a small canal. We watched as Venetians left their boats to enter the restaurant, and I fed scraps from our meal to a ragged-looking dog. We thought our cute canine companion was a stray until a door opened in a building next to the eatery and the pooch trotted in to greet its owner.

Our last activity in Venice was traveling to Marco Polo Airport before dawn via an incredibly romantic moonlit ride on a boat taxi.

Things were also going well with Maggie, and I was gratified to see she had developed a social conscience. Dismayed by the unnecessary Iraq War, Maggie became a volunteer for New Jersey Peace Action. And she cut off much of her hair for Locks of Love, the organization that provides wigs to ill, financially disadvantaged kids who've gone bald. I think growing up in a non-affluent household was one reason why Maggie became an unspoiled person.

Angus was happy, too. Though he undoubtedly missed his Indiana cornfield, he enjoyed munching on the grass in our backyard, scooting up trees, and leaping to try to catch fireflies (he never did). When Angus wanted to reenter the house, he often tore across the yard and slammed his front paws against the back door. Instant messaging!

But getting supplies at work was far from instant. Cost-cutting VNU required employees to order things like pens, pads, and paper clips from a cheaper outside vendor rather than buy them ourselves and get reimbursed. Using the vendor was a cumbersome process that involved filling out a long form and waiting for the supplies to be shipped. To avoid the hassle, I bought my own pens and took notes on photocopy paper rather than pads (keeping each set of notes together by folding the top page in half and using that page as a large made-out-of-paper "paper clip"). VNU reporters spotting a pristine manila folder dove for it like a fumbled football at an NFL playoff game.

One of my 2004 stories was about a contest "Doonesbury" cartoonist Garry Trudeau held offering $10,000 to anyone who could prove President Bush fulfilled his 1972 National Guard duty in Alabama. "I've been looking for something to do with a huge tax cut I didn't need," Garry told me. "Part of the blowback from Bush's largesse to the un-poor is that people like me have become fat cats!"

It was also in '04 that the "Doonesbury" strip's B.D. character lost his leg in Iraq and began an agonizing recovery that Trudeau would movingly and humorously chronicle over the next several years.

Trudeau spoke at the Association of American Editorial Cartoonists' April '04 convention in Lexington, Ky., as did *Hustler* publisher Larry Flynt. In 1988, the U.S. Supreme Court had affirmed the sleazy magazine's right to publish a graphic cartoon parody of Moral Majority leader Jerry Falwell, and the AAEC backed Flynt in that case for First Amendment reasons.

Speaking later in the convention, comedian Elayne Boosler referenced Flynt, a certain trashy tabloid, and a subway ride with this quip: "I love *Hustler* magazine. I like to hide the *New York Post* in something on my way home."

I also covered the National Society of Newspaper Columnists' June conference in New Orleans. My fondest memory of that gathering was seeing 80-something Dorothy Brush of Tennessee's *Crossville Chronicle* receive the NSNC's Columnist of the Year honor for never missing a deadline while battling lung cancer that was supposed to have killed her by early 2004. (Dorothy was still alive as I wrote this book!) The award presentation was at the fabulous Dooky Chase restaurant on a very modest New Orleans street that flooded when Hurricane Katrina devastated the city in 2005.

Then there was the July interview I did with maverick conservative Kathleen Parker after the widely syndicated columnist had the guts to do a piece calling many newspapers boring. She wrote that "the soul-snatching corporate culture has euthanized newsroom personalities."

Naturally, I had to call Kathleen up! "Did you worry about biting the hand that feeds you?" I asked in fascination.

"I never worry about who I'm going to offend because I'm always offending somebody," replied Parker, who would win the 2010 Pulitzer Prize for commentary. "People who read my column presumably want to hear my point of view, not a bedtime story."

And just before the presidential election in November, I asked dozens of cartoonists and columnists to predict what percentage of the vote candidates would receive. The winner, who guessed 51% for George W. Bush and 48% for John Kerry, was *Las Vegas Sun* editorial cartoonist Mike Smith from the city that knows something about betting. Among the close runners-up was congenial *Anniston* (Ala.) *Star* columnist legend George Smith — meaning people with common last names seem to make good forecasters. I never trusted weatherman Bob Vbwgpssen again.

I also did another "day in the life" feature — about the Associated Press just after its August move to new headquarters on West 33rd Street in Manhattan. The AP loved the article, and looking at it now makes me realize it's the first piece I ever wrote mentioning Barack Obama (I sat in on a news meeting in which AP editors discussed a story about Republican efforts to find a U.S. Senate candidate to oppose Obama in Illinois). But doing my AP story involved nearly 11 hours at the wire service and another 30 hours of writing and rewriting — while also churning out Web stories on other topics. With all those online responsibilities, I would soon become reluctant to do many massive features like the AP one. My editor would hold that against me in his yearly evaluations.

Another 2004 task was helping to choose winners of E&P's new "Editorial Cartoon of Month" feature. My editor asked me to surf the Web to find and print out dozens of cartoons, and then rank them in order of preference. I subsequently handed this stack to managing editor Shawn Moynihan, who ranked the cartoons in *his* order of preference. Shawn's picks and my picks differed, but often not by much. Then the stack went to my editor, who often chose a cartoon Shawn and I had not ranked very high.

CHAPTER TWENTY-EIGHT

2005: The Traveling Never Stopped Until It Did

Under the 2002-appointed editor, *E&P* won a number of Neal Awards, which are the trade-magazine world's Oscars — minus the glamour, box-office grosses, and paparazzi. Those Neals were nabbed mostly thanks to the excellent writing of staffers Jennifer Saba and Mark Fitzgerald. Also, *E&P* was among the most general-interest of the magazines eligible for the annual contest — which received entries from the likes of *Pork* and *Heavy Duty Trucking*. Judges may have favored us partly because they could easily understand *E&P*'s content!

Several stories I wrote in 2005 had an easy-to-understand premise: Conservative columnists got funding from the Bush administration, and never informed readers about the money until caught. They became known as "payola pundits," and attracted an affluent reader demographic (43rd presidents).

In early January, *USA Today* reported that Tribune Media Services columnist Armstrong Williams had received about $240,000 from the U.S. Department of Education to promote the No Child Left Behind law on his TV and radio shows — with the pundit also touting NCLB in several of his newspaper pieces. Williams defended himself by saying the money paid for an ad campaign airing on his broadcasts. TMS terminated Williams' contract — an action that contrasted greatly with Creators Syndicate keeping Robert Novak after he outed a CIA agent and Bill O'Reilly after that sexual-harassment charge.

In a Creators-distributed cartoon by conservative *Akron Beacon Journal* staffer Chip Bok, George W. Bush was shown writing as first lady Laura Bush asked: "Already editing your State of the Union speech, dear?" The president replied: "Nah. Armstrong Williams' next column."

Later in January, *The Washington Post*'s Howard Kurtz reported that Universal Press Syndicate columnist Maggie Gallagher had received $21,500 from the U.S. Department of Health and Human Services (HHS) to promote Bush's efforts to encourage (heterosexual) marriage. Gallagher mentioned those efforts in her column and also defended the president's proposal for a constitutional amendment banning same-sex marriage, wrote Kurtz. Gallagher responded that the $21,500 was to provide material about the benefits of (heterosexual) marriage, not to promote Bush's specific plan. But, unlike TMS with Williams, Universal kept Gallagher — and her client list remained at about 75. America's "liberal" daily papers sure are loyal!

Soon after the Gallagher revelations, Salon.com reported that self-syndicated "Ethics & Religion" columnist Michael McManus received about $10,000 from the HHS for subcontracted work to promote the Bush marriage initiative. McManus defended himself by saying the money was awarded to his Marriage Savers organization, not to him as a columnist.

I decided to ask a bunch of other syndicated writers what they thought of conservative pundits receiving federal largesse. "Taking money from a government agency should be a no-brainer. Don't!" replied *Providence* (R.I.) *Journal* columnist Froma Harrop in her typical no-nonsense way.

Apparently, Doug Bandow didn't get the Ethics 101 memo, because BusinessWeek.com would report in December 2005 that the columnist allegedly received thousands of dollars from corrupt Republican lobbyist Jack Abramoff to write op-ed pieces favorable to some of Abramoff's clients. Copley News Service quickly suspended Bandow, who then resigned from the syndicate.

You might be wondering why other media outlets broke the aforementioned payola stories. With all the Web stuff I had to do, it was hard to find time to unearth "scoops" the way I used to. I was more inundated reporter than investigative reporter.

While some columnists raked in the GOP dough, other syndicated creators struggled. Dailies continued to eliminate editorial cartooning positions; for instance, the *Los Angeles Times* sacked Michael Ramirez in 2005 (when it also axed longtime columnist Robert Scheer, who strongly opposed the Iraq War). Given that budget-slicing papers jettisoned about 2,000 people in 2005, cartoonists comprised a small portion of that total. But with perhaps 80 staff cartoonists left in the U.S. that year, any reduction in that number was huge.

Then, in January 2006, cartoonist Kevin "KAL" Kallaugher unwillingly took a buyout from the Baltimore *Sun* — which, like L.A.'s *Times*, was owned by the Tribune Co. But even as cost-cutting reigned at that media corporation, Tribune Co. CEO Dennis FitzSimons got a $41 million departing package two years later. Obscene.

One temporary exception to this dreary job picture involved the *South Bend* (Ind.) *Tribune* naming Ron Rogers its staff cartoonist in mid-2005. Ron was one of the few black creators ever to land such a post at a general-circulation daily (Tim Jackson was well-known for his cartoons in the *Chicago Defender*, an African-American paper).

But Indiana dailies gaveth and tooketh away. In 2006, the Munster *Times* would lay off cartoonist Stacy Curtis. "This profession has 'Titanic' painted on the side of it," lamented Curtis, who was escorted from the building the day of his firing even though he had been with the paper nearly 10 years and never did anything to deserve not getting two weeks' notice. Corporate-owned places are *so* humane.

Curtis did land on his feet as an illustrator of children's books — a genre also entered by syndicated cartoonists Tony Auth, Chip Bok, Berkeley Breathed, Steve Breen, Jerry Craft, Jim Davis, Guy Gilchrist, Lynn Johnston,

Mike Lester, Patrick McDonnell, Wiley Miller, Henry Payne, and Morrie Turner, among others. Doing children's books offered cartoonists a chance to draw bigger and more creatively — and potentially make more money — than working for newspapers. Some of these cartoonists also wrote the kid books they illustrated.

Meanwhile, non-staff cartoonists were hustling to make ends meet. One extreme example was entrepreneurial dynamo Dale Neseman, who drew a whopping 18 to 25 local cartoons a week for about 20 newspapers in a dozen states — getting many of his ideas by reading his client papers online.

But, as always, there were also fun things to write about. One thing I enjoyed was calling Pulitzer Prize recipients for comment each year on the day they won. In April 2005, I phoned Cleveland *Plain Dealer* columnist Connie Schultz.

Schultz, 47, sounded understandably giddy when I reached her in the *Plain Dealer* newsroom. Not only had she won journalism's biggest prize, but the Ohio native did it with a column launched only three years before.

This was the first time I ever spoke with Connie, but I immediately found her to be a warm person — like New York Times Syndicate sales rep Connie White. If you want to name your first daughter Connie, you'll get no argument from me, but a different name for your second daughter might avoid confusion.

Schultz's working-class roots — her father toiled in a factory — permeated her writing. One of Connie's Pulitzer-winning columns focused on a coat-check person at a party center who, after hard days of work, was forced to give all her tips to management. The piece embarrassed the party center into changing this reverse-Robin Hood policy.

"I received 1,200 responses to that column before noon," Schultz told me in her down-to-earth voice.

Also winning a 2005 Pulitzer was the Louisville, Ky., *Courier-Journal's* Nick Anderson, one of a growing number of editorial cartoonists coloring their work and adding other computer effects. Nick (who hides the names of his sons Colton and Travis in every drawing) later sent me a hilarious tongue-in-cheek greeting card with a cartoon of himself blissfully sleeping with a Pulitzer trophy so huge it nearly pushed his wife off the bed!

Detroit Free Press/Tribune Media Services columnist Mitch Albom didn't have as good an April as Anderson and Schultz. Albom was so busy (radio work, best-selling books, etc.) that he committed this faux pas: interviewing two NBA players about their plans to attend a Saturday college basketball game and then writing in the past tense about their experience at the game (the column had to be filed Friday for Sunday publication). But scheduling conflicts caused the two to miss the game!

Albom received lots of flak for what he did, and his column was suspended for roughly a month by the *Free Press*. But at least he apologized — and quickly.

Just before the Albom story broke, I wrote an article about a "Brenda Starr" strip picturing Arianna Huffington. After I asked Arianna what it was like to see herself in a comic, the TMS columnist mentioned that she and Ken Lerer were launching a site in May 2005 that would include blog posts (many by famous people), news, and more. At the time we talked, the site was tentatively titled The Huffington Report. But it would soon be renamed The Huffington Post — and become a runaway success.

Bob Koehler's TMS column isn't a runaway success sales-wise, but he's one of the best writers I had the privilege to cover in my many years at *E&P*. Eloquence, humanism, thoughtfulness, meticulous research — Bob's feature has it all, including moving essays about the death of his wife and raising his daughter as a single parent. Maybe some newspapers don't like the fact that Koehler is a "peace journalist"; his column frequently and skillfully debunks war propaganda.

Also, Bob courageously wrote several 2005 columns about possible voting irregularities that may have helped Bush win the 2004 presidential election. Koehler did those pieces in a careful, reasoned way — no doubt aware of how Bush backers dismissed everyone questioning the election as "conspiracy theorists." Koehler just wanted newspapers and other media to investigate those allegations more.

After I wrote about Bob's columns, I received many thank-you messages from Ohio poll workers and others who wondered about the 2004 results. Also, Brad Friedman of the excellent BradBlog.com (where I learned about Koehler's voting columns) invited me on his radio show to discuss the matter.

You may have noticed that I mentioned several TMS columnists in the last few pages. I didn't receive government money to do so, though I received government money *while* doing so. Yes, I got an income-tax refund the month I wrote this chapter.

I talked to yet another TMS columnist — Garrison Keillor of *Prairie Home Companion* fame — about the syndicated feature he would start in July 2005.

"Why take the plunge into newspapers?" I asked the Minnesota-based humorist in a phone interview.

"On my radio show, I can use 5,000 words if I want," he answered. "The newspaper column is 800 words. The beauty of it is the limitation of it."

That inspired me to write a one-word column someday.

It was also in 2005 that I first wrote about a *no*-word feature that soon became a newspaper-syndication phenomenon: "Sudoku" number puzzles. I never finished one of those puzzles myself, and the only explanation I can think of is I never started one either.

A *many*-worded '05 story of mine profiled "Among Friends" columnist/former Associated Press reporter Tad Bartimus, one of a small number of women who covered the Vietnam War. A month after Tad's 1973 arrival in Southeast Asia, she breathed in toxins (probably from Agent Orange) while visiting a defoliated area. Tad's health would never be the same — as she battled inflammations, pneumonia, asthma, and more before a move to a remote area of Hawaii helped her condition somewhat.

"How remote?" I asked.

"It takes two-and-a-half hours for me to drive to the grocery store, doctor, and dentist," she replied, adding with a chuckle: "52 miles, 652 turns, and 68 one-lane bridges!"

Um ... solving a Sudoku puzzle might be easier.

One bonus of profiling Bartimus was getting to ask Barbara Kingsolver — one of my favorite contemporary authors and a good friend of Tad's — to comment about the ex-APer's personal/topical column.

Kingsolver's *The Poisonwood Bible* masterpiece was among the books I read during a manic 19 days of travel in June 2005 — when I flew to Sacramento to cover the Association of American Editorial Cartoonists convention, flew home, drove 650 miles to Canada with my wife Laurel and daughter Maggie for a reunion of Laurel's extended family, drove back to New Jersey, flew to Texas to cover the National Society of Newspaper Columnists conference, and flew home. It was "The Trek Life" (to borrow the title of David Reddick's *Star Trek*-themed comic).

During the NSNC conference, attendees were bused to Dallas from our biosphere-like hotel complex in Grapevine to see the Sixth Floor Museum housed in the former Texas School Book Depository where authorities said Lee Harvey Oswald took aim at JFK on Nov. 22, 1963. Remember the iconic photo of Jack Ruby shooting Oswald, who was handcuffed to a law-enforcement guy wearing a white cowboy hat? That guy was Dallas police detective Jim Leavelle, who addressed the columnists at the museum.

In the photo, it looks like Leavelle was recoiling from the shooting as Ruby's bullet entered Oswald. But the speaker said he was trying to protect Oswald on that Nov. 24 day.

"I saw Ruby take the pistol out of his coat pocket," he remembered. "I knew what was happening. I was trying to pull Oswald behind me. If I had been further away, I would have had the leverage. All I ended up doing was turning his body."

The next day, Leavelle was involved in transferring Ruby. "I told him, 'You didn't do us any favors shooting Oswald,'" recalled the 84-year-old retired lawman. "He said, 'I just wanted to be a hero.'" Leavelle added that Ruby later came up with other reasons for what he did, such as sparing Jackie

Kennedy a trip back to Dallas for Oswald's trial and wanting to show that "Jews have guts."

After his talk, columnists gathered around Leavelle to ask questions as I watched on the periphery. A few minutes later, Leavelle mentioned that he kept a memento from Nov. 24, 1963 — and casually pulled it out of his pocket. It was the key to the handcuffs that attached him to Oswald.

Parents have to eventually unattach themselves (somewhat) from their kids, as was the case for me soon after I returned from Texas. My 15-year-old daughter Maggie was going to Europe for three weeks with other students on a "People to People" trip — visiting Spain, France, Switzerland, and Germany. This would be Maggie's first time overseas.

"You're going to love Europe," I told Maggie at the airport, hugging her and then surreptitiously wiping my eyes. I would not only greatly miss Maggie, but was also thinking about all the things my first daughter Abigail had missed out on.

By the time Maggie was traveling, a book about the work of a great French writer was sitting on our living-room bookshelf. *Colette and the Conquest of Self*, which my wife Laurel had been working on since the 1990s, was finally published in 2005! "Isn't this fun?" she said when opening a box containing copies of her book. *Conquest* was inspired by Laurel's Indiana University doctoral thesis, and many university libraries would be among the book's buyers.

Colette died four months after I was born, which means nothing except she might have been older than me.

I paid for Maggie's trip with a modest settlement I received after my 2004 car accident from the at-fault driver's insurance company. I probably would have obtained more money by taking the driver to court, but she seemed like a decent person who obviously didn't crash into my car on purpose. And I had an aversion to the legal process after what happened with Abigail.

"I trust you'll do the American thing and sue," columnist Cal Thomas had written wryly in a condolence email he sent the day after my accident. So I guess I need to prove my Americanism in another way, like foolishly calling the centrist Barack Obama a "socialist," as some right-wingers do.

Obama's presidential predecessor — Bush — was in the news in 2005 with his bumbling, callous response to Hurricane Katrina and the flooding of New Orleans. After that apocalyptic August disaster, one of the people I interviewed was New Orleans *Times-Picayune* columnist Sheila Stroup.

At the time of Katrina, Sheila was heading for France to celebrate her 40th wedding anniversary with husband Merwin — a retired airline pilot. Sheila's power and phone service were out, so I couldn't call her after she returned to her home north of Lake Pontchartrain. But I could email her questions.

"I'm using the computer by connecting a 200-foot extension cord to our next-door neighbor," explained Stroup, whose property was strewn with fallen trees but whose many animals (including three donkeys) weathered the storm.

Sheila was still trying to track down many residents she knew to find out if they had survived. "My heart broke for the people trapped in the Superdome," she added. "Most of them are good people left without resources."

I also interviewed the congenial Smiley Anders — whose award-winning daily "items" column had been a staple in the Baton Rouge *Advocate* since 1979 — to find out how things were going in his evacuee-filled city. He recalled overhearing a man who talked about losing his boat, TV, and other possessions in the hurricane. "It was like my last divorce," the man quipped.

But Smiley, who had four evacuees in his house at one point, relayed mostly serious tales about how generously or badly people acted after Katrina.

Meanwhile, several cartoonists launched a Web site to raise funds for hurricane relief. They included "Candorville" creator/"Rudy Park" artist Darrin Bell, "Rudy Park" writer Theron Heir (pen name of Pulitzer-winning *New York Times* reporter Matt Richtel), and "The Norm" creator Michael Jantze.

And when Hurricane Wilma hit in October 2005, I spoke with "Clear Blue Water" comic creator Karen Montague-Reyes about how she had to leave her Florida Keys home. That was the *seventh* time in two years a storm had forced Karen to flee — yet the cartoonist managed to keep making the deadlines on her partly autobiographical strip starring a large multiracial family.

Bush got lots of flak for his Katrina response *and* for his increasingly bloody Iraq War. When the number of American dead reached 2,000 in October 2005, the *Atlanta Journal-Constitution*'s Mike Luckovich did a brilliant editorial cartoon that involved hand-writing all 2,000 names in the shape of "WHY?" It took him more than 12 hours.

"I was trying to think of a way to make the point that this whole war is such a waste," Mike told me. "But I also wanted to honor the troops I believe our government wrongly sent to Iraq."

The cartoon helped Luckovich win his second Pulitzer the following April.

A feature the *Journal-Constitution* Web site launched in 2002 and Universal began syndicating in 2005 was "Woman to Woman," which featured the point-counterpoint views of liberal Diane Glass and conservative Shaunti Feldhahn. While intensely partisan columns can be fun to read, it was nice to see at least one feature give both sides in a less-confrontational way. You might say Shaunti and Diane (who died way too young in 2007 at age 42) were in a *civil* war between friends.

Meanwhile, Luckovich and other syndicated people were launching blogs that gave them another creative outlet, more interaction with readers, and ... a bigger workload. Among those joining the blogosphere in 2005 or soon after were columnist Michele Malkin, "Dilbert" comic creator Scott Adams, and editorial cartoonists Ted Rall, Tom Tomorrow, Chip Bok, Clay Jones, Jim Borgman, and Daryl Cagle. Cagle was an especially busy guy given that he also ran the Cagle Cartoons syndicate and a massive Web site posting the work of many cartoonists.

Earlier in this chapter, I mentioned that it was hard to find time for "scoops." I did end 2005 by breaking the news that widely syndicated humorist Dave Barry would pull the plug on his weekly *Miami Herald* column rather than return from a year-long sabbatical. Barry, via email, offered his usual funny answers to my questions. One example:

"If you resume your column, when might that happen?"

"Several weeks after my death."

And when I asked Dave what he thought about all those conservative columnists getting government money, he replied: "I think paying pundits is a terrible, terrible thing, unless for some reason I get back into punditry, in which case I will be all for it."

Joking aside, Barry's departure symbolized a major change in the syndication biz. Today, there are no syndicated humor columnists with remotely the newspaper readership that Barry or the 1996-deceased Erma Bombeck had. There *are* scores of funny writers out there, but many gravitate to cable TV programs (such as *The Daily Show* with Jon Stewart), the Web, and other media outlets that might offer a bigger, younger audience and (sometimes) more pay.

Even the humorists who manage to sign with a syndicate find that the diminished newspaper business means relatively few clients purchasing their work. Many papers are reluctant to spend money (except to highly pay their top execs!) and also know that readers can find funny writing for free on the Internet. So, these papers reason, why bother buying humor columns?

The endless availability of free Web content also affects syndicates' sales of serious columns, humor comics, and editorial cartoons. Newspapers buy fewer of these features, so syndicates offer fewer of them, and the downward spiral keeps spiraling downward.

The online age hasn't been a complete negative for syndicates. They save time and money by receiving, editing, promoting, and distributing features digitally. And syndicates sell features to newspaper Web sites, other Web sites, and the mobile-device market, but that revenue doesn't match what was earned when the daily print newspaper market was so robust decades ago.

CHAPTER TWENTY-NINE

2006:
Getting Hit With
a 'Bottle' Is
Great!

A group of private-equity firms acquired *E&P's* parent company VNU in 2006, and formed a replacement company. The purchase sent shudders through employees already battered by layoffs and other cuts, because private-equity firms are known for slashing staff and budgets in the hopes of selling a "leaner" company for a big profit several years later.

Earlier in '06, February was sabbatical-announcement month. Columnist Connie Schultz, the 2005 Pulitzer Prize winner, took a leave of absence to work on the U.S. Senate campaign of her husband — Rep. Sherrod Brown (D-Ohio). And Aaron McGruder announced a six-month break from his "The Boondocks" comic to devote more time to his *The Boondocks* TV show on the Cartoon Network.

One creator would return to newspapers and one wouldn't.

I also did a story about the growing number of bloggers who covered cartooning. Among those featured in the piece were Alan Gardner (Daily Cartoonist.com) and Tom Spurgeon (ComicsReporter.com).

Other bloggers writing about the field by 2006 or later included Daryl Cagle, Michael Cavna, Dirk Deppey, Mike Lynch, Heidi MacDonald, Eric Millikin, Tim O'Shea, Rob Tornoe, and Mike Rhode (Mike and cartoonist Dan Rosandich were among the people who suggested I write a book about my *E&P* experiences). Also, Josh Fruhlinger offered humorous snarky comments about syndicated strips in his "Comics Curmudgeon" blog.

So I had much more cartoon-covering competition in the 2000s than in the 1980s — not only from blogs, but from outlets such as the online "Rants & Raves" feature by R.C. Harvey, the *Stay Tooned!* magazine founded by John Read, the *Hogan's Alley* magazine edited by Tom Heintjes, the National Cartoonists Society newsletter edited by Frank Pauer, and the Association of American Editorial Cartoonists' *Notebook* magazine edited by J.P. Trostle, who was also news editor for the AAEC's EditorialCartoonists.com.

Why did I write about and/or link to my competition? Well, my competition also wrote about and/or linked to my coverage! And I figured that if another outlet had a story I didn't have, it was a service to my readers to tell them about that story while crediting the original source. I just had to make sure I generated enough good content of my own to keep people reading *E&P* in addition to the other outlets — and I did.

The AAEC apparently thought so, too. I was covering the organization's banquet at the end of its June meeting in Denver when AAEC president Clay Bennett prepared to announce that year's winner of the Ink Bottle Award for service to editorial cartooning. I sat in the audience taking notes, dazed from the 18-hour days I had spent attending sessions and frantically writing stories on a laptop in my hotel room as I munched veggie subs from a nearby eatery (some high-paid execs who now owned *E&P* ate fancy meals on the company dime; I did not).

As I jotted down Clay's remarks, I suddenly got a strange feeling. He was talking about someone who had covered editorial cartooning for a long time, and saying other nice things about a person who sounded suspiciously like ... me.

Uh-oh, I thought to myself, in a near panic. Conflict-of-interest alert! I shouldn't be honored by a group I cover!

Then Clay announced my name, and the 200 or so people in the audience stood and applauded as I somehow stumbled toward the podium through a sea of high-fives.

I didn't step onto the podium, though; I was just hoping to accept the plaque and slink back to my seat. But a beaming Clay urged me to get behind the microphone and say a few words.

The honor was such a big (and happy) shock that it should have rendered me mute, but I managed to blurt out a couple of sentences. I said I wasn't sure if it was right to accept the award, but quickly added that I was very thankful for it.

I felt doubly good that spring because, just before an April family trip to Florida for my mother's 80th birthday, I learned that I had helped *The Montclair Times* win a New Jersey Press Association prize for top editorial section. (I would later help *Times* editor Mark Porter and managing editor Lillian Ortiz win that same award twice more.)

Meanwhile, Ann Coulter was tops in "joking" references to the killing of people. For instance, the conservative columnist said in January 2006 that someone should "put rat poison" in liberal Supreme Court Justice John Paul Stevens' "crème brûlée." Then, in June, Coulter "quipped" that Rep. John Murtha (D-Pa.) was "the reason soldiers invented 'fragging'" (the killing of officers by their own soldiers). She made this mean-spirited remark after Murtha, a hawkish ex-Marine officer, came out against the Iraq War that Coulter avidly supported.

But Universal Press Syndicate stood by its pundit, and most of Coulter's 100 or so newspapers kept printing her. Also, she continued to sell lots of books, earn tons of money in speaking fees, and appear as a guest on many TV programs. Being a thin blonde in addition to being a conservative undoubtedly helped Coulter's wallet stay fat.

"I can't believe all those papers still publish her," said my wife Laurel, who was far from naïve but liked to think the best of people and institutions.

"Most papers have conservative owners," I replied. "A lot of reporters are centrist or liberal, but they're not the ones deciding which columns to buy."

That's a big reason why talented conservative columnists Kathleen Parker, Cal Thomas, and George Will amassed well over 1,000 papers between them while talented liberal columnists E.J. Dionne Jr., Eugene Robinson, and Bob Herbert (when he was with *The New York Times*) ran in far fewer publications.

I was so disgusted with Coulter's "humorous" death wishes that I wrote a column for *E&P*'s Web site criticizing the Universal writer. Coulter's fan base responded as maturely as I expected, with dozens of emails cursing me out and suggesting I join Rep. Murtha and Justice Stevens in the land of the non-living.

Then Universal president Lee Salem sent a rebuttal that was posted on our site. In it, he said Coulter wrote in the satirical tradition of Jonathan Swift's "A Modest Proposal" and that Universal also supported liberal creators when they did controversial work.

I might have missed it, but I didn't remember any of those liberal creators "joking" about killing people.

Soon, I drove with Laurel to Boston to cover the National Society of Newspaper Columnists conference — where the NSNC named Coulter the "winner" of its Sitting Duck Award "for cheapening political discourse in America." The organization said the "honor" was given "reluctantly because we know Ms. Coulter is desperate for any kind of attention!"

Also, conference keynoter Arianna Huffington said Coulter is "one of the most toxic people on the American cultural scene," but added that she could see why Coulter's writing was compelling to some people. "People are so used to manufactured political speech that there's kind of a longing for someone to say something, no matter how crazy," Arianna explained.

During the conference, the NSNC *re*-presented its Lifetime Achievement Award to Art Buchwald — with Art's daughter Jennifer accepting it on her miraculous father's behalf.

Why "miraculous" and "*re*-presented"? The famous political humorist had refused dialysis and entered a Washington, D.C.-area hospice in February 2006. With the expectation that he would die in weeks, Buchwald ate junk food and received a steady stream of goodbye visits and phone calls from his countless admirers in high and not-so-high places. NSNC president Suzette Martinez Standring traveled to the hospice in February to personally present Art with the lifetime honor — which he had been named to receive before he fell ill — and wrote a moving guest column about her visit for *E&P*'s Web site. (Suzette later authored an excellent 2008 how-to book called *The Art of Column Writing* that included advice from Buchwald and others.)

But Buchwald didn't die in 2006 and Jennifer, speaking to the NSNC audience on July 2 of that year, said: "Dad is alive and well and arrived at Martha's Vineyard today for the summer!"

The audience was also shown brief videotaped remarks by the honoree himself. "My theory is that dying is easy, parking is tough," quipped Buchwald, who would resume his column and write one more book before passing away in January 2007. After his death, *Boston Globe* columnist Ellen Goodman told me: "Humor today has much more of a cynical edge. Art's humor was more that of a loyal opposition.... He was a delightful guy, wonderfully amusing company, and deliciously insecure."

Boston's Old Granary Burial Ground was within yards of the NSNC conference hotel, and it was an amazing experience to see the graves of Paul Revere, John Hancock, Samuel Adams, Crispus Attucks, Benjamin Franklin's parents, and civilized discourse (thanks, Ann Coulter!).

In the fall of 2006, Aaron McGruder buried his "Boondocks" comic, while the other on-sabbatical creator — Connie Schultz — saw her husband Sherrod Brown win that U.S. Senate seat. She also worked on a book (titled ... *and His Lovely Wife*) about her experiences as a non-stereotypical spouse on the campaign trail, and resumed her Cleveland *Plain Dealer* column in January 2007.

Connie said some people wrongly thought she might give up her column to be a senator's wife. "I'm separate and distinct from my husband," she said. "Women have their own opinions, and I'm one of them."

Props to Schultz for that comment, and props to Broadway theaters for having props. But no props to Connie's employer, because the *Plain Dealer* endorsed Brown's Republican opponent!

Also that fall, my daughter Maggie was named co-editor-in-chief of the Montclair High School newspaper — and handled that job well while applying to colleges. One of her journalistic strengths was spotting typos — sumting aye'm gud att az wel.

Meanwhile, layoffs continued under my company's new ownership (though *E&P*'s already-decimated staff was spared — at least during '06). And employees got health insurance that took a bigger bite out of our paychecks and required us to fork over co-pays of $30.

Also, when Mac-equipped staffers tried to get reimbursed for travel expenses, we had to use a complex online form designed for PCs — resulting in so many glitches that they formed their own nation-state. It now could take two hours to keyboard expenses when the simple paper forms of the past took just minutes to fill out. But the online system probably allowed the company to pay fewer people in its outsourced accounting department.

After I *finally* completed the form, it got digitally routed to my editor — who often waited a week or two before approving it. By the time I was reimbursed for expenses that could run $1,000-plus a trip, I had sometimes already drained my own bank account to make the payment before my corporate AmEx card's deadline.

It was all like a "Dilbert" comic without the humor.

Then there were the company-wide "town hall meetings" for employees who had no time for such meetings — because most of us were doing the work of two or more people. Execs droned on about this and that at the gatherings, and the editors and publishers of various magazines were forced to jump through hoops giving upbeat reports when things were far from upbeat. A number of employees (myself included) started skipping some of the meetings in order to do actual work. Given that hundreds of people attended those "town hall" soirees, our absences may not have been noticed.

The company also kept sending employees emails about the importance of profitability even as we were getting squeezed to achieve that profitability. And these messages often contained annoying corporate lingo about the company's "core values," about "working smarter" to make up for all the (dumb) layoffs, and about "facilitating execution" of "strategic initiatives" to "grow our business going forward." Anyone could see that the rich private-equity owners just wanted to shrink the company as much as possible and then sell all or part of it so they could become even richer.

CHAPTER THIRTY

2007: Controversy and Conferences

Cartoonist Lynn Johnston told me in 2001 that she might end "For Better or For Worse" in 2007, so I contacted her in late 2006 to see if that was still the case. She surprised me — and readers of my January '07 story — with the news that her 28-year-old comic would continue as a hybrid of old and new material starting that September. Insiders told me Lynn had wanted to pull the plug on "FBorFW" until Universal Press Syndicate (averse to losing a lucrative feature running in more than 2,000 newspapers) suggested the strip go into reruns a la "Peanuts." Lynn countered with the hybrid idea.

"What will the hybrid involve?" I asked Lynn.

The cartoonist — who was doing something with little precedent in comic history — hadn't figured out all the details yet. "I'll be flying by the seat of my eraser," she quipped.

Part of the reason Johnston wanted to ease up on her "FBorFW" workload was to spend more hours with her longtime husband Rod, who had retired from dentistry. But Rod shocked Lynn by suddenly leaving her for another woman in April 2007 — and by the time Johnston told me about this betrayal five months later, she had decided to work harder on the hybrid "FBorFW" than originally planned. As it turned out, Lynn would chronologically revisit past episodes with a mix of repeated and new material — and draw the new material in her old, comparatively looser style. The cartoonist ended up retaining a large chunk of her newspaper clients.

It was for better and better for Long Island, N.Y., *Newsday* editorial cartoonist Walt Handelsman in April 2007, when he won his second Pulitzer Prize on the strength of both his print work and his brilliant seriocomic Web animations. Walt had spent about 250 hours teaching himself to do his multimedia extravaganzas for Newsday.com starting in late 2005.

This was the first time in the 85-year history of the Pulitzer cartooning category that online animations helped someone win. And the two other '07 cartooning Pulitzer finalists — Mike Thompson of the *Detroit Free Press* and Nick Anderson of the *Houston Chronicle* — were also cited for both their print and animation work.

A number of editorial cartoonists had been using sound and movement for years. Indeed, Mike Shelton and Jocelyne Leger collaborated on online animations starting in the early 1990s, when they were with California's *Orange County Register*. But the genre really hit the journalistic mainstream in 2007.

That spring, my daughter Maggie got accepted into the wonderful but pricey Barnard College, which is affiliated with Columbia University in

Manhattan. Given that Columbia didn't accept me into its Graduate School of Journalism 30 years earlier, I was delighted not to bequeath that rejection gene.

Barnard was Maggie's first choice, but I couldn't come close to affording its yearly price tag of $45,000-plus. So we waited anxiously for the financial-aid letter that was due a few days later.

It arrived in the mail when I was alone in the house, taking a day off from *E&P*. But the letter was addressed to Maggie, so I didn't feel comfortable opening it. Eventually, I reached her on her cell to get her okay.

"Tell me! What does it say?" she asked in a voice that mixed excitement and terror.

I sliced open the envelope and quickly scanned the numbers. "Omigod!" I croaked. "Omigod! "We'll ... we'll only have to pay about $10,000 this year!"

"Omigod!"

So Maggie was Barnard-bound.

But first there was her chaotic Montclair High graduation. It was raining hard that June evening, so Laurel and I joined other attendees in the school auditorium — the alternate site for when bad weather prevented use of the school amphitheater. Then the rain let up enough for the ceremony to be held outside after all. Laurel and I walked to the amphitheater — and all the seats and standing room were taken by other parents, grandparents, and siblings. So we were forced to return to the auditorium to watch the ceremony on closed-circuit TV. Then, as diplomas were given out after the speeches, the skies opened again and everyone scrambled inside.

To top it off, I had to drive 90 miles to Philadelphia that night to cover the National Society of Newspapers Columnists conference starting early the next morning (we would take Maggie out for a graduation dinner the day after I returned). I arrived in the City of Brotherly Love well past midnight.

I should've just skipped the meeting, but *E&P* always wanted plenty of content for its Web site. The NSNC conference certainly generated numerous stories, including one about a speech by blunt conservative Bill O'Reilly.

"Newspapers are dying, and there are two reasons why," the Fox News host/syndicated columnist told NSNC attendees. "One reason is the Internet. The other is ideology." O'Reilly contended that many papers are losing circulation because they've allowed the "liberal" ideology of their editorial pages to "bleed into news coverage."

Though I didn't say this in my story, I thought it strange that O'Reilly described editorial pages as "liberal" when most of those pages had supported President Bush and the Iraq War, and were running more conservative columnists than liberal ones.

O'Reilly ended up liking my story about his talk. Where did I go wrong?!

Things lightened up when humorist Dave Barry addressed attendees. After his prepared speech, former NSNC president Suzette Standring asked: "Can you discuss humor that's based on stereotypes?"

"Only a woman would ask that question," Barry shot back, as the room erupted in laughter.

Later in the conference — ably hosted by *Philadelphia Daily News* columnist Stu Bykofsky — the NSNC's 2007 Sitting Duck Award went to a U.S. attorney general who conveniently "forgot" things when testifying in front of Congress. "We're giving the award to Alberto Gonzales, but can't remember why," deadpanned NSNC president Mike Argento of the *York* (Pa.) *Daily Record*.

The following month, the Association of American Editorial Cartoonists held a big bash to mark its 50th anniversary. I drove to Washington, D.C., with Maggie — who hadn't accompanied me to a cartoonist or columnist meeting since she was 11.

We heard remarks from people such as legendary White House correspondent-turned-columnist Helen Thomas, Democratic presidential candidate Dennis Kucinich, and the president himself ... yes, AAEC president Rob Rogers of the *Pittsburgh Post-Gazette*.

Why were the 2007 heads of the AAEC and the NSNC both from Pennsylvania? Another question Alberto Gonzales never answered.

With job losses threatening U.S. cartoonists, AAECers also spent two hours brainstorming possible ways to counteract their profession's shrinkage. Session co-leader Milt Priggee — who had been laid off several years earlier by *The Spokesman-Review* of Spokane, Wash. — said: "Will the AAEC become an organization of freelancers? That's where we might be going." Attendees agreed on several good suggestions, such as commissioning an AAEC poll to show how popular editorial cartoons are with newspaper readers. But layoffs would continue to mount.

As of mid-2007, the already tightly staffed *E&P* was still spared from its parent company's periodic spasms of profit-pumping layoffs — but other cost-cutting measures did affect our magazine. For instance, the company decided to save money by giving up several floors of its Manhattan office building and squeezing staffers into cubicles that were so much smaller that I kept banging my right elbow into a partition (the pain came in handy for staying awake during late nights of unpaid overtime!). If this workspace downsizing involved shared sacrifice, there might have been a "we're all in this together" vibe. But top company execs and magazine editors got to keep their separate offices.

I had accumulated so much stuff since 1983 that it took me two weeks to pare things down before packing what remained into boxes that would be moved to my new storage-space-challenged cubicle about 30 yards away. I did a lot of this pre-move sorting in the evening, but it still cut into time I usually spent writing stories. So some days I would do, say, six Web pieces rather than seven — lazy me!

"No one else is taking so long to pack," my editor told me.

"I've been here longer than other people," I replied. More years = more stuff seemed like an obvious equation to me. And given that I had recently sent back 15 stories from the editorial cartoonists' convention, I was hardly a slacker.

The company also tried to save money by denying E&P a much-overdue update of its Web site — which had an old-fashioned look, no blogs, no video, and no way for readers to post comments under stories. The site still got more than a million hits during many 2007 months, but it might have attracted more traffic and more ads if it didn't look so ... 2004.

There was no updating problem for editorial cartoonist Marshall Ramsey of the Jackson, Miss., *Clarion-Ledger*. In August 2007, the two-time Pulitzer finalist posted his 3,000[th] entry for a blog he had started just 14 months before. "I should be tested for steroids," joked the steroid-free Ramsey when he somehow found a few minutes to be interviewed by me.

Later that month, I drove Maggie and her stuff to Barnard for the college-move-in day that's so emotional for parents everywhere. She ended up with the top bunk in a three-person dorm room, but otherwise seemed more happy than nervous about starting campus life. And Maggie chatted easily with the two roommates (from Connecticut and Alaska) she was meeting for the first time. I thought back to how scared and socially inept I was during my freshman year at Rutgers, and happily concluded that the Astor family had evolved.

I'm convinced that my migration from painfully shy to fairly confident — a process my E&P successes helped bring about — was a big reason why I raised a daughter much more sure of herself than I was at Maggie's age. If that sounds like "pop psychology," well, I *am* a dad.

Also, 2007 was the publishing year for two major cartoonist biographies: R.C. Harvey's *Meanwhile* about "Terry and the Pirates"/"Steve Canyon" creator Milton Caniff, and David Michaelis' *Schulz and Peanuts* about you know who.

Before the Charles Schulz book was published into bestsellerdom that October, I read an uncorrected proof and did a lengthy phone interview with Michaelis. I thought the seven-years-in-the-making *Schulz and Peanuts* was researched to the max and wonderfully written. It had many positive things to say about the cartoonist, but also painted a darker picture of Schulz than I had sensed from my times meeting and talking with the "Peanuts" creator. For instance, the book had a good deal of content about the cartoonist's melancholy behavior, his occasional alleged meanness, and an affair he had as his first marriage unraveled.

So before publishing my story, I contacted the cartoonist's widow Jeannie to ask if she liked or disliked the book — and she emailed me this statement: "What I'm grateful about is the research David was able to do over several critical years right after Sparky died, digging into archives and interviewing people who are no longer here." Jeannie said this research would "be available for future researchers and biographers."

I included these comments in the story, not grasping that Jeannie was diplomatically offering faint praise. That's one problem with the email interviews I used sparingly; you don't always catch nuances that might lead to necessary follow-up questions.

Sure enough, Jeannie called after my story was published to say it gave Michaelis' book too much credence and suggested I speak with Schulz's son Monte for a follow-up piece. I conducted *that* interview by phone.

Monte told me his father wasn't as melancholy as Michaelis made him out to be, that too many pages were devoted to Schulz's affair, and that too few pages focused on the cartoonist's happy second marriage to Jeannie and his positive relationships with his children and friends.

Michaelis countered that he wasn't trying to besmirch Schulz; the biographer said he had to go where the research took him.

After this battle of words, I was ready for a vacation. I had been with *E&P* long enough to get four weeks off a year, but could rarely take even a week at a time because of the workload. So when Laurel was invited to give a paper at an Emile Zola Society conference in Aix-en-Provence, I was thrilled to tag along but could only spare three weekdays to attach to the weekend in the south of France. That contracted time frame helped cause a frenetic (but fun) sojourn.

After arriving at Marseille's airport, we wanted to visit the city's port area before going to Aix. So we headed to the airport's luggage-check counter, got there at 12:05 p.m., and ... found it was closed for lunch from noon to 2! We then decided to leave our suitcases at Marseille's train station, but that luggage checkroom was closed because of a railroad strike.

"Why don't we just bring our bags with us to the port?" said Laurel, ever the can-do trooper.

So we bumped our bags down the broken escalator of the metro station, boarded the subway to the port, emerged at about 1:50 p.m., and looked for the restaurant a friend of Laurel's had recommended. We spotted it and ... watched the steel gate get pulled down. We tried several other eateries (all closed for lunch, too) before giving up and taking a bus to Aix.

The next morning, I watched Laurel give her paper in both English and French as part of a four-person panel that also included professors from France, Sweden, and Australia. Laurel was a little nervous at first, but soon gained confidence as she expertly analyzed the part of *The Silent Rooms* that French-Canadian novelist Anne Hébert set in Provence.

We did return to Marseille another day, and took a boat to the rocky island of If to see the former prison that figures so prominently in Alexandre Dumas' *The Count of Monte Cristo* — the best novel about revenge ever (though no high-ranking execs were harmed).

During our last full day in France, we had a great lunch with Laurel's friend and former dissertation advisor Margot Gray, who was living in Aix for a year with her husband Oz and two sons as she ran a prestigious study-abroad program for Indiana University. Then Laurel and I joined conference attendees on a bus to see the Provence countryside and the Mont Sainte-Victoire peak that novelist Zola's childhood friend Paul Cézanne often painted.

No one was told we had an arduous hike ahead of us, so I was wearing dress shoes and some of the female attendees had on heels. We stumbled up mountain paths for about two hours before reaching a dam that Zola's father designed in the mid-1800s. One hiker was Zola's great-granddaughter, so that was cool!

The next morning, Laurel and I flew from Marseille to Paris with barely enough time for the connecting flight to New Jersey's Newark airport. (Given the short amount of vacation we had because of my *E&P* workload, we didn't want to schedule a lot of time in airports waiting for planes.) We reached the gate ... just after the plane door closed. We tried to book another flight, and — sure enough — most Air France agents were at lunch as we waited on line for more than an hour.

There were no other planes to Newark until the next day, so we instead flew to New York's JFK airport, from where we had to ride two buses and a taxi before getting home five hours after the plane landed. "Taking the long way," as the Dixie Chicks sang. Our cat Angus, annoyed that we showed up nine hours after the pet sitter last fed him, hasn't read Zola to this day.

Soon after Aix, I did a story marking the 30th anniversary of daughter succeeding late mother on "Hints from Heloise." The gracious thank-you note Heloise sent was handwritten — an increasing rarity in the 2000s. I often sent people handwritten notes, too, but Heloise's penmanship (penwomanship?) was better.

There was nothing gracious about the continued cost-cutting at my magazine's parent company. In the fall of 2007, *E&P*'s talented and friendly photo editor Daniela DiMaggio was laid off after seven years — bringing our editorial staff down to nine (remember, it was 21 in 2000!). Daniela's departure left even more work for art/design director Reiko Matsuo — and the writers, too, because we now had to find our own story images and get them sent to us.

But the company didn't give writers' email systems enough storage capacity, so I had to always quickly move the art I received into online folders or delete the art right after forwarding it to Reiko so my system wouldn't become full and prevent new emails from flowing in. Managing those photos and cartoons wasn't a big problem at the office, but I also had to access the system from home Saturdays and Sundays to prevent it from reaching its capacity. Thanks, private-equity investors, for making weekends special!

It was around this time that the company also reorganized the classified-ad departments of various magazines — which may have caused sales of those ads to plummet even faster. Among the people losing their jobs was *E&P* classified account manager Michele MacMahon, who had been with us since the late 1990s — and was as nice and competent an employee as any company could hope to have.

As the company jettisoned hardworking people like Michele and Daniela, it continued to hire high-paid executives with amorphous-sounding titles — and to proudly announce these appointments in emails to the demoralized layoff survivors. This was beyond tone-deaf.

CHAPTER THIRTY-ONE

2008:
More Syndicate and
Newspaper
Shrinkage

During her first year at Barnard College, my daughter discovered she absolutely loved New York City. The excitement, the culture, the cows chewing A-Rod's stray $100 bills on the Yankee Stadium grass....

Maggie also began writing for the *Columbia Daily Spectator*. She would eventually be elected to the newspaper's managing board as head copy editor and decide to pursue a career in journalism — proving the adage that the Apple computer doesn't fall far from the tree.

I had mixed feelings about Maggie working in an imploding profession. Newspapers were getting rid of many more people than they were hiring, and there weren't nearly enough online media jobs to compensate. But the print or online media outlets that *do* hire the occasional person often prefer lower-salaried young adults over graying writers like me. Maggie ended up being one of the fortunate ones, landing a nicely paid job as a *New York Times* copy editor in 2012. Fortunate, yes, but she's also an excellent copy editor and writer — and a very hardworking woman.

In April 2008, there were rumors *E&P*'s parent company would slash jobs yet again. So it was alarming when my magazine's editor asked staffers to gather in his office. Would I finally get the ax?

From what I understood, the company mandated the layoff numbers, and then the heads of each magazine picked the specific people to fire. That didn't bode well for me, because my relationship with my editor was not ideal — and I had received a mixed employee review earlier in '08. It was the same old allegedly not-doing-enough-work stuff, even though I now wrote as many as a dozen online stories and items a day in addition to print articles.

If I was possibly going to get fired in a few minutes, I decided to at least tell my editor that I'd be speaking later that month at the New York Comic Con — which would draw 60,000 people to Manhattan's Javits Center. *Your Career in the Comics* author Lee Nordling had invited me to be part of his future-of-comics panel along with King Features comics editor Brendan Burford, Universal Press assistant acquisitions editor Lucas Wetzel, Web cartoonist extraordinaire Brad Guigar, and newspaper cartoonist extraordinaire Mark Tatulli — who does the delightfully creepy "Lio" pantomime feature and the sunnier "Heart of the City."

At the meeting, my editor announced that there would indeed by an *E&P* layoff of ... online editor Pauline Millard.

This reduced *E&P*'s editorial staff to eight and threw another nice person's life into turmoil. But how could a magazine with an active Web site function without Pauline? By giving others more work, of course.

Shawn Moynihan was made online editor in addition to managing editor. To give him more time for online duties, I was assigned to take over his job of writing obituaries for the print magazine. Also, I was told to post other staffers' stories on the Web site when Shawn wasn't available, do my own inserting of HTML code when creating Internet links, and do more non-syndicate stories for the site.

Fifty-hour-plus workweeks ensued, and gastroenterologists everywhere rejoiced at the predicted coming of ulcers for our shrunken editorial staff.

So I spoke at the New York Comic Con as an *E&P* employee rather than ex-employee, and did fine. My strongest memory of that Saturday morning in the Javits Center was seeing "Spider-Man" legend Stan Lee — still looking rakish at age 85 — being hurriedly escorted to an appearance followed by many hyper-excited fans. It was almost like Beatlemania 1964!

In 1968, the Beatles went to India. Forty years later, *E&P*'s parent company outsourced most of its IT department to that lower-wage country in order to increase profits. If we needed our computers fixed now, it nearly always had to be done over the phone — meaning it usually took the tech person longer to figure out what was wrong. And many in-house IT staffers lost their jobs; I remember one soon-to-be-laid-off guy with young children criticizing the company's heartless outsourcing.

"I thought I had job security if I knew computers," he said bitterly, as he gave me a new keyboard. All those lunches while working probably jammed the thing up.

Yes, as the recession worsened in 2008, it was becoming quite a year for layoffs. In May, Creators Syndicate announced it was buying the 1955-founded Copley News Service, which resulted in most of the 21 CNS employees losing their jobs.

When I interviewed some Copley cartoonists about the sale, I was struck by how much they loved and respected CNS vice president/editor Glenda Winders, who is also an excellent writer. Nothing beats high praise when forced to leave a place after 20-plus years (except maybe a good severance package!).

There was now one fewer major syndicate for me to cover, but this hardly made a dent in my workload since I was also writing so much non-syndicate stuff.

The company also sliced travel budgets again, so I got to cover just one meeting in 2008 — the editorial cartoonists in San Antonio. The most intense part of that June convention was attending a talk by severely wounded Iraq War veterans, including one soldier with a badly burned face and another who struggled to the podium on two artificial legs. They were brave, and their inspiring remarks drew a standing ovation, but it infuriated me that the president who sent them to Iraq barely served during the Vietnam War and that Vice President Dick Cheney got five deferments to avoid going to Southeast Asia.

John Branch, the soft-spoken *San Antonio Express-News* editorial cartoonist who skillfully hosted the convention, lost his job several months later. Among the 15 or so other cartoonists getting laid off or taking buyouts in 2007, 2008, and 2009 were Stuart Carlson of the *Milwaukee Journal Sentinel,* Bill Day of the Memphis *Commercial Appeal,* Steve Greenberg of California's *Ventura County Star,* Lee Judge of *The Kansas City Star,* and Dwane Powell of North Carolina's Raleigh *News & Observer.*

In a few cases, cartoonists continued drawing for their papers on a freelance basis (with less pay and benefits, of course). And many continued to draw for syndication, though they couldn't make a living with that alone.

Also, the Denver *Rocky Mountain News* folded in 2009 — putting cartoonists Ed Stein and Drew Litton out of work. Drew, a sweetheart of a guy, was one of America's few sports cartoonists.

And, to top it off, ultra-talented cartoonist Ann Telnaes left print syndication in June 2008 to concentrate on doing animations for WashingtonPost.com.

By the time the smoke cleared from the carnage, there were perhaps 55 staff cartoonist positions left in the U.S. — compared to several hundred in earlier decades. One needed a time machine to get a job in the field, though there's always the dilemma of whether to buy or lease one of those temporal contraptions.

Nearly 16,000 U.S. newspaper journalists were laid off or pressured to take buyouts in 2008, several newspaper chains filed for bankruptcy in '08 or '09, and other daily papers joined the *Rocky Mountain News* in going out of business. Heck, only 1,422 dailies remained in 2008 — 223 fewer than the 1,645 in 1988. And many of the 1,422 survivors lost readers, with the 20 biggest U.S. papers suffering a collective circulation decline of 8% from 2004 to 2008.

Meanwhile, most dailies reduced their news holes, which meant fewer stories and less space into which syndicates could sell features. And ad revenue nosedived from nearly $45.4 billion in 2007 to less than $27.6 billion in 2009, according to the Newspaper Association of America.

All this was wreckage from the bad economy, Web competition, years of bland content that turned off younger readers, and years of profits of which too much was given to executives and shareholders and not enough given to staffers and invested back in the product.

And newspaper woes continued to have a negative impact on *E&P.* The magazine's circulation plummeted from about 20,000 in 1996 to 12,000 or so in 2008 (though "pass-along" readership remained well over 12,000). And our Web site still wasn't getting enough ad revenue.

Not surprisingly, newspaper woes and the recession influenced many stories I wrote in 2008. For instance, I did several Web pieces quoting financial columnist Don McNay, who astutely analyzed all things economic.

One of my print features focused on how workplace-themed columns and comics were addressing the recession. That story gave me a chance to interview people such as Mildred Culp, the congenial writer who launched two features an impressive 22 years apart — "WorkWise" (1982) and the Q&A-formatted "WorkWise Interactive" (2004).

I also did a print article about syndicated creators who worked "day jobs" to survive. For instance, "Maintaining" cartoonist Nate Creekmore delivered packages for FedEx, columnist Bob Koehler served as an assistant editor at his syndicate, and "Tell Me a Story" writer Amy Friedman did things like teaching.

"Many people think you're rich" when they learn you're syndicated, said Friedman. "Would that it be so!"

Then I wrote a story about the irony of newspapers saving money by dropping syndicated features that offered money-saving advice to budget-crunched readers. One example involved Michelle Singletary's excellent "The Color of Money" column losing some clients.

"It's crazy to cut something people want to read," Singletary told me. "Personal-finance columns are the very definition of 'news that you can use.'"

But newspaper owners prefer cash they can stash.

I did do one 2008 print story that had a positive economic element — the reported $6.7-million advance for *The Last Lecture* book by Dr. Randy Pausch and *Wall Street Journal* columnist Jeff Zaslow that was published in April 2008 and became a huge bestseller. Dr. Pausch was the terminally ill professor (he died in July 2008) who gave an amazingly inspirational and humorous speech at Carnegie Mellon University in September 2007. CMU alum Zaslow attended that talk, and wrote a column and narrated a Web video that went viral.

And to think the Michigan-based Zaslow almost didn't cover that speech in Pittsburgh. "My wife said, 'You can't go,'" Jeff told me, because one of their daughters might need a ride somewhere. "My editors said I could do a 'phoner.' But I was drawn to the lecture."

Yet even Zaslow had a backstory that showed how economically brutal the newspaper business can be. As you might recall from Chapter 9, Jeff co-won the 1987 contest to replace Ann Landers at the *Chicago Sun-Times*. He went on to write great columns for the paper, and do all kinds of community-service things (such as raise money for needy children to get school supplies) that eventually earned him the National Society of Newspaper Columnists' first Will Rogers Humanitarian Award in 2000. The *Sun-Times* thanked Zaslow by laying him off in 2001.

Jeff, who wrote or co-wrote several other best-selling books after *The Last Lecture*, died tragically in a February 2012 car accident. Despite his literary fame, he had remained a friendly, helpful, down-to-earth guy.

An important non-economic 2008 story was one I broke in January about eight African-American cartoonists planning to draw similar Sunday comics on Feb. 10. The idea was to satirically protest the belief of some editors that so-called "black strips" are interchangeable — an erroneous notion that gives many papers the excuse to publish no more than one or two of these comics.

"Candorville" creator Darrin Bell, who co-organized the Feb. 10 action with "Watch Your Head" creator Cory Thomas, told me that comics by cartoonists of color are obviously as different from each other as those by white creators.

When I also contacted several white cartoonists to get reaction, some supported the protest. "So far, we as a nation haven't found a way out of the cultural shorthand that the symbolic 'everyman' is both white and male," astutely observed "Rhymes With Orange" creator Hilary Price in a story I did for *E&P*'s Web site.

Although the site still didn't have video, it finally got a couple of blogs in September 2008. One was business-oriented; the other covered a wider swath of the newspaper world — and I was a contributor to the latter.

And boy did I contribute. Between Sept. 2 and Oct. 20, I wrote 85 posts — in addition to my usual Web stories and print articles. One day, I wrote 18 stories and blog posts! By the time I left the office after 10 p.m. that evening, I felt like a zombie from *Night of the Living Dead*.

At least Laurel and her California sister Sheila were toiling on something for themselves rather than for an overwork-the-workers corporation: a "cozy" mystery novel set in the Midwest called *Death in the Museum*.

About 10 of my 85 blog pieces weren't posted by my editor for reasons unknown to me. One possibility: A few of the unpublished posts were on somewhat sentimental topics (such as the death of a columnist's dog), and my editor often preferred political-type topics.

Still, doing the blog posts was mostly fun. I was good at humor writing, and my pieces were often humorous. One could also blog about things that weren't necessarily story-worthy but made for interesting reading. For instance, I did several posts spotlighting presidential election odds provided by Benjamin Eckstein, the "America's Line" columnist better known for sports odds. "Yes we can" say that Ben predicted Barack Obama's victory well before November.

For *E&P*'s November issue, I spent part of October writing a story about the "Doonesbury" comic's Rick Redfern getting laid off from his well-paying *Washington Post* reporting job and launching an unpaid blog. (Actually, "unpaid blog" is almost redundant, like "wet water.")

Yes, even cartoon characters weren't immune from "The Great Recession," which had arrived thanks to the greed and irresponsibility of financial institutions that got obscenely bailed out anyway. I guess one reason Republicans give Wall Street almost everything it wants is because the GOP supports its loyal southern base, and Wall Street is in southern Manhattan.

With America in economic distress, would my company "downsize" even more?

CHAPTER THIRTY-TWO

Still 2008:
The 'E' in 'E&P'
Means 'Exit'

On Oct. 21, 2008, I arrived at work a little late after narrowly missing a train. I was told my editor wanted to see me, and could only assume he didn't want to MapQuest the short stroll to my desk.

As I trudged to the editor's office, I thought about how I had worked at *E&P* long enough for my salary to creep up to a decent level for the pricey New York area, meaning that this salary might be seen as a tempting target — despite my experience and institutional memory.

But I also recalled fearing I might be laid off in April 2008 — and had dodged that bullet. Maybe there was hope. Plus I had been toying with the idea of taking Laurel's advice and hunting for a new job.

I entered the editor's office, and saw a soulless-looking young corporate type I didn't recognize waiting with him.

"Sit down," said the editor, and before I hit the chair, he quickly added: "We're letting you go." After that, I was too dazed to remember much else he said.

E&P's editorial staff would now be down to seven — exactly a third of what it was in 2000. And, after stumbling out of the editor's office, I soon learned I was one of about 20 company employees axed that day.

As I sat stunned at my desk, the editor called a brief meeting of surviving staffers to announce my layoff. Then those staffers came to my cubicle to offer hugs and sympathy, as I had done so many times when other people were sacked. Several non-*E&P*ers also visited during the rest of the day; some of them were among the 20 pink-slipped that morning.

"It's almost a relief to get fired from this place," said one, and I had to agree.

But I felt a little dumb that I wouldn't be leaving on my own terms. As my wife Laurel's brother-in-law Anthony Thomas so eloquently emailed the next day: "You should feel happy when you're finally thrown out of prison but mostly you feel thrown out."

I *did* still love covering cartoonists and columnists, I *did* like my co-workers, and a person gets used to a place after 25 years. Also, I had never been laid off from a job before.

It was financially terrifying to become unemployed in an imploding economy and a shrinking media profession. What would I do next? Start a jitney service to transport all those readers moving from print to the Web? Launch a business in which unemployed journalists took relaxing baths for overworked journalists who only had time for showers?

But, seriously, I thought about my daughter Maggie being at an expensive college for nearly three more years. Plus Laurel and I were in the process of adopting a Guatemalan child named Maria. (Our little girl is wonderful.) Tuition and toddler expenses while being unemployed? Laurel's community-college professor salary not that high for the pricey New York area? This was going to be interesting....

I picked up the phone and called Laurel.

"I've been laid off."

Silence. Then: "Oh, Dave! That's awful! How stupid can they be?"

"Pretty stupid."

"You'll find something better," said the ever-optimistic Laurel after a few seconds. "We'll get through this."

Then I contacted Maggie.

"I don't know what to say," was her shocked reaction.

With the knowledge that I'd at least be getting severance pay for a while, I started boxing up my stuff — eventually filling 18 cartons to ship home with the mailing help of kind company staffer Norma Lamicella. Then I prepared to notify people I covered that I had been let go, because *E&P* almost never wrote stories about its own layoffs — even while reporting on the many layoffs devastating the newspapers it covered. Double-standard operating procedure.

I signed into my work email — and found it had been cut off (*E&P* publisher Charles McKeown would intervene to get it restored a couple days later). After muttering a few curses, I remotely accessed my home email and — in a two-hour keyboarding frenzy — wrote approximately 200 cartoonists, columnists, syndicate executives, and others to tell them I was canned effective Oct. 31.

Soon, I was flooded with (and greatly touched by) replies lamenting my departure and praising my work. I ended up getting nearly 400 emails — including 200 or so from people I hadn't even contacted.

Some excerpts: "I cannot tell you how devastated I am by your news" ... "What a loss for *E&P*" ... "You are a class act who didn't deserve this" ... "Our industry is committing suicide" ... "You have done a wonderful job covering our industry" ... "I can't think of anyone else on the planet who knows more about syndicates" ... "You're one of the few people who got it right."

I printed out the emails and showed them to my editor's supervisor.

"Wow! I've never seen an outpouring of support like this," the executive told me as I sat in her huge office. But this very well-paid person — who weirdly always had a smile on her face as she oversaw round after round of layoffs — did absolutely nothing to save my job. Cost-cutting was king.

Also, many cartoon bloggers posted wonderful pieces, and I was truly thankful for their tributes and the words of people commenting under the pieces. DailyCartoonist.com blogger Alan Gardner actually called me "the founding father of syndication reporting," a title the real founding fathers would have puzzled over when they gathered in Philadelphia more than two centuries ago for some 76ers b-ball and beer in pricey souvenir cups.

Several days later, National Society of Newspaper Columnists Web site editor Sheila Moss posted two very complimentary stories about me by former NSNC president Suzette Standring and *Fort Worth Star-Telegram* columnist Dave Lieber. Then the organization devoted much of its November 2008 newsletter to yours truly. Newsletter editor Bob Haught, formerly of *The Oklahoman*, even called me "the columnist's columnist"!

So when the NSNC asked me to run for the archivist position on its board in 2009, how could I say no? Besides, the two previous archivists (Linda Caillouet and Ben Pollock) were both writers from a state that begins with "A" (Arkansas) — the same first letter as my last name and the word archivist. Which made me wonder: Which NSNC position might be the right alphabetical fit for great *Stamford* (Conn.) *Advocate* humor columnist Jerry Zezima?

NSNCers elected me archivist in June '09, and reelected me two years later.

I admired the NSNC and enjoyed their conferences during the many years I covered the group. I also loved covering other organizations, including the Association of American Editorial Cartoonists and the National Cartoonists Society. Most members of these groups are creative, *non-corporate* people who are nice to be around.

Anyway, all the positive publicity in the days after my Oct. 21, 2008, layoff might have influenced *E&P*'s editor to take the very unusual step of writing a story about someone he laid off. His article about me was posted on *E&P*'s Web site soon after the two NSNC stories appeared on Columnists.com.

"I can't believe the site actually mentioned something that doesn't put *E&P* in a good light!" one of my co-workers exclaimed, sounding more surprised than if a three-headed ferret had become our ad manager.

One of my favorite layoff reactions came later in 2008, when Kim Campbell, director of public relations for "Garfield" cartoonist Jim Davis' Paws Inc., emailed me at home to say that Jim had told her: "If we subscribe to *E&P*, let's cancel it. If we don't, let's subscribe … AND THEN CANCEL IT!"

A month after I left, *E&P* art/design director Reiko Matsuo sent me the December 2008 issue. It was beyond weird not seeing my name on the masthead for the first time since early 1983.

And when Laurel and I walked out the door after visiting our very good friends Barbara and Mickey Abrash in a Manhattan building just two short blocks north of the *E&P* office, I averted my eyes like Dracula seeing a wooden stake.

As the economy continued to worsen in 2008 and beyond, there was a long stretch of unemployment for me — though I knew someone who knew someone who imagined they had a job interview. I spent quality time with Angus the cat, and continued writing my "Montclairvoyant" column for *The*

Montclair Times — even winning both first and second place for that weekly topical-humor feature in the New Jersey Press Association's 2009 contest. Also, I became a humor blogger for the widely read Huffington Post in 2009 and started writing about books for HP in 2011. Those posts were unpaid, but the site's vast audience helped my book pieces (http://www.huffingtonpost.com/dave-astor) attract a large following — more than 1,450 "fans" and many hundreds of comments by April 2012.

Yes, my freelance earnings were far from a full-time salary, so the biggest laughs I got were from tellers who saw my bank balance. Still, writers need to write as much as dentists need to dent.

And you won't be surprised to learn that after my play, novel, and children's book didn't succeed, I managed to author a memoir that will conclude ... now.